Manual de práctica que acompaña

Entrevistas

An Introduction to Language and Culture

Second Edition

Volume 1

Manual de práctica que acompaña

Entrevistas

An Introduction to Language and Culture

Second Edition

Volume 1

Robert L. Davis
University of Oregon

H. Jay Siskin
Cabrillo College

Alicia Ramos
Hunter College

Rosario Murcia
University of Oregon

Wayne A. Gottshall
Late of University of Oregon

Boston Burr Ridge, IL Dubuque, IA Madison, WI New York
San Francisco St. Louis Bangkok Bogotá Caracas Kuala Lumpur
Lisbon London Madrid Mexico City Milan Montreal New Delhi
Santiago Seoul Singapore Sydney Taipei Toronto

This is an EBI book

Manual de práctica que acompaña
Entrevistas
An Introduction to Language and Culture

Published by McGraw-Hill, an imprint of the McGraw-Hill Companies, Inc., 1221 Avenue of the Americas, New York, NY 10020.

5 6 7 8 9 0 QPD/QPD 0 9 8 7

ISBN 978-0-07-255862-3
MHID 0-07-255862-8

Editor-in-chief: *Emily G. Barrosse*
Executive editor: *William R. Glass*
Sponsoring editor: *Christa Harris*
Development editor: *Allen J. Bernier*
Supplements development editor: *Fionnuala McEvoy*
Director of development: *Scott Tinetti*
Project manager: *David Sutton*
Production supervisor: *Rich DeVitto*
Compositor: *The GTS Companies/York, PA Campus*
Typeface: 10/12 *Palatino*
Printer: *Quebecor, Dubuque*

Grateful acknowledgment is made for the use of the following material:

Readings:
Page 19 Excerpt reproduced with permission from *South America on a Shoestring*, 6th edition, © 1997 Lonely Planet Publications; **Page 46** From *http://www.incostarica.net/docs/people;* **Page 46** From *Costa Rica Handbook* by Christopher P. Baker. Used by permission of Moon Travel Handbooks; **Page 67** *Faces of Latin America* by Duncan Green, Latin America Bureau, 1997. © Latin America Bureau. Used by permission; **Page 93** Reprinted from *Culture Shock! Spain* by Marie Louise Graff with permission from Graphic Arts Center Publishing Company, Portland, Oregon and Times Editions Pte. Ltd., Singapore. All rights reserved; **Page 118** From *Dominican Republic Handbook* by Gaylord Dold. Used by permission of Moon Travel Handbooks; **Page 140** Excerpts from *The Old Patagonian Express* by Paul Theroux. Copyright © 1979 by Paul Theroux. Reprinted by permission of Houghton Mifflin Company. All rights reserved; **Page 160** From *Mexico Handbook* by Joe Cummings & Chicki Mallan. Used by permission of Moon Travel Handbooks; **Page 183–184** From *The Hispanic Almanac: From Columbus to Corporate America*, Nicolas Kanellos ed., Visible Ink Press 1994. Reprinted by permission of Visible Ink Press

Realia:
Page 95 Hernani Homes, Javea, Spain; **Page 96** INVESCOSTA

http://www.mhhe.com

Contents

Note to Students

This Volume 1 of the *Manual de práctica que acompaña Entrevistas: An Introduction to Language and Culture,* Second Edition, offers you activities designed to reinforce the vocabulary, grammar, and cultural points presented in your *Entrevistas* textbook.

After a set of initial review and preparation activities, the sections of the *Manual* mirror the main structure of the *Entrevistas* textbook. This organization will provide you with additional vocabulary and grammar review and practice. In **Parte 2** of each chapter, **Análisis cultural** (called **Se dice que...** in the First Edition) offers a short reading and an activity that, like the similarly named section in the textbook, may challenge your assumptions about the Spanish-speaking world.

Additionally, you will find a **Portafolio cultural** section (called **A ti te toca** in the First Edition) that now includes a composition activity **(Redacción)** and a cultural research activity **(Exploración).** These two activities will allow you to demonstrate your comprehension of the cultural themes of the chapter as you expand your knowledge of the country or region of focus. Thus, for each chapter, you will find the following sequence of activities.

Repaso y anticipación

Parte 1

Vocabulario

Entrevista 1

Forma y función

Pronunciación y ortografía

Parte 2

Vocabulario

Entrevista 2

Forma y función

Análisis cultural

Portafolio cultural

You will find several types of activities in this workbook.

- **Vocabulary practice activities** allow you to make meaningful associations of new words with previously studied material or with situations that are familiar to you.
- **Mechanical activities** help you to review and practice how a grammar point works in expressing meaning.
- **Open-ended writing activities** allow you to integrate the material you have studied and convert it into meaningful communication in Spanish.
- **Listening activities** help you develop the important skill of aural comprehension.
- **Pronunciation and orthography activities** (denoted by a headphones icon in the margin) help you isolate problems in your pronunciation and spelling that may impede effective communication with Spanish speakers.
- **Cultural activities** allow you to integrate and consolidate your increasing knowledge about the cultures of the regions where Spanish is spoken.

The following suggestions should help you to use this *Manual* successfully.

- You will benefit most if you complete the *Manual* activities immediately after the material is presented and practiced in your class. That is, do not wait until the end of the chapter to complete all the activities in the *Manual*!
- Especially while doing the grammar activities, remember that it is more important to know *why* a given answer is correct than just to guess the right one.
- Activities may seem challenging at first, but do not avoid them. For example, the listening activities allow you to repeat a particular item of speech until you have mastered it completely.
- Even if your teacher does not assign some exercises, such as the cultural activities, you may find these among the most interesting and informative ones.
- Try to complete the activities with your textbook closed. One effective way of proceeding is to review the textbook material first, then test your understanding by working in the *Manual.*
- Most of the answers are given in the Answer Key at the back of the *Manual;* check them immediately after you have completed an activity. It is a good idea to mark with a highlighter pen the items you could not answer correctly. This will help you study and review before chapter tests. If you do not understand a particular answer given, consider two possibilities: (1) you are very creative and thought of an idea the authors did not anticipate, or (2) you may need further explanation of the vocabulary or grammar point in question. In either case, ask your instructor for more details.
- For further practice with the material covered in each chapter, use the *Entrevistas* Interactive CD-ROM, and visit the *Entrevistas* Online Learning Center at **www.mhhe.com/entrevistas2**.

See also the general suggestions regarding language study in the preface to your *Entrevistas* textbook ("A Letter to the Student").

In conclusion, we hope that this *Manual* helps you make progress in communicating successfully in Spanish, as well as understanding more about the cultures of Spanish-speaking regions. We wish you **buena suerte** on your journey!

Robert L. Davis
H. Jay Siskin
Alicia Ramos
Rosario Murcia
Wayne A. Gottshall

CAPÍTULO

1

Anticipación

A. Saludos y despedidas (*Greetings and farewells*). Under each of the following drawings, write the letter of the most appropriate expression for the situation. Remember to consider issues of formality and familiarity.

1. 

2. _____

3. _____

4. _____

a. Buenos días. ¿Cómo está usted?
b. ¡Hola! ¿Qué tal?
c. Adiós. Nos vemos, ¿eh?
d. Hasta luego, mamá.

❖ ***B. ¿Formal o informal?**

Paso 1. Name two situations in which you might address someone as **usted.**

1. ____
2. ____

*The answers to activities or parts of activities with this symbol (❖) are *not* included in the Answer Key at the back of this *Manual.*

Paso 2. What would you say in these situations to someone whom you address as **usted?**

1. greeting in the morning ______________________________
2. to find out his/her name ______________________________
3. to find out how he/she is doing ______________________________

PARTE 1

Vocabulario

Los saludos; El alfabeto español; El origen y la nacionalidad

A. Saludos y despedidas. Listen to the following dialogues and indicate whether the speakers are saying hello **(Se saludan)** or good-bye **(Se despiden)** to each other. You will hear the answers on the audio program.

	SE SALUDAN.	SE DESPIDEN.
1.	☐	☐
2.	☐	☐
3.	☐	☐
4.	☐	☐
5.	☐	☐

B. ¿Formal o informal? Listen to the dialogues and indicate whether the speakers are using formal or familiar address. If you can't tell, check **No sé.** You will hear the answers on the audio program.

	FORMAL	INFORMAL	NO SÉ.
1.	☐	☐	☐
2.	☐	☐	☐
3.	☐	☐	☐
4.	☐	☐	☐
5.	☐	☐	☐

C. Una conversación incompleta. Complete the following conversations with appropriate expressions.

1. ROSA: ¿Cómo _______ __________________ usted, señor?

   SEÑOR ROMÁN: _______ __________________ Joaquín Román.

   ROSA: Mucho gusto, señor Román.

   SEÑOR ROMÁN: ____________________________________, Rosa.

2. SEÑORA MUÑOZ: Buenos días, señor Millán. ¿Cómo está usted?

   SEÑOR MILLÁN: __________________ bien, gracias. ¿Y __________________, señora Muñoz?

   SEÑORA MUÑOZ: ____________________________________.

3. MARIFLOR: ¡Hola, Jaime! ¿Cómo ________________?

   JAIME: Muy bien, ¿y ______?

   MARIFLOR: Bien, gracias. Hasta mañana.

   JAIME: ________________.

D. El alfabeto. Listen as five Spanish words are spelled out. Write down the letters of each word, then try to guess its meaning.

MODELO (*you hear*) a-ele-efe-a-be-e-te-o
(*you write*) alfabeto
(*you guess*) alphabet

LA PALABRA (*WORD*) ESPAÑOLA	SU SIGNIFICADO (*ITS MEANING*)
1. ___ ___ ___ ___ ___ ___ ___ ___ ___	________________
2. ___ ___ ___ ___ ___ ___ ___	________________
3. ___ ___ ___ ___ ___ ___ ___ ___	________________
4. ___ ___ ___ ___ ___ ___ ___ ___ ___ ___ ___	________________
5. ___ ___ ___ ___ ___ ___ ___ ___ ___ ___	________________

E. ¿Quién es? Indicate whether the statements you hear apply to a man **(un hombre)** or a woman **(una mujer).** If it could be either, check **hombre o mujer.**

MODELO (*you hear*) Es inglés.
(*you check*) Un hombre.

	UN HOMBRE	UNA MUJER	HOMBRE O MUJER
1.	☐	☐	☐
2.	☐	☐	☐
3.	☐	☐	☐
4.	☐	☐	☐
5.	☐	☐	☐
6.	☐	☐	☐
7.	☐	☐	☐

F. ¿De dónde es? State the person's nationality, based on his/her country of origin. **¡OJO!** (*Careful!*) Be certain that the adjective of nationality reflects the gender of the person.

MODELOS Hans es de Alemania. →
Él es alemán.
Marisol es de España. →
Ella es española.

1. Giulietta es de Italia. Ella es ________________________________.
2. Yumiko es de Japón. Ella es ________________________________.
3. José es de Puerto Rico. Él es ________________________________.
4. Mao He es de China. Él es ________________________________.
5. Camille es de Francia. Ella es ________________________________.
6. ¿Y yo? Yo soy de ________________________. Soy ________________________.

❖ **G. ¡Lo mejor (*The best*)!** In your opinion, where do the best of the following products come from? Follow the model.

MODELO el mejor vino →

El mejor vino es de Francia. (El mejor vino es francés.)

1. el mejor té ________________
2. el mejor café ________________
3. la mejor pizza ________________
4. el mejor queso (*cheese*) ________________
5. la mejor cámara ________________

Entrevista 1

A. Sonido y significado

Paso 1: Sonido. The sentences in this activity are based on the interview with Jairo Bejarano Carrillo. First, read each sentence silently and make sure you understand its meaning. Then, listen as the speaker pronounces each sentence in phrases. Repeat the phrase in the interval provided until you can say it smoothly. **¡OJO!** You can pause the audio program if you need more time to practice each sentence.

Jairo Bejarano Carrillo
Bogotá, Colombia

1. Yo soy de Bogotá, Colombia.
2. **Bejarano** se escribe B-E-J-A-R-A-N-O.
3. Mi padre y mi madre son colombianos, pero (*but*) no son de Bogotá.
4. Son de pueblos pequeños. Sus apellidos son de origen español.

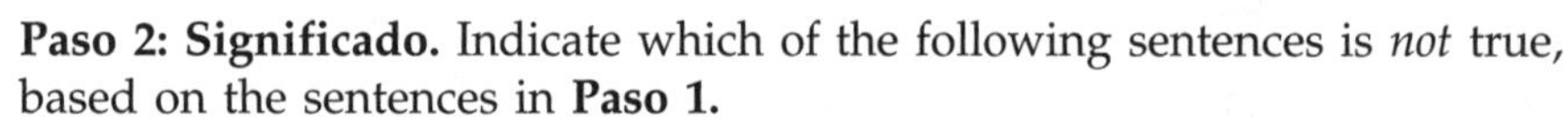

Paso 2: Significado. Indicate which of the following sentences is *not* true, based on the sentences in **Paso 1.**

a. ☐ **Bejarano** se escribe con **B de burro.**
b. ☐ Jairo es colombiano.
c. ☐ Los padres de Jairo son de Bogotá.

B. Respuestas lógicas. First, read the questions and divided responses from the interview with Jairo. Then, listen to the interview and match the first and last part of his responses.

PREGUNTAS Y RESPUESTAS PARTE 1

1. ¿Cómo te llamas?

   «Mi nombre _____.»

2. ¿Cómo se escribe tu (*your*) nombre?

   «**Jairo** _____.»

3. ¿Cómo se escriben tus apellidos?

   «**Bejarano** se escribe _____.»

4. ¿De dónde eres?

   «Yo soy _____.»

5. ¿De dónde son tus padres?

   «Mi padre y mi madre son colombianos, pero no son de Bogotá. _____.»

RESPUESTAS PARTE 2

a. de Bogotá, Colombia
b. es Jairo Bejarano Carrillo
c. Son de pueblos pequeños. Sus apellidos son de origen español
d. se escribe J-A-I-R-O
e. con **B de burro:** B-E-J-A-R-A-N-O. Y **Carrillo:** C-A-R-R-I-L-L-O

C. ¿Entendiste? Answer the following questions in complete sentences, based on the interview with Jairo.

1. ¿De dónde es Jairo?

   ____

2. ¿Cuáles (*what*) son sus (*his*) apellidos?

   ____

3. ¿De dónde son sus padres?

   ____

❖ **D. Preguntas para ti.** You will hear three questions. Write down your personal answers.

1. ______________________________
2. ______________________________
3. ______________________________

Forma y función

1.1 Subject Pronouns

Clínica de gramática

Subject pronouns are the words that indicate the subject of the sentence—the person or thing performing the main action.

Los pronombres de sujeto			
SINGULAR		PLURAL	
yo	I	**nosotros/nosotras**	we
tú	you (*familiar*)	**vosotros/vosotras**	you all, you guys (*familiar*)
usted	you (*formal*)	**ustedes**	you (*formal*)
él	he	**ellos**	they (*masculine*)
ella	she	**ellas**	they (*feminine*)

¿De quién hablamos? Indicate which pronoun corresponds to the following subjects.

	ELLA	ÉL	NOSOTROS	VOSOTROS	USTEDES	ELLOS
1. el señor Pérez	☐	☐	☐	☐	☐	☐
2. Marta	☐	☐	☐	☐	☐	☐
3. mi mamá y yo	☐	☐	☐	☐	☐	☐
4. los señores Ortiz	☐	☐	☐	☐	☐	☐
5. tus amigos y tú	☐	☐	☐	☐	☐	☐

A. ¡A escuchar! Listen to each of the statements, then write the subject pronoun you hear. You will hear the answers on the audio program.

1. ______________ 3. ______________ 5. ______________ 7. ______________

2. ______________ 4. ______________ 6. ______________ 8. ______________

B. ¿Quién? Indicate which pronoun corresponds to the following people.

	ÉL	ELLA	ELLOS	ELLAS
1. Ricky Martin	☐	☐	☐	☐
2. Henry Cisneros y Antonia C. Novello	☐	☐	☐	☐
3. Antonio Banderas y Jimmy Smits	☐	☐	☐	☐
4. Gloria Estefan y Tito Puente	☐	☐	☐	☐
5. Jennifer López y Christina Aguilera	☐	☐	☐	☐
6. Salma Hayek	☐	☐	☐	☐
7. Laura Esquivel y Ana María Matute	☐	☐	☐	☐
8. tu profesor(a) de español	☐	☐	☐	☐

C. ¿Tú o usted? Read the following questions and indicate whether they address **tú** or **usted.**

	TÚ	USTED
1. ¿Cómo te llamas?	☐	☐
2. ¿Cómo está?	☐	☐
3. ¿Cómo se llama?	☐	☐
4. ¿Cómo estás?	☐	☐
5. ¿De dónde es?	☐	☐
6. ¿De dónde eres?	☐	☐

D. ¿Quién es? Decide which subject pronoun is appropriate for the following situations and write it in the space provided.

1. You and your friend are speaking about yourselves. ______________
2. You are speaking about your grandfather. ______________
3. You are speaking to your friends Paco and Fernando from Colombia and referring to them. ______________

4. You are speaking about your neighbor Mrs. Fernández. ______________

5. You are speaking to your friends Elisa and María from Spain and referring to them. ______________

6. You are speaking directly to your dog Missy. ______________

1.2 The Verb **ser**

Clínica de gramática

In Spanish, there is a distinct verb form for most of the subject pronouns. The following table shows the present tense forms of the irregular verb **ser** (*to be*).

ser					
SINGULAR			PLURAL		
(yo)	**soy**	I am	(nosotros/as)	**somos**	we
(tú)	**eres**	you (*fam.*) are	(vosotros/as)	**sois**	you (*fam.*) are
(usted)	**es**	you (*form.*) are	(ustedes)	**son**	you (*form.*) are
(él/ella)	**es**	he/she/it is	(ellos/as)	**son**	they (*m./f.*) are

¿Quién es? Indicate which verb form corresponds to the following subject pronouns.

	SOY	ERES	ES	SOMOS	SOIS	SON
1. tú	☐	☐	☐	☐	☐	☐
2. nosotros	☐	☐	☐	☐	☐	☐
3. ustedes	☐	☐	☐	☐	☐	☐
4. usted	☐	☐	☐	☐	☐	☐
5. ella	☐	☐	☐	☐	☐	☐
6. yo	☐	☐	☐	☐	☐	☐
7. vosotras	☐	☐	☐	☐	☐	☐

A. ¡A escuchar! Listen to each of the following statements about famous people. Indicate whether the statement is **cierto** (*true*) or **falso** (*false*), then write the form of **ser** that you hear. You will hear the answers on the audio program.

MODELO (*you hear*) Rosie Pérez es alemana.
(*you check*) falso
(*you write*) es

	CIERTO	FALSO	
1.	☐	☐	______________
2.	☐	☐	______________
3.	☐	☐	______________
4.	☐	☐	______________
5.	☐	☐	______________

B. ¿Cuál es la forma correcta? Write the correct form of the verb **ser.**

1. Nosotros ______________ estadounidenses.
2. Ustedes ______________ mexicanos.
3. ¿Usted ______________ española?
4. Ella ______________ china.
5. ¿Tú ______________ canadiense?
6. Vosotros ______________ colombianos.
7. Yo ______________ puertorriqueña.

C. ¿De dónde son? Write a sentence using the verb **ser** that tells where the following people are from.

MODELO Mi (*my*) novio/a (*boyfriend/girlfriend*) →
Mi novio es de Georgia.

1. yo ____
2. mi mejor amigo/a ____
3. mi profesor(a) de español ____
4. mis abuelos (*grandparents*) ____
5. mi hermano/a (*brother, sister*) / hijo/a (*son/daughter*) ____

D. Hispanos famosos. Write a complete sentence in Spanish using the verb **ser.**

MODELO Rubén Blades **/** Panamá →
Rubén Blades es de Panamá.

1. Andy García y Jimmy Smits **/** Estados Unidos

   ____

2. Ricky Martin **/** Puerto Rico

   ____

3. Enrique y Julio Iglesias **/** España

   ____

4. Fernando Botero **/** Colombia

   ____

5. Julia Álvarez **/** la República Dominicana

   ____

6. Isabel Allende **/** Chile

   ____

E. Paco y Tomás. Complete the following dialogue with the correct form of the verb **ser.**

PACO: ¿De dónde ___________[1] tú?

TOMÁS: Yo ___________[2] de San Francisco.

PACO: ¿De dónde ___________[3] tus padres y tus hermanos?

TOMÁS: Mi mamá ___________[4] de México y mi papá ___________[5] de Los Ángeles.

Mis hermanos y yo ___________[6] de California.

F. Frases revueltas (*scrambled*). Unscramble the following phrases and write complete sentences. **¡OJO!** Use the correct form of the verb **ser.**

1. Pedro **/** de **/** ser **/** Perú

   ____

2. ¿de **/** ser **/** dónde **/** tus amigos?

   ____

3. de Atlanta **/** ser **/** tú

   ____

4. España **/** de **/** mi profesora de español **/** ser

   ____

5. ser **/** ustedes **/** México **/** de

   ____

6. ¿dónde **/** vosotros **/** ser **/** de?

   ____

G. Una conversación. Complete the following conversation with the missing information.

LUIS: Hola, ¿cómo estás?

MARISELA: Bien, gracias, ¿y tú?

LUIS: Muy bien. ¿______________________________[1]?

MARISELA: Me llamo Marisela Guntermann.

LUIS: ¿Cómo se escribe **Guntermann?**

MARISELA: ______________________________[2] G-U-N-T-E-R-M-A-N-N.

LUIS: ¿______________________________[3]?

MARISELA: Soy de California.

LUIS: ¿______________________________[4]?

MARISELA: Mi familia es de Chile, pero mi apellido es alemán.

Pronunciación y ortografía

Vowels and Consonants

Study the explanation of vowel and consonant sounds in your textbook before doing these practice activities.

A. Las vocales. Listen to and repeat the following words, paying special attention to the sound of the underlined vowels. **¡OJO!** A vowel has the same sound in both stressed and unstressed syllables.

1.	banana	Canadá	Panamá	fantástico
2.	excelente	energético	heterogéneo	perenne
3.	difícil	imbécil	mínimo	crítico
4.	horóscopo	contexto	Carolina	teléfono
5.	universidad	música	cultura	gusto

B. Las vocales. Remember that Spanish has short, clear vowels. Listen and circle each word you hear. Is it English or Spanish? You will hear the answers on the audio program.

	ENGLISH	SPANISH
1.	see	sí
2.	say	se
3.	pasta	pasta
4.	dodo	dodo
5.	use	use

C. Las consonantes. Listen to and repeat each of the following words, paying close attention to the pronunciation of the underlined consonants.

1.	jefe (*chief, boss*)	hijo	Jaime	ejemplo (*example*)
2.	maravilloso (*marvelous*)	se llama	llegar (*to arrive*)	tortilla
3.	hora (*hour*)	helado (*ice cream*)	bahía (*bay*)	ahora (*now*)
4.	señora	año (*year*)	pequeño (*small*)	castaño (*brown*)
5.	general	geografía	biología	gigante (*giant*)

D. Dictado. You will hear ten cognates, words with similar sounds and meanings in Spanish and English. Write each word you hear and try to guess the meaning.

MODELO (*you hear*) teléfono
(*you write*) teléfono (*telephone*)

1. ______________________ 6. ______________________
2. ______________________ 7. ______________________
3. ______________________ 8. ______________________
4. ______________________ 9. ______________________
5. ______________________ 10. ______________________

Vocabulario

Los días y los números (1–31); Las descripciones

A. ¡Bingo! You will hear a series of letters and numbers for each of the following bingo cards. Circle each letter/number combination you hear. How many winning cards do you have?

1.

B	I	N	G	O
1	3	6	8	10
4	7	11	12	13
15	18	14	22	16
23	20	24	26	17
27	31	30	28	19

2.

B	I	N	G	O
2	3	6	5	7
5	11	8	10	17
9	15	12	14	18
21	19	13	16	20
22	25	29	30	31

3.

B	I	N	G	O
1	5	3	2	6
8	10	11	9	12
13	16	18	17	14
19	21	23	20	22
25	30	24	26	29

B. ¿Qué día? Listen as Mrs. Álvarez tells her students which day of the week and date they give their class presentations. Write each student's name from the list on the corresponding date.

Andrés, Felipe, Javier, María, Pilar, Sara, Tomás

MARZO

lunes	martes	miércoles	jueves	viernes	sábado	domingo
		1	2	3	4	5
6	7	8	9	10	11	12
13	14	15	16	17	18	19
20	21	22	23	24	25	26
27	28	29	30	31		

C. La aritmética. Write the math problems you hear, then solve them. Spell out each answer next to the problem.

VOCABULARIO ÚTIL

y	+ (*plus*)
menos	− (*minus*)
son	= (*equals*)

MODELOS (*you hear*) dos y dos son
(*you write*) 2 + 2 = 4, cuatro
(*you hear*) diez menos tres son
(*you write*) 10 − 3 = 7, siete

1. ______________________
2. ______________________
3. ______________________
4. ______________________
5. ______________________

D. Capitales del mundo hispano. You will hear average high and low temperatures for the month of January in various capital cities. Fill in the blanks with the appropriate numbers.

	TEMPERATURA MÁXIMA	TEMPERATURA MÍNIMA
1. Buenos Aires (Argentina)	30 °C	________ °C
2. Caracas (Venezuela)	________ °C	________ °C
3. La Paz (Bolivia)	________ °C	________ °C
4. Madrid (España)	________ °C	________ °C
5. Ciudad de México	________ °C	________ °C
6. Santiago de Chile	________ °C	________ °C

E. El número siguiente. Write out the number that immediately follows the number you hear.

MODELO (*you hear*) veintiocho
(*you write*) veintinueve

1. ______________________
2. ______________________
3. ______________________
4. ______________________
5. ______________________
6. ______________________
7. ______________________

F. Antónimos y sinónimos. Give an antonym (≠) or a synonym (=) for each of the following words. **¡OJO!** Use the same gender in your answer.

1. antipático ≠ ______________
2. buena ≠ ______________
3. bonito = ______________
4. pequeña ≠ ______________
5. perezosa ≠ ______________
6. gordo ≠ ______________
7. guapa = ______________

G. Descripciones. You will hear a series of incomplete sentences. Check the form of the following adjectives that could complete the descriptions. You will hear the complete sentence on the audio program.

MODELO (*you hear*) Tengo el pelo…
(*you check*) negro

1.	☐ perezoso	☐ perezosa	☐ perezosos	☐ perezosas
2.	☐ castaño	☐ castaña	☐ castaños	☐ castañas
3.	☐ encantador	☐ encantadora	☐ encantadores	☐ encantadoras
4.	☐ corto	☐ corta	☐ cortos	☐ cortas
5.	☐ pequeño	☐ pequeña	☐ pequeños	☐ pequeñas
6.	☐ bonito	☐ bonita	☐ bonitos	☐ bonitas

❖ **H. Un cuento de hadas (*A fairy tale*).** Imagine that you are casting the movie version of a fairy tale. What sort of person would you look for to fill each role? Write at least two lines to describe each character's appearance and personality. Use your imagination!

VOCABULARIO ÚTIL

tiene *he/she has*
tienen *they have*

MODELO the villain →
Tiene el pelo corto y negro. Tiene los ojos azules. Es guapo, pero es malo.

1. the heroine

____

____

2. the hero

____

____

3. the parents of the heroine, who betray her to the villain

____

____

4. the hero's best friend, who deceives him in the end

____

____

I. Busco… (*I'm looking for . . .*)

Paso 1. Read the following personal ads that Victoria finds in today's paper. (The check boxes are for **Paso 3.**)

☐ Juan: Soy independiente, enérgico e impulsivo. Busco una mujer tradicional y reservada.
☐ Leonardo: Mi mujer ideal es romántica, generosa y sincera. Tiene el pelo rubio y los ojos azules.
☐ Roberto: Tengo los ojos verdes y el pelo castaño. Soy muy inteligente y ambicioso. Busco una mujer práctica, organizada y sincera.

Paso 2. Now listen to Victoria talk about what she is looking for in an ideal partner. Take notes as you listen.

____

____

____

____

Paso 3. Reread the personal ads from **Paso 1,** and check which person Victoria would probably call.

Entrevista 2

A. Sonido y significado

Paso 1: Sonido. The sentences in this activity are based on ideas from the interview with Stella Amado Carvajal. First, read each sentence silently and make sure you understand its meaning. Then, listen as the speaker pronounces each sentence in phrases. Repeat the phrase in the interval provided until you can say it smoothly. **¡OJO!** You can pause the audio program if you need more time to practice each sentence.

Stella Amado Carvajal
Duitama, Boyacá, Colombia

1. Duitama es una ciudad moderna con un paisaje (*countryside*) alrededor (*surrounding*) muy verde.
2. Los colombianos son amables y hospitalarios.
3. La gente (*people*) de Duitama, somos reservados y formales, pero alegres.
4. Soy una colombiana típica del altiplano (*high plain*). Tengo el pelo castaño y los ojos oscuros.

Paso 2: Significado. Indicate which of the following sentences is *not* true, based on the information in **Paso 1.**

a. ☐ Stella es de Bogotá.
b. ☐ Los colombianos en general son simpáticos.
c. ☐ Stella es muy similar a otros colombianos de la región.

B. Respuestas lógicas. First, read the questions and divided responses from the interview with Stella. Then, listen to the interview and match the first and last part of her responses.

PREGUNTAS Y RESPUESTAS PARTE 1

1. ¿Cómo es su ciudad?

   «Duitama es una ciudad moderna _____.»

2. ¿Cómo son los colombianos?

   «Los colombianos somos amables, alegres, _____.»

3. ¿Cómo es la gente de Duitama?

   «La gente de Duitama, somos _____.»

4. ¿Es usted una colombiana típica?

   «Soy una colombiana típica del altiplano. Tengo el pelo castaño, _____.»

RESPUESTAS PARTE 2

a. hospitalarios y muy trabajadores
b. los ojos oscuros y la piel clara
c. con un paisaje alrededor muy verde
d. reservados, formales, pero alegres.

C. ¿Entendiste? Answer the following questions in complete sentences, based on the interview with Stella.

1. ¿Cómo se llama la ciudad de Stella?

   ______

2. ¿Cómo es la ciudad de Stella?

   ______

3. ¿Cómo son los colombianos en general?

   ______

4. ¿Cómo es Stella físicamente?

   ______

❖ **D. Preguntas para ti.** You will hear three questions. Write down your personal answers.

1. ______
2. ______
3. ______

Forma y función

1.3 Gender and Number Agreement

Definite and Indefinite Articles

Clínica de gramática

The following table shows the different forms of the definite article (= English *the*) and the indefinite articles (= *a, an, some*). The form required depends on the noun that the articles appear with.

Los artículos definidos e indefinidos

	SINGULAR		PLURAL	
Masculine	**el** pueblo	*the town*	**los** pueblos	*the towns*
Feminine	**la** casa	*the house*	**las** casas	*the houses*
Masculine	**un** pueblo	*a town*	**unos** pueblos	*some towns*
Feminine	**una** casa	*a house*	**unas** casas	*some houses*

¿Masculino o femenino, singular o plural? Indicate whether the following nouns are **masculino** or **femenino** and **singular** or **plural.**

	MASCULINO	FEMENINO	SINGULAR	PLURAL
1. un perro	☐	☐	☐	☐
2. unos gatos	☐	☐	☐	☐
3. las familias	☐	☐	☐	☐
4. una ciudad	☐	☐	☐	☐
5. la niña	☐	☐	☐	☐
6. un profesor	☐	☐	☐	☐
7. la madre	☐	☐	☐	☐
8. los ojos	☐	☐	☐	☐
9. las muchachas	☐	☐	☐	☐

A. ¡A escuchar! Listen to the following descriptions. Then mark the corresponding article **definido** (*definite*) or **indefinido** (*indefinite*). **¡OJO!** Remember that definite articles **(el, la, los, las)** are for specific or definite people or things, whereas indefinite articles **(un, una, unos, unas)** are for nonspecific or indefinite people or things. You will hear the answers on the audio program.

MODELOS (*you hear*) El niño es colombiano.
(*you check*) definido
(*you hear*) Es una señora encantadora.
(*you check*) indefinido

	DEFINIDO	INDEFINIDO		DEFINIDO	INDEFINIDO
1.	☐	☐	5.	☐	☐
2.	☐	☐	6.	☐	☐
3.	☐	☐	7.	☐	☐
4.	☐	☐	8.	☐	☐

B. ¿Cómo son? Complete each sentence with the correct form of the definite article **(El, Los, La, Las).**

1. _____ comida (*food*) de Colombia es deliciosa.
2. _____ profesor de mi clase es bueno.
3. _____ libros de español son difíciles (*difficult*).
4. _____ profesoras son inteligentes.
5. _____ estudiante es buena.

C. Definiciones. Complete each sentence with the correct form of the indefinite article **(un, unos, una, unas).**

1. Es _____ persona interesante.
2. Es _____ hombre grande.

3. Son _____ muchachas italianas.
4. Son _____ actores guapos.
5. Es _____ músico romántico.

Adjectives

Clínica de gramática

Adjectives, like articles, must agree with the nouns they modify. They can have up to four different forms: masculine singular, masculine plural, feminine singular, and feminine plural. Review the three types of adjective agreement patterns in your textbook.

Los adjetivos

	SINGULAR	PLURAL
Masculine	El pueblo es pequeño.	Los pueblos son pequeños.
Feminine	La casa es pequeña.	Las casas son pequeñas.

Así son. Complete the following table with the correct forms of the adjectives to agree with the nouns given.

	alegre	antipático/a	encantador(a)	alto/a
1. los estudiantes				
2. la mujer				
3. la gente			*encantadora*	
4. las señoras				
5. el profesor	*alegre*			
6. los muchachos				
7. mi amigo				

A. ¡A escuchar! Listen to each description, then mark the corresponding person or thing being described. You will hear the answers on the audio program.

1. ☐ el hombre ☐ la mujer
2. ☐ el padre ☐ la madre
3. ☐ los niños ☐ las niñas
4. ☐ el pueblo ☐ los pueblos
5. ☐ la casa ☐ las casas

B. ¿Cómo son? Complete each sentence with the correct adjective.

1. María es ______________________ (guapo/guapa).
2. Mis amigos son ______________________ (encantador/encantadores).

3. Mi papá es ________________ (rubio/rubia).

4. Yo tengo (*I have*) los ojos ________________ (azul/azules).

5. Mi mamá es muy ________________ (trabajador/trabajadora).

C. Singular y plural. Rewrite each sentence, changing the noun, adjective, article, and verb from singular to plural or from plural to singular.

MODELOS Es un hombre alto. →
Son unos hombres altos.
Las casas son bonitas. →
La casa es bonita.

1. Es una amiga amable. ________________
2. Los profesores son inteligentes. ________________
3. Las clases son interesantes. ________________
4. Es un cantante (*singer*) famoso. ________________
5. El autor colombiano es de Bogotá. ________________
6. Son unas estudiantes trabajadoras. ________________

❖ **D. ¿Cómo son estas personas famosas?** Complete each sentence with the correct form of an appropriate adjective from the list. **¡OJO!** Don't forget to make sure that the adjectives agree with the nouns they describe both in number and gender.

arrogante, inteligente, lógico, moderno, práctico, romántico, tradicional

1. Edward James Olmos es un actor ________________.
2. Rubén Blades es un músico ________________.
3. Julia Roberts es una actriz ________________.
4. Barbara Walters y Diane Sawyer son periodistas (*journalists*) ________________.
5. Brad Pitt y Tom Cruise son actores ________________.

❖ **E. Retratos (*Portraits*).** Describe the following people. Use the verb **ser** and at least two appropriate adjectives. **¡OJO!** Use the correct form of **ser** and watch for number and gender agreement.

MODELO mi novio/a / esposo/a (*husband/wife*) →
Mi novia es simpática, inteligente y rubia.

1. yo ________________
2. mi mejor (*best*) amigo/a ________________
3. mi profesor(a) de español ________________
4. los estudiantes de mi clase ________________
5. mis padres/hijos (*children*) ________________

❖ Análisis cultural

The following quote about Colombia from a major travel guide will add to your knowledge of the geography of Colombia. Use this information as well as what you have learned in this chapter and from personal experience to answer the questions that follow the quote.

> "Colombia's geography is among the most varied in South America, as are its flora and fauna. The inhabitants form a palette of ethnic blends uncommon elsewhere on the continent and include a few dozen Indian groups, some of which still have traditional lifestyles. In effect, it's a country of amazing natural and cultural diversity and contrast, where climate, topography, wildlife, crafts, music, and architecture change within hours of overland travel—it's as if Colombia were several countries rolled into one."
>
> Source: *Lonely Planet on a Shoestring: South America*

1. Based on what you have learned so far in this chapter, with which of the preceding generalizations about Colombia do you agree?

   ____

   ____

2. Consult a geographical map of Colombia. In which ways is Colombia a country of amazing natural diversity?

   ____

   ____

3. What sorts of cultural diversity have you observed in this chapter?

   ____

   ____

4. In which ways is Colombia "several countries rolled into one"? Which other countries do you think it resembles? Why?

   ____

   ____

   ____

5. What more would you like to learn about Colombia?

   ____

   ____

❖ PORTAFOLIO CULTURAL

The **Portafolio cultural** section in each chapter of this *Manual* will provide you with a unique composition activity **(Redacción)** and several suggestions for a research activity **(Exploración),** for which you will need to consult the Internet, the library, and other sources. You should include the results of each **Redacción** and **Exploración** activity in your portfolio and submit them to your professor for feedback and evaluation, according to his/her instructions.

Redacción: ¡Venga (*Come*) a ___!

A. Antes de escribir (*Before writing*). For this chapter, you will create a travel brochure to attract tourists to your country, region, or favorite place. Your description will include geographical information and should emphasize the special identity of the place you choose. Complete the following steps on separate sheets of paper.

Paso 1. Choose a destination to write about, then describe its geographical location in Spanish. You can use expressions from the following list.

VOCABULARIO ÚTIL

Geographical Coordinates:

al este de	*to the east of*
al norte de	*to the north of*
al oeste de	*to the west of*
al sur de	*to the south of*
cerca de	*close to*

Landmarks:

el bosque (lluvioso)	*(rain) forest*
en la costa caribeña/atlántica/pacífica	*on the Caribbean/Atlantic/Pacific coast*
el Golfo de México	*Gulf of Mexico*
la isla	*island*
el Mar Caribe	*Caribbean Sea*
las Montañas Rocosas	*Rocky Mountains*
el Océano Atlántico/Pacífico	*Atlantic/Pacific Ocean*
el parque nacional	*national park*
la playa	*beach*

MODELO Colombia: en la costa caribeña, al norte de Ecuador y Perú

Paso 2. Which of the following expressions describes your destination? Ask your instructor to help you with additional expressions.

un lugar (*place*) de belleza (*beauty*) natural
un lugar encantador/divertido (*fun*)/tranquilo
un lugar histórico/moderno/popular/típico
un paraíso (*paradise*)

Paso 3. Make a list of the geographical features that describe your destination. You can select words from the following list or look up additional words you might need.

árido, lluvioso (*rainy*), montañoso (*mountainous*), tropical, el bosque, la costa, el desierto, el golfo, la montaña, la playa, el río (*river*), el valle (*valley*)

MODELO Es un país tropical, con playas bonitas y bosques lluviosos.

Paso 4. How would you describe the people who live in your destination? List at least four adjectives to describe them. **¡OJO!** In Spanish the word **gente** (*people*) is feminine and singular (not plural). Use feminine, singular adjectives to describe **la gente.**

La gente de _____ es…

1. ______________________________ 3. ______________________________

2. ______________________________ 4. ______________________________

B. ¡A escribir! Now, on a separate sheet of paper, create your brochure. Write the text and add maps, drawings, and/or photos, with captions in Spanish.

MODELOS ¡Venga a Colombia!

¡Es un país diverso, con montañas y playas!

¡Los colombianos son amables y divertidos!

¡La gente de Colombia es hospitalaria y moderna!

C. ¡A corregir (*Let's correct*)! Before you turn in your brochure, check the following points.

☐ Agreement of definite and indefinite articles
☐ Adjective agreement—number
☐ Adjective agreement—gender
☐ Punctuation (Don't forget the inverted question marks and exclamation points!)

WWW Exploración

Choose and complete *one* of the following research activities. Then, based on your instructor's directions, present your results to the class and/or create a short report to include in your portfolio.

1. Use the Internet and other resources such as encyclopedias and almanacs to trace the history of the indigenous population in Colombia. What percentage of the country's inhabitants did they constitute during the colonial years? What has been the governmental policy toward indigenous people during the course of the country's history? Which indigenous groups still live in Colombia today and where? Under what economic, social, and political conditions do they live? Organize and write a brief essay of your findings. Make comparisons between the history of Colombia's indigenous population and that of the United States.
2. Interview a native Colombian in your community. Where is he or she from? What are his/her city or region and its inhabitants like? How does he/she characterize a "typical" Colombian? How is he/she similar to or different from the Colombians you have heard from in this chapter? Prepare a transcript of this interview and summarize the major points.
3. Using the Internet, travel guides, and information provided by Colombian government agencies (the Tourist Board, embassies, or consulates), plan a visit to Bogotá and/or Duitama. How will you get there? What will you pack for your trip? What will you see and do? Create a written itinerary, with photos if you wish.
4. Find more information in your library or on the Internet about Colombia. Here are some ideas and key words to get you started:

   - greetings and formality in Colombia (comparison and contrast with other Spanish-speaking countries)
   - **el Departamento de Boyacá, Colombia**
   - **el palenquero** (a Colombian creole language)
   - Colombia's diversity: the Amazon region, Caribbean culture, **la Cordillera de los Andes,** and so on
   - Colombian music and dance: **la cumbia, el vallenato,** and so on

CAPÍTULO 2

Repaso y anticipación

❖ A. En la universidad

Paso 1. Imagine that you are in a study-abroad program. The registration process during your term abroad requires that international students fill out a special data form. Provide the information requested.

INFORMACIÓN PERSONAL

Nombre: ______

Apellido(s): ______

Nacionalidad: ______

Número de pasaporte (o de identidad): ______

Número de teléfono local: ______

Paso 2. On the reverse side of the personal data form are blank lines for a self-description. Provide any pertinent information (for example, you may comment on your height, coloring, personality traits, your origins, your home city or town). Write short phrases or whole sentences, as you prefer, but remember that the adjectives should agree in gender and number with the nouns they modify.

INFORMACIÓN PERSONAL

Autodescripción:

______

______

______

______

______

B. Un examen de aptitud. In this case, registration involves a short aptitude test. Spell out the missing numbers in the following mathematical reasoning section.

1. cinco, diez, ________________, veinte, veinticinco, treinta
2. tres, seis, doce, ________________
3. treinta, veintisiete, veintitrés, dieciocho, ________________, cinco
4. tres, seis, nueve, doce, quince, dieciocho, ________________, veinticuatro
5. siete, ________________, dieciocho, veintidós, veinticinco

C. Los estudiantes internacionales. At the opening assembly for new international students, you meet classmates from all over the world. Following the model, explain the origin and nationality of the following students. **¡OJO!** Remember that adjectives of nationality must agree in number and gender with the people they describe.

MODELO Charles (Francia) → Es de Francia. Es francés.

1. Lynne Ann (Estados Unidos) ________________
2. Pedro (España) ________________
3. Hilga y Ann (Alemania) ________________
4. John (Inglaterra) ________________
5. Francesca (Italia) ________________
6. David (Puerto Rico) ________________
7. Alberto (México) ________________
8. Lina (China) ________________

PARTE 1

Vocabulario

Los estudios universitarios; El horario; Preguntas para el estudiante típico

A. Las materias. Complete the following sentences with the appropriate class subject.

1. En la clase de ________________, los estudiantes dibujan (*draw*) mucho.
2. En la Facultad de Ciencias Sociales, hay clases de ________________ y de ________________.
3. Para mí (*For me*), la clase de ________________ es muy difícil y la clase de ________________ es muy aburrida.

4. En la clase de _______________ española, los estudiantes leen (*read*) *Don Quijote.*
5. ¡Me gustan mucho las computadoras! Voy a tomar (*I'm going to take*) una clase de _______________.
6. Los estudiantes de la clase de _______________ están en el laboratorio para un experimento de gases y líquidos.
7. Madame Crochet, una profesora de lenguas de París, enseña _______________ en la universidad.

❖ **B. ¿Y tú?** Listen to the following questions about your studies. Answer briefly in Spanish. You will hear each question two times.

1. En mi universidad, _______________
2. _______________
3. _______________
4. _______________ es más (*more*) práctica.

C. Al contrario (*On the contrary*). Flor is describing the courses she is taking, but you have an entirely different point of view. Complete each sentence, using the opposite of the word in italics.

MODELO FLOR: La historia es *fácil.* →
TÚ: En mi opinión, la historia es difícil.

FLOR: El diseño es *obligatorio.*
TÚ: ¡Al contrario! El diseño es _______________[1].
FLOR: Las ciencias sociales son *interesantes.*
TÚ: ¡No es verdad! Las ciencias sociales son _______________[2].
FLOR: El cálculo es *inútil.*
TÚ: ¡No tienes razón! El cálculo es _______________[3].
FLOR: La informática es *optativa.*
TÚ: ¡Al contrario! La informática es _______________[4].
FLOR: Las lenguas son *difíciles.*
TÚ: ¡No tienes razón! Las lenguas son _______________[5].

D. Preguntas y respuestas. Choose an appropriate answer from column B for each question in column A.

A

1. _____ ¿Por qué estudias español?
2. _____ ¿Cómo es tu (*your*) universidad?
3. _____ ¿Cuántas horas trabajas por semana?
4. _____ ¿Quién es la profesora de español?
5. _____ ¿Cuál es tu clase favorita?
6. _____ ¿Cómo llegas a la universidad?

B

a. Se llama señora Clinch.
b. Me gusta mucho la clase de diseño.
c. Voy en autobús.
d. Es muy grande y un poco impersonal.
e. Porque es una lengua muy útil.
f. Trabajo quince horas por semana.

E. ¿A qué hora? Write complete sentences stating at what time these classes meet.

MODELO 

Historia de la música →

La clase de historia de la música es a las nueve y media de la mañana.

1. 

Arte precolombino

____

2. 6:00

Introducción a la filosofía

____

3. 

Química orgánica

____

4. 

Arquitectura posmodernista

____

5. 7:30

Psicología adolescente

____

F. El horario de Luz. Explain at what time Luz does the following activities based on her schedule.

Hoy es el _______ de ____________ de 200 ___	
8:00	
9:00	**universidad**
	clase de informática
10:00	
11:00	**clase de diseño**
12:00	**cafetería**
	librería
1:00	
	oficina de profesora Quiñones
2:00	
3:00	**gimnasio**
4:00	**clase de historia de Costa Rica**
5:00	
	laboratorio de lenguas
6:00	
7:00	
8:00	**casa**

MODELO llega a la universidad →
Luz llega a la universidad a las nueve.

1. habla con una profesora

   ____

2. practica deportes

   ____

3. escucha CDs en francés

   ____

4. entra en la clase de informática

   ____

5. dibuja triángulos y rectángulos

____

6. regresa a casa

____

G. Preguntas. Fill in the blank with the correct question word, based on the answer.

MODELO —¿__________ horas trabajas por semana?
—Trabajo diecinueve horas por semana. →
Cuántas

1. —¿__________ estudia Roger?

   —Estudia en su casa.

2. —¿__________ son los estudiantes de la universidad?

   —Son trabajadores y serios.

3. —¿__________ es la profesora de español?

   —La profesora de español es la señora Martínez.

4. —¿__________ son las vacaciones?

   —Son en junio, julio y agosto.

5. —¿__________ es la matrícula (*tuition*) de la universidad?

   —Es $20.000 por año.

6. —¿__________ son tus clases favoritas?

   —Mis clases favoritas son el español y la química.

❖ **H. Más preguntas.** Using words from each column, write four questions that you would like to ask your instructor. Be discreet!

¿a qué hora?	es	su (*your*) autor (*author*) favorito
¿de dónde?	regresa	los exámenes (*exams*)
¿quién?	prepara	deportes
¿cómo?	practica	la clase de español
¿cuál?	llega	su mejor (*best*) friend
¿cuándo?	enseña	a/en la universidad

MODELO ¿Cuándo llega usted a la universidad?

1. ____
2. ____
3. ____
4. ____

Entrevista 1

A. Sonido y significado

Paso 1: Sonido. The sentences in this activity are based on the interview with Silvana Quesada Nieto. First, read each sentence silently and make sure you understand its meaning. Then, listen as the speaker pronounces each sentence in phrases. Repeat the phrase in the interval provided until you can say it smoothly. **¡OJO!** You can pause the audio program if you need more time to practice each sentence.

Silvana Quesada Nieto
San José, Costa Rica

1. La universidad está dividida (*divided*) en facultades.
2. Para el bachillerato (*undergraduate degree*), los estudiantes estudian aproximadamente cuatro años.
3. Los estudiantes están obligados (*required*) a llevar estudios generales: ciencias, letras y un idioma (*language*).
4. Hay tres períodos de clases: el primero (*first*) de siete a doce del día, el segundo en la tarde y el nocturno de siete a nueve.

Paso 2: Significado. Indicate which of the following sentences is *not* true, based on the sentences in **Paso 1.**

a. □ Silvana trabaja en una escuela en San José.
b. □ Para los estudiantes costarricenses, es posible estudiar de la mañana a la noche.
c. □ En Costa Rica, los estudiantes universitarios llevan clases que no son de su carrera.

B. Respuestas lógicas. First, read the questions and divided responses from the interview with Silvana. Then, listen to the interview and match the first and last part of her responses.

PREGUNTAS Y RESPUESTAS PARTE 1

1. ¿De dónde es usted?

   «Yo soy tica o costarricense, y trabajo _____.»

2. ¿Es grande la universidad?

   «La universidad tiene aproximadamente 15.000 estudiantes y está dividida en facultades: _____.»

3. ¿Cuántos años estudian los costarricenses en la universidad?

   «Bueno, depende del estudiante. Para el bachillerato aproximadamente _____.»

4. ¿Cuántos cursos llevan los estudiantes?

   «Generalmente llevan seis cursos _____.»

5. ¿Hay clases obligatorias?

   «Algo importante es que los estudiantes están obligados a llevar estudios generales que consisten en _____.»

6. ¿Cuándo son las clases?

   «Hay tres períodos de clases: el primero en la mañana de siete a doce del día, el segundo en la tarde de una a seis _____.»

RESPUESTAS PARTE 2

a. cuatro años, para la licenciatura, cinco o seis años, depende del estudiante
b. una materia de ciencias, una de letras y una de idioma, y éste (*this*) es un requisito para todos los estudiantes
c. la Facultad de Educación, la Facultad de Ciencias y Letras, la Facultad de Filosofía, entre otras
d. en la Universidad Nacional de Heredia
e. y cada curso puede ser de tres a cuatro horas por semana
f. y el nocturno que es de siete a nueve o un poquito más

C. ¿Entendiste? Answer the following questions in complete sentences, based on the interview with Silvana.

1. ¿Dónde trabaja Silvana?

   ____

2. ¿Cuántos años es el bachillerato en Costa Rica?

   ____

3. En general, ¿cuántos cursos llevan los estudiantes costarricenses?

   ____

4. ¿Qué clases obligatorias llevan los estudiantes en Costa Rica?

   ____

5. ¿Cuántos períodos de estudio hay en el sistema costarricense?

   ____

❖ **D. Preguntas para ti.** You will hear three questions. Write down your personal answers.

1. ______________________________
2. ______________________________
3. ______________________________

Forma y función

2.1 Regular -ar Verbs; Negation

Clínica de gramática

Spanish verbs have a distinctive set of personal endings for each of the three verb conjugations (verbs whose infinitives end in **-ar**, **-er**, or **-ir**). These endings let you know who or what the subject of the sentence is even when the subject is not stated explicitly. The endings are attached to the stem of the verb. Here are the present tense endings for the verb **usar** (*to use*).

usar: STEM **us-**

(yo)	uso	(nosotros/as)	us**amos**
(tú)	us**as**	(vosotros/as)	us**áis**
(usted, él/ella)	us**a**	(ustedes, ellos/as)	us**an**

Práctica. Complete the following table with the correct forms of the verbs indicated.

	yo	tú	usted, él/ella	nosotros/as	vosotros/as	ustedes, ellos/as
1. trabajar						
2. hablar					*habláis*	
3. escuchar						
4. practicar			*practica*			
5. estudiar						
6. enseñar						
7. llegar						*llegan*

A. ¿Estudiante o profesor(a)?

Paso 1. You will hear some people describe what they do related to the university. Indicate whether a statement relates more to a typical student **(estudiante)** or instructor **(profesor[a]).**

1. ☐ estudiante ☐ profesor(a)
2. ☐ estudiante ☐ profesor(a)
3. ☐ estudiante ☐ profesor(a)
4. ☐ estudiante ☐ profesor(a)
5. ☐ estudiante ☐ profesor(a)
6. ☐ estudiante ☐ profesor(a)

Paso 2. Listen to the statements from **Paso 1** again and write down the *infinitive* of the verb you hear in each sentence.

1. ______ 4. ______
2. ______ 5. ______
3. ______ 6. ______

B. Una mañana típica. Complete Rolando's monologue with the correct form of each verb in parentheses to find out how Rolando and his wife, Emilia, typically spend their mornings.

«Mi esposa (*wife*) Emilia y yo (enseñar) ________________[1] en la universidad. Yo (enseñar) ________________[2] literatura y Emilia (enseñar) ________________[3] ciencias políticas. A las seis de la mañana, yo (preparar) ________________[4] el café para los dos. Emilia (escuchar) ________________[5] las noticias (*news*) y yo (estudiar) ________________[6] las lecciones de mis clases. Normalmente, (hablar: nosotros) ________________[7] de nuestros (*our*) planes para el día. Yo (llegar) ________________[8] a la universidad a las siete y media y (entrar) ________________[9] en mi primera clase a las ocho. Emilia y sus (*her*) estudiantes (participar) ________________[10] en un grupo político por la mañana. Los estudiantes (usar) ________________[11] el tiempo (*time*) para estudiar y expresar ideas políticas. Emilia no (entrar) ________________[12] en clase hasta (*until*) las once.»

C. La vida de dos estudiantes. Complete each sentence with the correct form of the verb in parentheses.

1. Rodrigo y su novia ________________ (estar) despiertos (*awake*) a las siete de la mañana.
2. Ella ________________ (preparar) el café y, a las ocho de la mañana, los dos ________________ (tomar) el desayuno juntos (*together*).
3. Mientras (*While*) Rodrigo ________________ (escuchar) música, su novia ________________ (practicar) yoga.
4. Rodrigo y su novia ________________ (llevar) tres cursos.
5. Rodrigo ________________ (estudiar) español y su novia medicina. ¡Son muy buenos estudiantes!

D. Las clases. Complete the following conversation between Eduardo and Marta with the correct form of the verb in parentheses.

MARTA: Eduardo, ¿(llevar: tú) ________________[1] cinco clases este semestre?

EDUARDO: No, Marta. Este semestre (llevar: yo) ________________[2] cuatro clases, pero (trabajar: yo) ________________[3] veinte horas por semana.

MARTA: Ah, ¿sí? ¿(Trabajar: Tú) ________________[4] en la biblioteca?

EDUARDO: Sí.

MARTA: ¿A qué hora (llegar: tú) ________________[5] a la biblioteca?

EDUARDO: (Llegar: Yo) ________________[6] a las tres de la tarde. (Regresar: Yo) ________________[7] a la residencia a las siete y media. ¿Y tú? ¿(Llevar) ________________[8] muchas clases?

MARTA: Sí, (llevar) ________________[9] seis clases. ¡(Estudiar: Yo) ________________[10] mucho! Pero me gustan mis clases. Son interesantes.

EDUARDO: ¡Ay! ¡Casi son las tres (*It's almost three*)! (Hablar: Nosotros) ________________[11] pronto. ¡Hasta luego!

MARTA: Adiós, Eduardo.

E. ¡No! Jacobo can't seem to get it right when he asks his new classmate, Alicia, the following questions. She always answers **no.** Write out her answers to Jacobo's questions. First, negate the information from the question, then correct it using the information in parentheses.

MODELO JACOBO: Alicia, ¿escuchas música rock?
ALICIA: (salsa) →
No, no escucho música rock. Escucho salsa.

JACOBO: ¿Estudias biología?
ALICIA: (psicología y francés) ______
______

JACOBO: ¿Practicas francés en el laboratorio?
ALICIA: (con amigos franceses) ______
______

JACOBO: ¿Hablas francés con tus amigos en la residencia?
ALICIA: (en la cafetería) ______
______

JACOBO: ¿Llevas muchas clases?
ALICIA: (tres clases) ______
______

JACOBO: ¿Trabajas en la librería?
ALICIA: (en la biblioteca) ______
______

JACOBO: ¿Regresas a la residencia estudiantil a las nueve?
ALICIA: (a las diez) ______
______

❖ **F. Un día típico.** Write four sentences that describe a typical day for you, for a friend of yours, and/or for you and your friend. Use verbs from the following list.

entrar, escuchar, estudiar, hablar, llegar, llevar, practicar, regresar, trabajar

MODELOS Mi amigo y yo llegamos a la universidad a las ocho de la mañana.
Yo llego a la universidad a las ocho, pero mi amigo llega a las nueve.

1. ______
2. ______
3. ______
4. ______

2.2 Question Formation

Clínica de gramática

Information questions in Spanish begin with an inverted question mark and a question word, which always carries a written accent mark. Make sure you know the meanings of the following interrogatives.

¿Cómo?	¿Dónde?	¿Quién(es)?
¿Cuál(es)?	¿Qué?	¿A qué hora?
¿Cuánto/a(s)?		

Preguntas. Complete the following table with the interrogative word or phrase you would use to find out each type of information.

1. location	*¿Dónde?*
2. time	
3. quantity	
4. a person	
5. a definition	
6. which one of a set	
7. in what manner	

A. ¿Qué preguntan?

Paso 1. Listen to each question, then write the letter that corresponds to the information requested in the question.

MODELO ¿Dónde está la librería? →
b. (a location)

1. _____
2. _____
3. _____
4. _____
5. _____
6. _____
7. _____

a. a time
b. a location
c. a quantity
d. a person
e. what
f. which one
g. characteristics/qualities

Paso 2. Read the following statements. Then listen to each question from **Paso 1** again and write the letter that corresponds to the appropriate answer.

MODELO ¿Dónde está la librería? →
h. Está al lado de la Facultad de Ciencias.

1. ____
2. ____
3. ____
4. ____
5. ____
6. ____
7. ____
8. ____

a. Trabajo en la cafetería.
b. Es alto y simpático.
c. Es la clase de español.
d. Es Juanita.
e. Estudio arquitectura.
f. Es a las 9:00.
g. Llevo cuatro clases.
h. Está al lado de la Facultad de Ciencias.

B. La pregunta es... Read each of the following responses, then write a question that requests the italicized information. Use question words from the list.

cómo, cuál(es), cuándo, cuánto/a(s), dónde, qué, quién(es)

MODELO Los estudiantes usan *cuatro* libros en la clase de biología. →
¿Cuántos libros usan los estudiantes en la clase de biología?

1. Los estudiantes usan las computadoras *por la noche.*

 ____

2. *Elisa y Gustavo* practican alemán en el laboratorio de lenguas.

 ____

3. Llevo *cinco* clases este semestre.

 ____

4. *Estoy bien,* gracias.

 ____

5. Nola estudia en *la biblioteca.*

 ____

6. La profesora Quintero enseña *matemáticas.*

 ____

C. Preguntas revueltas. Unscramble and rewrite the following questions so that they make sense. **¡OJO!** Add any necessary punctuation and accent marks.

1. a la residencia / regresas / cuando

 ____

2. lleváis / cuantas / clases

 ____

3. los estudiantes / están / como

 ____

4. quienes / Ricky Martin y Gloria Estefan / son

 ____

5. trabaja / donde / Lorena

____

6. son / las clases / cuales / obligatorias

____

❖ **D. Entrevista.** Imagine that you work for the campus newspaper and have been assigned to interview a typical student. Make a list of at least five possible questions about what the student does on a normal day. Use question words you have learned and verbs from the list.

escuchar, estudiar, llegar, llevar, participar, practicar, regresar, trabajar

MODELO ¿Cuántas clases llevas?

1. ______________________________
2. ______________________________
3. ______________________________
4. ______________________________
5. ______________________________

Pronunciación y ortografía

Intonation in Questions; Spelling Conventions in Questions

Read and study the information in your textbook before you complete the following activities.

A. ¡Repitan, por favor! Listen to each of the following statements and questions. Then repeat, trying to imitate the intonation of the native speaker.

1. Rosa, ¿dónde estudias generalmente?
2. En Costa Rica hay muchas oportunidades para estudiar.
3. ¿Cuánto es la matrícula en tu universidad?
4. ¿Dónde está la cafetería?
5. Los estudiantes costarricenses trabajan mucho.
6. Por la noche estudiamos en la biblioteca.

B. ¿Preguntas? Listen to each sentence, then indicate whether you hear a statement **(afirmación)** or a question **(pregunta).** You will hear the answers on the audio program.

1. ☐ afirmación ☐ pregunta
2. ☐ afirmación ☐ pregunta
3. ☐ afirmación ☐ pregunta
4. ☐ afirmación ☐ pregunta
5. ☐ afirmación ☐ pregunta

C. Correcciones. Edit the following questions to include the proper punctuation and accent marks.

MODELOS Que libros usas →
¿Qué libros usas?
Es a las ocho la clase →
¿Es a las ocho la clase?

1. Donde trabajas

____

2. Es muy grande la universidad

____

3. Cuantas clases llevas

____

4. Hay muchas clases obligatorias

____

5. Quien trabaja en un restaurante

____

Vocabulario

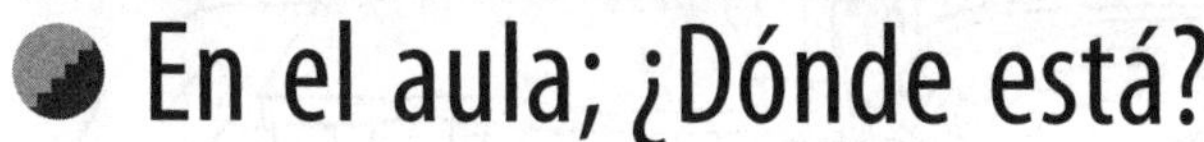

En el aula; ¿Dónde está?

A. ¿Qué hay en el aula?

Paso 1. Fill in the blanks with the name of the objects indicated in the drawing. **¡OJO!** Remember to include the definite article **(el/la/los/las).**

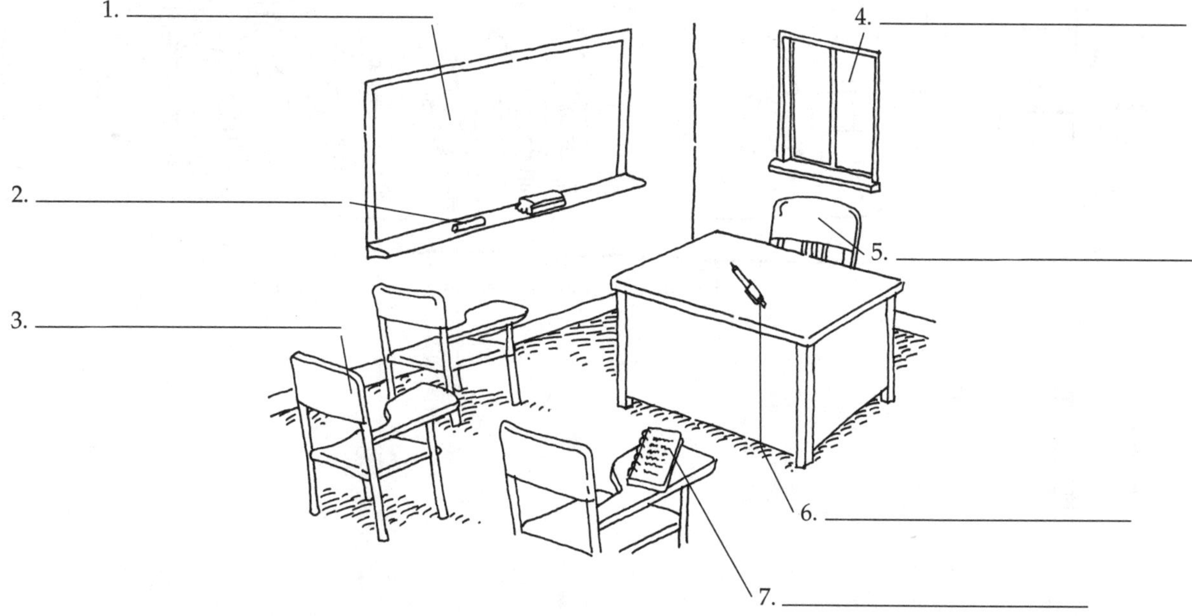

Paso 2. Listen to each of the following statements, then indicate whether it is true **(cierto)** or false **(falso),** based on the drawing in **Paso 1.** You will hear the answers on the audio program.

	CIERTO	FALSO
1.	☐	☐
2.	☐	☐
3.	☐	☐
4.	☐	☐
5.	☐	☐
6.	☐	☐

B. La respuesta lógica. Listen to each question, then check the most logical answer. You will hear the correct answers on the audio program.

MODELO (*you hear*) ¿Cuántos estudiantes hay en el aula?
(*you read*) ☐ una pizarra y quince pupitres ☐ dieciséis
(*you mark*) dieciséis

1. ☐ un libro y unos cuadernos ☐ el pupitre y la silla
2. ☐ en el cuaderno ☐ en la pizarra
3. ☐ a la profesora ☐ el bolígrafo y el lápiz
4. ☐ Hay dos tizas. ☐ No hay.
5. ☐ el estudiante ☐ el pupitre

C. ¿Dónde está?

Paso 1. Study the following drawing. Then listen to each statement and indicate whether it is true **(cierto)** or false **(falso)** based on the drawing.

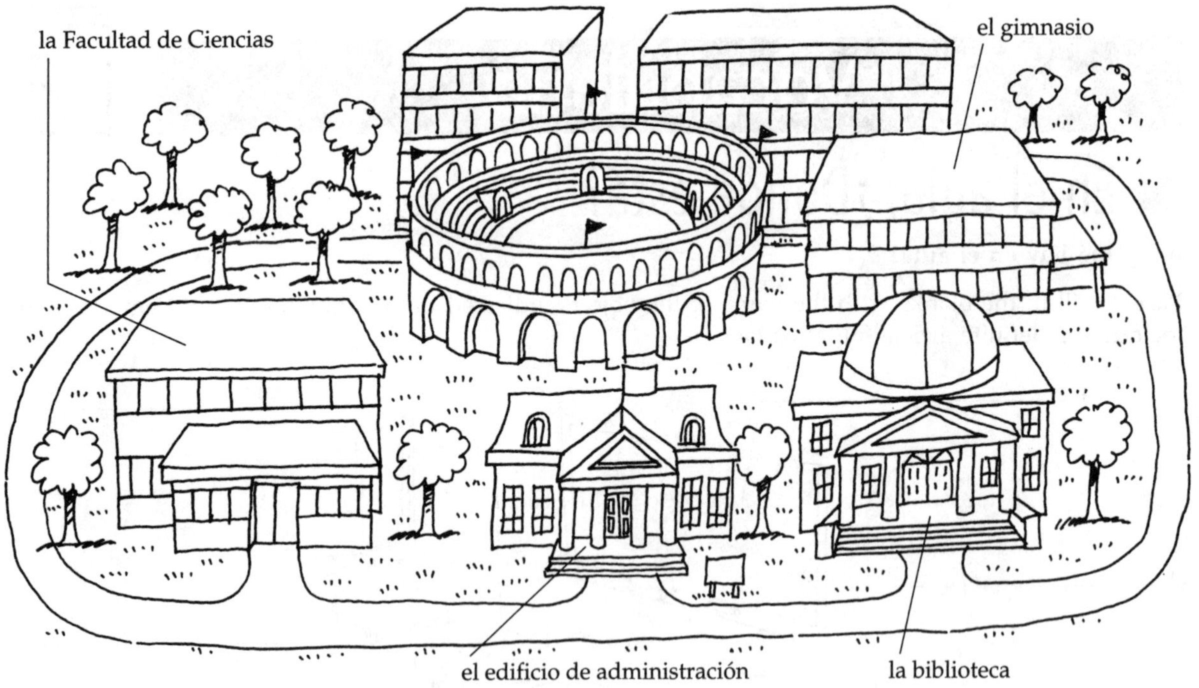

	CIERTO	FALSO
1.	☐	☐
2.	☐	☐
3.	☐	☐
4.	☐	☐
5.	☐	☐

Paso 2. Now listen to the sentences again in order to correct the false statements. Write each corrected statement on the blank lines given. You can listen more than once if you like.

1. ______________________________
2. ______________________________
3. ______________________________
4. ______________________________
5. ______________________________

D. ¿Qué lugar (*place*) es? Match the descriptions in column A with the building in column B.

A

1. _____ Hay libros, bolígrafos y otros objetos para la venta (*for sale*).
2. _____ Hay partidos de fútbol en este lugar.
3. _____ Hay cursos de química en este edificio.
4. _____ Hay cursos de literatura en este edificio.
5. _____ La oficina del presidente de la universidad está en ese (*this*) edificio.
6. _____ Es necesario guardar silencio en este lugar.

B

a. la biblioteca
b. la Facultad de Letras
c. el edificio de administración
d. el estadio
e. la librería
f. la Facultad de Ciencias

Entrevista 2

A. Sonido y significado

Paso 1: Sonido. The sentences in this activity are based on ideas from the interview with Érika Claré Jiménez. First, read each sentence silently and make sure you understand its meaning. Then, listen as the speaker pronounces each sentence in phrases. Repeat the phrase in the interval provided until you can say it smoothly. **¡OJO!** You can pause the audio program if you need more time to practice each sentence.

Érika Claré Jiménez
San José, Costa Rica

1. Si trabajás,* necesitás* un horario flexible. Tomás* dos clases al día, dos horas cada (*each*) clase.
2. No existen residencias dentro de la universidad, pero hay personas que alquilan cuartos (*rent rooms*) a estudiantes.
3. Los estudiantes comen (*eat*) en pulperías, que son puestos de comida (*food stands*).
4. Si alquilás* un cuarto, la comida está incluida.
5. En el tiempo libre, vamos a la playa, vamos a cafés a chismear (*gossip*) y tomamos un traguito (*drink*) con los amigos.

*Verb forms marked with an asterisk in this **Entrevista** section correspond to the subject pronoun **vos,** which is used in Costa Rica and elsewhere instead of **tú.** See your textbook for more information.

Paso 2: Significado. Indicate which of the following sentences is *not* true, based on the information in **Paso 1.**

a. ☐ Los estudiantes costarricenses toman cuatro horas de clases cada día.
b. ☐ Los estudiantes comen en cafeterías en la universidad.
c. ☐ Hay muchas actividades para el tiempo libre.

B. Respuestas lógicas. First, read the questions and divided responses from the interview with Érika. Then, listen to the interview and match the first and last part of her responses.

PREGUNTAS Y RESPUESTAS PARTE 1

1. ¿Dónde estudias?

   «Yo estudio _____.»

2. ¿Trabajas y estudias?

   «Bueno, depende mucho de la persona. Si trabajás,* necesitás* un horario flexible… y _____.»

3. ¿Dónde viven (*live*) los estudiantes?

   «No existen residencias en la universidad, _____.»

4. ¿Dónde comen los estudiantes?

   «Hay varias opciones: Existen las pulperías, que son puestos de comida, también restaurantes que son específicos para los estudiantes, _____.»

5. ¿Y qué hacen en el tiempo libre?

   «Hay muchas cosas… Vamos a la playa, que queda a como hora y media, vamos a cafés a chismear con los amigos, _____.»

RESPUESTAS PARTE 2

a. y si sos* (eres) un estudiante que alquila un cuarto, entonces por lo general la comida está incluida
b. por ejemplo tomás* dos clases al día, lo cual quiere decir (*which means*) dos horas cada clase, es un total de cuatro horas
c. y también existen muchos bares para tomarnos un traguito. Y también existen conciertos de todo tipo
d. pero existen personas que alquilan cuartos a estudiantes o también viven con sus padres
e. en la Universidad de Costa Rica

C. ¿Entendiste? Answer the following questions in complete sentences, based on the interview with Érika.

1. ¿En qué universidad estudia Érika?

   ____

2. Según Érika, ¿dónde viven muchos estudiantes?

   ____

3. ¿Dónde comen muchos estudiantes?

   ____

4. ¿Qué actividades son populares entre (*among*) los estudiantes costarricenses?

   ____

❖ **D. Preguntas para ti.** You will hear three questions. Write down your personal answers.

1. ____
2. ____
3. ____

Forma y función

2.3 The Verb **ir; ir a** + Infinitive

Clínica de gramática

Here are the present tense forms of the irregular verb **ir** (*to go*).

ir			
(yo)	**voy**	(nosotros/as)	**vamos**
(tú)	**vas**	(vosotros/as)	**vais**
(usted, él/ella)	**va**	(ustedes, ellos/as)	**van**

Mañana. Complete each sentence with the correct form of the verb **ir** to tell what you and/or your roommate **(compañero/a de cuarto)** are going to do tomorrow.

Mañana…

1. yo ______________ a trabajar a las seis de la mañana.
2. mi compañero/a de cuarto ______________ a estudiar con un amigo.
3. nosotros ______________ a cenar juntos a las siete de la tarde.
4. yo ______________ a mirar la televisión después de cenar.
5. mi compañero/a de cuarto ______________ a hablar por teléfono con su mamá.
6. más tarde, nosotros ______________ al cine con algunos amigos.

A. La vida estudiantil. Read the following statements. Then listen to each question and choose the corresponding statement. You will hear the answers on the audio program.

1. ____
2. ____
3. ____
4. ____
5. ____
6. ____

a. Va al edificio de administración.
b. Van seis estudiantes.
c. Van a mirar un video.
d. Voy a las nueve de la mañana.
e. No, solamente vamos a llevar tres.
f. Vamos a estudiar en la cafetería.

B. Nuestros planes. Complete Felipe's monologue with the correct forms of the verb **ir** to find out where he and his roommate are going tomorrow.

«Mi amigo Esteban y yo tenemos (*have*) muy poco tiempo libre (*very little free time*) mañana. Yo ________________[1] a clase a las ocho mañana y Esteban ________________[2] a trabajar a las ocho y media. Nosotros ________________[3] a la biblioteca a las once para estudiar. Yo ________________[4] a preparar un proyecto (*project*) para la clase de historia y Esteban y Pedro, otro (*another*) amigo, ________________[5] a estudiar para un examen de química. A las seis, nosotros ________________[6] a la cafetería. Después (*Later*), yo ________________[7] a trabajar en la oficina de la residencia estudiantil y Esteban y Pedro ________________[8] a regresar a la biblioteca.»

C. ¿Adónde vamos? Listen to the following statements, then indicate whether the action typically takes place on campus **(en la universidad)** or off campus **(fuera de la universidad).** You will hear the answers on the audio program.

	EN LA UNIVERSIDAD	FUERA DE LA UNIVERSIDAD
1.	☐	☐
2.	☐	☐
3.	☐	☐
4.	☐	☐
5.	☐	☐
6.	☐	☐

D. Vamos a... Form sentences using the following information. Use **ir a** + *infinitive* in each sentence to express what the subject is going to do.

MODELO Juanita / estudiar / la residencia →
Juanita va a estudiar en la residencia.

1. Leonardo / trabajar / las tres de la tarde

____

2. María y Dolores / ir / clase / las nueve de la mañana

____

3. vosotros / llegar / a la residencia / las dos de la tarde

____

4. yo / usar / la computadora / por la tarde

____

5. tú / escuchar / música / por la noche

____

6. nosotros / hablar / con la profesora / la una

____

E. ¿Adónde vas? Answer each question to explain where you and/or someone else might go to do the activity indicated.

MODELOS ¿Adónde vas para comprar (*to buy*) libros? →
Voy a la librería.
¿Adónde van ustedes para comprar libros? →
Vamos a la librería.

1. ¿Adónde van ustedes para practicar la pronunciación del español?
   ______
2. ¿Adónde vas para estudiar para los exámenes?
   ______
3. ¿Adónde van ustedes para escuchar música?
   ______
4. ¿Adónde va el profesor / la profesora para preparar las lecciones?
   ______
5. ¿Adónde van los estudiantes para hablar con el profesor / la profesora?
   ______
6. ¿Adónde va la clase de química para hacer experimentos?
   ______

❖ **F. El lunes próximo (*Next Monday*)**

Paso 1. On a separate sheet of paper, make a chronological list of at least five activities that you plan on doing next Monday. Include the corresponding time of day. **¡OJO!** When making a list of planned activities, you should use the infinitive of the verb.

VOCABULARIO ÚTIL

cenar	practicar deportes
comer en la cafetería	hacer la tarea (*to do homework*)
estudiar	trabajar
ir a ______	¿ ?

MODELO 8:00 A.M. ir a la universidad
8:30 A.M. estudiar en la biblioteca
11:30 P.M. comer en la cafetería con una amiga
1:00 P.M. trabajar
5:00 P.M. regresar a casa

Paso 2. Now write out your answer to the question: **¿Qué vas a hacer el lunes próximo?**

MODELO El lunes próximo, voy a ir a la universidad a las ocho. A las ocho y media, voy a estudiar en la biblioteca. A las once y media,...

____

____

____

____

____

2.4 The Verb **estar**

Clínica de gramática

Here are the present tense forms of the verb **estar. Estar** is often translated into English as *to be* and is used to express location **(*estoy en la universidad*)** and health **(*estoy bien*).**

	estar		
(yo)	**estoy**	(nosotros/as)	**estamos**
(tú)	**estás**	(vosotros/as)	**estáis**
(usted, él/ella)	**está**	(ustedes, ellos/as)	**están**

¿Dónde están estas personas? Complete each sentence with the correct form of the verb **estar** and a logical phrase to tell where these people are.

MODELO Los profesores →

Los profesores están en su oficina.

1. La biblioteca ______________________________.
2. Yo ______________________________.
3. El bolígrafo ______________________________.
4. Tú ______________________________.
5. Mis amigos ______________________________.
6. Luisa y yo ______________________________.
7. Ustedes ______________________________.
8. Juan y José ______________________________.

A. ¡A escuchar! Listen to each statement, then check whether the speaker is referring to the health **(salud)** or location **(lugar)** of someone or something. You will hear the answers on the audio program.

	SALUD	LUGAR
1.	☐	☐
2.	☐	☐
3.	☐	☐
4.	☐	☐
5.	☐	☐
6.	☐	☐

B. ¿Dónde están? Complete each sentence with the correct form of the verb **estar.**

1. Mis amigos ______________ en la cafetería.
2. Yo ______________ en clase ahora.
3. Nosotros ______________ cerca de la Facultad de Letras.
4. Tú ______________ en el laboratorio de lenguas.
5. María ______________ en la biblioteca.
6. Ustedes ______________ en la librería.

C. ¿Cómo están hoy? Complete each sentence with the correct form of the verb **estar** to describe how the following people are feeling today.

Hoy…

1. mi mejor amiga ______________ enferma (*ill*).
2. mis compañeros de clase ______________ nerviosos.
3. nosotros ______________ cansados (*tired*).
4. tú ______________ muy relajada.
5. yo ______________ descansado (*rested*).
6. ustedes ______________ deprimidos (*depressed*).

❖ **D. A las ocho…** Write five sentences using **estar** to explain where different people you know, including yourself, are at different times of the day. Use the following expressions of time. **¡OJO!** Note the use of **de** and **por** in the following expressions.

a la(s) (+ *time*) **de** la mañana/tarde/noche (*specific time*)
por la mañana/tarde/noche (*general time*)

MODELOS Yo estoy en clase a las nueve de la mañana.
El profesor está en casa por la noche.

1. ____
2. ____
3. ____
4. ____
5. ____

❖ Análisis cultural

The following quotes come from travel guides in print and on the Internet. Both concern Costa Rican attitudes toward education. Use this information and what you have learned in this chapter about Costa Rica to answer the questions that follow the quotes.

"Education and public health are high-priority items in Costa Rica. As a result, the literacy rate is quite high, and infectious diseases have been largely eradicated in even the most rural parts of the country. Costa Rica has no army, but does maintain a small national guard unit. Expenditures for national security amount to only 2.6 percent of the national budget, one-tenth of what is spent by the central government on education."

Source: *www.incostarica.net/docs/people*

"A progressive people, **Ticos** revere education. 'We have more teachers than soldiers' is a common boast, and framed school diplomas hang in even the most humble homes."

Source: *Costa Rica Handbook*

1. What types of educational institutions have you seen described in this chapter?

____

____

2. What aspects of the Costa Rican government demonstrate that education is a high-priority item in Costa Rica? How are these aspects similar or different from policies in your country?

____

____

3. Why do you think the attitude of families and individuals toward education makes a difference in the literacy rate of a country? How is Costa Rica an example of this?

____

____

4. What is your impression of the system of higher education in Costa Rica?

____

____

5. How important is the issue of education in your country? Do you think it should receive more/less investment and attention?

____

____

❖PORTAFOLIO CULTURAL

Redacción: Un mensaje a Costa Rica

A. Antes de escribir. For this chapter, you will compose a letter or e-mail message to students of the Universidad Nacional de Costa Rica (UNa) describing your university. Your description should include aspects of your campus, course offerings, and student life. When possible, compare your university to UNa. You may wish to post your message on a class website or begin an electronic exchange with students from UNa.

Paso 1. The best writers always plan their compositions before writing. To begin, prepare most of the ideas and vocabulary you will need to describe your university. Do this before you begin writing to avoid excessive use of your Spanish-English dictionary as you write. The lists you make now will serve as your dictionary when you write.

On a separate sheet of paper, make a list of categories you will describe, keeping your audience in mind. What will UNa students who have never been to this country like to know? Under each category heading, jot down nouns, adjectives, and other expressions you might use. Here are some possible categories and words to get you started.

universidad: campus, edificios, nacional, estatal (*state*), privado, público, grande, pequeño
cursos: biología, lenguas (etcétera), difícil, fácil
horario: por la mañana/tarde/noche
estudiantes: número de (etcétera)

Paso 2. Use the categories you have developed to compare your university and UNa. On a separate sheet of paper, create a comparison table with columns for **mi universidad** and UNa.

Paso 3. Use the table you created in **Paso 2** to form complete sentences that describe, compare, and contrast the two universities.

MODELOS Mi universidad es parecida a la UNa porque hay como quince mil (*thousand*) estudiantes en las dos.

Mi universidad es diferente de la UNa porque hay treinta mil estudiantes en mi universidad.

Paso 4. Write down the greeting, introduction, and closing you might use in your message. Remember that e-mail messages can be less formal than letters.

MODELOS (*greeting*) Querido amigo: / Querida amiga: (*letter*) / Hola: (*e-mail*)
(*introduction*) Me llamo… y soy estudiante de…
(*closing*) Cordialmente (*Cordially*), (*letter*) / Hasta pronto, (*e-mail*)

B. ¡A escribir! Now organize and modify your sentences to form two short paragraphs. In the first paragraph, describe your university. In the second, compare it to the UNa. You may also add a third paragraph in which you ask questions about UNa and student life there. Add your greeting, introduction, and conclusion.

C. ¡A corregir! Before you turn in or send your message, check the following points.

☐ Adjective/noun agreement (gender and number)
☐ Subject/verb agreement
☐ Punctuation and accents for questions

WWW Exploración

Choose and complete *one* of the following research activities. Then, based on your instructor's directions, present your results to the class and/or create a short report to include in your portfolio.

1. Visit two university websites from Costa Rica. Look for information about each university. Where are the universities located? How many students attend each? What fields of study are available? Are there any classes available for foreign students wishing to learn Spanish? Which would you prefer to attend if you were given the opportunity? Why? Create a profile of each university with visuals, such as campus photos, charts, and so on, from the websites. Make comparisons between the two universities and your own.
2. Locate a student on campus or in your community who is from Costa Rica or another Spanish-speaking country. Interview the student, asking him/her to compare the educational experiences in this country with experiences in his/her country of origin. Which system offers more options for study? Which is more rigorous? Which is more costly?
3. Choose two other countries in the Spanish-speaking world. Use the Internet, encyclopedias, almanacs, and other print resources to compare the educational systems of those two countries with that of the one in Costa Rica. How are they similar or different in structure? How do the literacy rates compare? Can you find any historical or political factors to explain differences in literacy rates?
4. Find more information in your library or on the Internet about Costa Rica. Here are some ideas and key words to get you started:

    - biodiversity and national parks in Costa Rica
    - ecotourism in Costa Rica
    - volcanos: Turrialba, Arenal, Irazú, Poás, Rincón de la Vieja, Miravalles
    - remnants of Costa Rica's indigenous population: the Bribri, Cabecar, and others
    - the role of women in Costa Rican history, government, and/or society

CAPÍTULO

3

Repaso y anticipación

A. Una estudiante internacional en Ecuador

Paso 1. An international exchange student in Ecuador introduces herself to other classmates. Complete her introduction with the appropriate form of each verb in parentheses.

«¡Hola! Yo (ser) ____________[1] Chris. Mi familia (ser) ____________[2] de Irlanda, pero yo (ser) ____________[3] estadounidense. Yo (estudiar) ____________[4] español en Ecuador y (ir) ____________[5] a llevar tres clases. Mi amiga y yo también (ir) ____________[6] a hacer excursiones (*to take trips/tours*) por Ecuador. Mi familia (estar) ____________[7] en Ecuador esta semana, pero mis padres (regresar) ____________[8] a los Estados Unidos el domingo.»

Paso 2. Chris's friends are eager to learn more about her, so they ask many questions. Complete their questions with the appropriate interrogative words from the list.

¿Cómo?, ¿Cuál(es)?, ¿Cuándo?, ¿Cuánto/a(s)?, ¿Dónde?, ¿Qué?, ¿Quién(es)?

1. ¿____________ está tu familia?
2. ¿____________ es tu clase favorita?
3. ¿____________ carrera estudias?
4. ¿____________ regresas a tu país (*country*)?
5. ¿____________ es tu profesor(a) de español en Ecuador?

❖ **B. Las actividades**

Paso 1. Indicate which of the following activities you do alone **(solo/a),** which you engage in with your family or friends **(con la familia o amigos/as),** and which do not apply to you (NA).

	SOLO/A	CON LA FAMILIA O AMIGOS/AS	NA
1. usar la computadora	☐	☐	☐
2. estudiar	☐	☐	☐
3. escuchar música	☐	☐	☐
4. hablar	☐	☐	☐
5. regresar a casa	☐	☐	☐
6. trabajar	☐	☐	☐
7. practicar el español	☐	☐	☐
8. enseñar	☐	☐	☐

Paso 2. Now complete the following sentences based on your answers in **Paso 1.** You may include more than one activity per sentence.

1. Yo ______________________________ solo/a.
2. Mis amigos/as y yo ______________________________ juntos (*together*).
3. Mi familia ______________________________ juntos.
4. Yo no ______________________________.

❖ **C. Los planes.** Write sentences to describe three things you and/or other people plan to do this week. Use the **ir a** + infinitive structure in each sentence.

MODELO (*someone else and you*) →
Por la tarde, la profesora y yo vamos a hablar en la cafetería.

1. (*you*) ______________________________
2. (*someone else and you*) ______________________________
3. (*someone else*) ______________________________

PARTE 1

Vocabulario

La familia y los parientes; Los números y la edad

A. La familia

Paso 1. Write the name of the family member described. **¡OJO!** Be sure to use the correct gender.

MODELO el hijo de mi hermana → mi sobrino

1. la madre de mi padre ______________________________
2. el hijo de mi madre ______________________________
3. el esposo de mi hermana ______________________________
4. la hermana de mi padre ______________________________

Paso 2. Now write your own definitions for family members using the items in **Paso 1** as models.

1. mi primo
____
2. mi sobrina
____
3. mi abuelo
____
4. mis nietos
____

5. mi tío

____

6. mi cuñada

____

B. La familia de Victoria. Read the following statements. Then listen to the description of Victoria's family. Check off whether each statement is true **(cierto)** or false **(falso)**. You will hear the answers on the audio program.

VOCABULARIO ÚTIL

solamente	*only*	tiene	*he/she has*
ninguno	*none*	así que	*such that*
todos	*all*	tengo	*I have*

	CIERTO	FALSO
1. Hay cuatro personas en la familia de Victoria.	☐	☐
2. El hermano de Victoria está casado.	☐	☐
3. Victoria tiene cinco tíos y una tía.	☐	☐
4. Los tíos de Victoria tienen (*have*) hijos pequeños.	☐	☐
5. Victoria solamente tiene una prima.	☐	☐

C. ¿Cuántos años?

Paso 1. Listen to Ignacio describe his family. As you listen, match each person with the appropriate age. You can listen more than once if you like.

1. _____ Ignacio
2. _____ el padre de Ignacio
3. _____ la madre de Ignacio
4. _____ el abuelo de Ignacio
5. _____ Margarita

a. 59
b. 71
c. 65
d. 21
e. 92

Paso 2. Spell out the numbers from **Paso 1.**

1. Ignacio tiene _______________________ años.
2. El padre de Ignacio tiene _______________________ años.
3. La madre de Ignacio tiene _______________________ años.
4. El abuelo de Ignacio tiene _______________________ años.
5. Margarita tiene _______________________ años.

❖ **Paso 3.** Now write down the names and ages of five family members or people you know. Spell out the numbers.

1. ____
2. ____
3. ____
4. ____
5. ____

D. Un poco sobre Ecuador. Here are some facts about Ecuador. Spell out the numbers that appear in parentheses.

MODELO El ____________________ (25) por ciento de la población ecuatoriana es de origen indígena. →
El veinticinco por ciento de la población es de origen indígena.

1. ______________________________ (100) centavos ecuatorianos = 1 dólar.*
2. La temperatura media en enero es de ______________________________ (15) grados centígrados.
3. El ______________________________ (50) por ciento de la población trabaja en el sector agrícola.
4. El ______________________________ (94) por ciento de la población es católica.
5. Hay ______________________________ (21) provincias en Ecuador.

Entrevista 1

A. Sonido y significado

Paso 1: Sonido. The sentences in this activity are based on the interview with Cynthia Cevallos Mendoza. First, read each sentence silently and make sure you understand its meaning. Then, listen as the speaker pronounces each sentence in phrases. Repeat the phrase in the interval provided until you can say it smoothly. **¡OJO!** You can pause the audio program if you need more time to practice each sentence.

Cynthia Cevallos Mendoza
Quito, Ecuador

1. Mi familia viene de Quito, la capital de Ecuador, pero tengo familia en otras ciudades.
2. Mi familia es mi papá y mi mamá. También tengo dos hermanos.
3. Mi hermana está soltera. Mi hermano está casado y tiene un niño pequeño.
4. En mi familia, siempre estamos en comunicación a pesar de que (*in spite of the fact that*) cada uno trabaja y estudia.

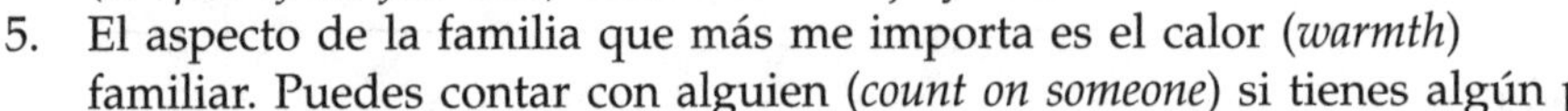

5. El aspecto de la familia que más me importa es el calor (*warmth*) familiar. Puedes contar con alguien (*count on someone*) si tienes algún problema.

Paso 2: Significado. Indicate which of the following sentences is *not* true, based on the sentences in **Paso 1.**

a. ☐ Cynthia tiene una familia unida.
b. ☐ Cynthia tiene dos sobrinos.
c. ☐ La familia es muy importante para Cynthia.

B. Respuestas lógicas. First, read the questions and divided responses from the interview with Cynthia. Then, listen to the interview and match the first and last part of her responses.

---

*In September 2000, the Ecuadorian sucre was withdrawn as an official currency and replaced by the U.S. dollar.

PREGUNTAS Y RESPUESTAS PARTE 1

1. ¿De dónde viene tu familia?

   «Mi familia viene de Quito, la capital de Ecuador. _____.»

2. ¿Cómo es tu familia?

   «Mi familia es mi papá y mi mamá. Mi papá se llama Manolo y tiene 52 años, mi mamá se llama Blanca y tiene 53 años. _____.»

3. ¿Son varones los dos?

   «Tengo una hermana y un hermano. Mi hermana se llama Milene, tiene 26 años y está soltera. Mi hermano se llama Manolo, _____.»

4. ¿Cómo es la relación entre ustedes?

   «Es una relación muy unida. Estamos siempre en comunicación a pesar de que cada uno trabaja y estudia. _____.»

5. ¿Qué aspecto de la vida familiar te importa más?

   «El aspecto de la familia que más me importa es el calor familiar: saber de que puedes contar con alguien si tienes algún problema o _____.»

RESPUESTAS PARTE 2

a. Estamos siempre en contacto y tratamos de hacer cosas juntos
b. simplemente para conversar, saber que siempre tienes alguien con quien contar
c. También tengo dos hermanos
d. tiene 23 años, está casado y tiene un niño pequeño
e. También tengo familia en Guayaquil y en otras ciudades del país

C. ¿Entendiste? Answer the following questions in complete sentences, based on the interview with Cynthia.

1. ¿De dónde es Cynthia?

   ____

2. ¿Cuántos hermanos tiene?

   ____

3. ¿Cómo se llaman sus hermanos?

   ____

4. ¿En qué situaciones es importante para Cynthia la familia?

   ____

❖ **D. Preguntas para ti.** You will hear three questions. Write down your personal answers.

1. ______________________________
2. ______________________________
3. ______________________________

Forma y función

3.1 Expressing Possession

Clínica de gramática

The verb **tener** (*to have*) is used to express possession, just like its English equivalent. Here are the present tense forms of the irregular verb **tener.**

	tener		
(yo)	**tengo**	(nosotros/as)	**tenemos**
(tú)	**tienes**	(vosotros/as)	**tenéis**
(usted, él/ella)	**tiene**	(ustedes, ellos/as)	**tienen**

¿Quién lo tiene (*Who has it*)? Complete the following table with the correct forms of the verb **tener.**

	tener		**tener**
1. yo		8. tú	
2. Juan y yo		9. mi novio y yo	
3. los estudiantes		10. nosotras	
4. mi mamá		11. mi tío	
5. mis amigos		12. la profesora	
6. usted		13. los jóvenes	
7. vosotros		14. ustedes	

A. ¿Qué tienes? Complete each sentence with the correct form of the verb **tener.**

1. Nosotros __________________ buenas universidades en este país.
2. Tú __________________ dos hermanos muy simpáticos.
3. Yo sólo __________________ cinco minutos más para acabar (*finish*) el examen. ¡Ay!
4. La señora Rosa todavía (*still*) __________________ dos abuelos que viven aquí.
5. Tus amigos __________________ una familia grande y muy linda.
6. Ustedes no __________________ clase de español hoy.

B. Datos familiares. Listen to the following statements. Then indicate whether each statement demonstrates that these people have family or not. You will hear the answers on the audio program.

	SÍ	NO
1. Laura	☐	☐
2. Ángel	☐	☐
3. Yo	☐	☐
4. Samuel y Rodrigo	☐	☐
5. Nosotros	☐	☐

C. ¡Cuántos parientes tienen! Complete each sentence to indicate how many relatives the following people have. **¡OJO!** Use the correct form of the verb **tener.**

MODELO Nora **/** tres hijos →
Nora tiene tres hijos.

1. Lisa **/** dos hermanos
______
2. Samuel y Mary **/** tres sobrinos
______
3. mis padres **/** cinco hijos
______
4. mi madre **/** un primo
______
5. mi hermano y yo **/** veinte primos
______
6. yo **/** quince tíos
______

D. ¿Cuántos años tienen? Complete each sentence with the verb **tener** and spell out the number indicated.

MODELO Nosotros ______ años. (26) →
Nosotros tenemos veintiséis años.

1. Mi abuela ______ años. (69)
2. Los gemelos ______ años. (23)
3. Yo ______ años. (19)
4. Mi hermana y yo ______ años. (35)
5. Tú ______ años. (47)
6. Vosotros ______ años. (54)

E. ¿De quién es? Read the following questions. Then write an answer based on the information given in parentheses.

MODELO (*you read*) ¿De quién es el libro? (mi padre)
(*you write*) Es de mi padre.

1. ¿De quién es la casa? (mis padres)

____

2. ¿De quién son los perros? (Ana)

____

3. ¿De quién son los gatos? (el padre de mi novia)

____

4. ¿De quién es la niña? (mi hermano)

____

5. ¿De quién es la clase? (el profesor Martínez)

____

F. ¿Quién tiene… ? Based on the information given, write sentences that explain who has the missing items.

MODELO Juan **/** libro **/** María →
Juan tiene el libro de María.

1. Jorge **/** gato **/** Gabriela

____

2. Teresa y Rogelio **/** el perro **/** Juanito

____

3. tú y yo **/** coche **/** Heriberto

____

4. vosotros **/** los libros **/** el profesor

____

5. yo **/** la paciencia **/** mis padres

____

3.2 Possessive Adjectives

Clínica de gramática

In addition to the verb **tener,** Spanish can also express possession by using possessive adjectives. These forms are used before nouns and must agree with the noun they modify.

Los adjetivos posesivos

mi(s)	my	**nuestro/a/os/as**	our
tu(s)	your (*fam.*)	**vuestro/a/os/as**	your (*fam. pl.*)
su(s)	your (*form.*), his, her, its	**su(s)**	your (*form. pl.*), their

La familia. Complete the following table with the correct forms of the possessive adjectives.

	primos	hermana	padres	tía	abuelos
1. mi					
2. tu					
3. su			*sus padres*		
4. nuestro					
5. vuestro					*vuestros abuelos*

A. ¿De quién? Listen to each statement. Then check the word(s) that correctly identify the owner expressed in the statement. **¡OJO!** In some cases, more than one answer is correct. You will hear the correct answers on the audio program.

MODELO (*you hear*) Sus libros están en la mochila.
(*you see*) ☐ yo ☐ Pedro y yo ☐ ella
(*you check*) ella

1. ☐ yo ☐ vosotros ☐ María y Elena
2. ☐ ellos ☐ tú ☐ usted
3. ☐ ellas ☐ Juan ☐ nosotros
4. ☐ ella ☐ tú ☐ Pedro y Ana
5. ☐ Elena ☐ ellos ☐ tú
6. ☐ ellas ☐ tú ☐ Felipe y tú

B. ¿De quién es? Complete each sentence with the correct form of the possessive adjective given.

MODELO _____ abuelo tiene muchos años. (mi) → Mi

1. ________________ hermana es soltera. (vuestro)
2. ________________ padres trabajan mucho. (su)
3. ________________ sobrina es joven. (tu)
4. ________________ amigas son de Ecuador. (nuestro)
5. El hermano de Marcos y Linda es ________________ mejor amigo. (su)

C. Descripciones. The following sentences are missing the possessive adjective. Listen to the statement that explains possession in order to complete each of the sentences with the correct possessive adjective. You will hear the answers on the audio program.

MODELO (*you hear*) Tengo dos hermanos.
(*you read*) _____ hermanos son guapos y jóvenes.
(*you write*) Mis

1. _____ hermana trabaja en la Facultad de Ciencias de la universidad.
2. _____ sobrino va a la escuela este año porque tiene cinco años.
3. _____ amigos de Bogotá, Colombia, llegan mañana.
4. _____ abuela practica el quechua con los niños.
5. _____ primos son encantadores.
6. _____ perros van a una escuela de disciplina para perros.

Pronunciación y ortografía

Written Accents (I)

Read and study the information in your textbook before you complete these activities.

A. El acento

Paso 1. Listen to the following words and underline the stressed syllable. **¡OJO!** These words are listed here without the necessary accent marks!

1. fa-mi-lia
2. u-ni-co
3. co-mi-co
4. re-la-cion
5. di-vor-cia-do
6. pe-si-mis-ta
7. tra-ba-ja-dor
8. to-le-ran-te

Paso 2. Now, based on your answers in **Paso 1,** determine which words require accent marks. Review the rules of stress in your textbook, then rewrite each word, inserting the necessary accent marks.

1. ______________________________
2. ______________________________
3. ______________________________
4. ______________________________
5. ______________________________
6. ______________________________
7. ______________________________
8. ______________________________

B. Las reglas (*rules*)

Paso 1. The words in this list follow the two rules of stress you have learned. Check which rule (1 or 2) each word follows.

	REGLA 1	REGLA 2
1. persona	☐	☐
2. menor	☐	☐
3. novecientos	☐	☐
4. entonces	☐	☐
5. universidad	☐	☐
6. sobrinos	☐	☐
7. español	☐	☐
8. estudiantil	☐	☐

Paso 2. Now look at the following words that break the rules of stress. Check which rule (1 or 2) each of the words breaks.

	REGLA 1	REGLA 2
1. también	☐	☐
2. está	☐	☐
3. difícil	☐	☐
4. bolígrafo	☐	☐
5. miércoles	☐	☐
6. fácil	☐	☐
7. lápiz	☐	☐
8. lápices	☐	☐

C. Nuevas palabras (*words*)

Paso 1. The stress patterns and use of written accents is very regular in Spanish. Therefore, if you know the rules, you should be able to pronounce unfamiliar words correctly. Use the rules you have learned to find and underline the stressed syllables in the following words.

1. sig-ni-fi-ca
2. ab-do-men
3. ca-lle-jón
4. ám-bar
5. e-le-men-tal
6. la-bra-dor
7. lí-der
8. au-to-mó-vil
9. in-fe-rior
10. cár-cel
11. cas-ca-bel
12. hin-ca-pié
13. te-nis
14. Pa-rís
15. úl-ti-mo

Paso 2. Now, pronounce each word from **Paso 1** aloud, then listen to it on the audio program.

Vocabulario

La familia en transición; Las actividades familiares

A. La familia de Antonio. Complete each sentence about Antonio's family with the most logical choice.

1. El padre de Antonio no vive con su familia porque sus padres están _____.

   ☐ jubilados ☐ solteros ☐ divorciados

2. El segundo esposo de su madre es su _____.

   ☐ hermanastro ☐ padrastro ☐ tío

3. Antonio tiene una tía que no está casada y tiene dos hijos. Ella es una madre _____.

   ☐ gregaria ☐ soltera ☐ jubilada

4. El padre de Antonio ya no trabaja porque está _____.

   ☐ jubilado ☐ divorciado ☐ casado

5. Los hijos de la segunda esposa de su padre son sus _____.

   ☐ madrastras ☐ primos ☐ hermanastros

B. ¿Dónde? Match each activity with the most logical place.

1. _____ salir a bailar
2. _____ dar un paseo
3. _____ leer libros y estudiar
4. _____ mirar la televisión
5. _____ beber vino

a. en un parque
b. en casa (*at home*)
c. en una discoteca
d. en un bar
e. en una biblioteca

C. Jubilados. Listen to Rosalinda and Ester talk about their retired parents, then match each set of parents with the corresponding activities. You can listen more than once if you like.

	LOS PADRES DE ESTER	LOS PADRES DE ROSALINDA
1. llevar clase	☐	☐
2. bailar	☐	☐
3. mirar televisión	☐	☐
4. echar siestas	☐	☐
5. visitar a amigos	☐	☐
6. discutir	☐	☐
7. hablar por teléfono	☐	☐
8. comer en restaurantes	☐	☐
9. dar paseos	☐	☐

❖ **D. ¿Qué te gusta?** Write five sentences explaining which of the following activities you like to do. Include information about when or with whom you like to do them.

beber vino/cerveza	discutir la política	mirar la televisión
comer	echar una siesta	salir a bailar
dar un paseo	escribir cartas/poemas	visitar a parientes
descansar	leer revistas (novelas, el periódico)	

MODELO bailar → Me gusta bailar con mis amigos.

1. ______
2. ______
3. ______
4. ______
5. ______

E. ¿Qué verbo? Complete each sentence with the most logical infinitive from the following list.

bailar, beber, comer, dar, discutir, echar, leer, llevar, mirar

1. ¿Cuántas clases vas a ______ el próximo semestre?
2. Me gusta ______ la televisión por la tarde.
3. El sábado, los estudiantes de mi clase de español vamos a una discoteca a ______.
4. ¿Te gusta ______ vino con la cena?
5. No tengo tiempo para ______ siestas durante la semana.
6. —¿Por qué no te gusta ______ paseos en el parque?

   —Porque en este momento tengo que ______ muchos libros para mi clase de historia.

F. Las familias multigeneracionales. The following passage describes the multigenerational family, a type of family that is frequently encountered in Ecuador. Read the passage, then indicate which lettered sentence in the text expresses the general ideas that follow the passage. **¡OJO!** Two of the sentences express ideas that do not occur in this passage; mark these with an X.

VOCABULARIO ÚTIL

hasta	*even*	herencia	*inheritance*
viviendo	*living*	incluso	*even*
trabajando	*working*	vecinos	*neighbors*
empresa	*business*	cuidar	*to take care of*

Las familias multigeneracionales en Ecuador

[a]En nuestro país existe un buen porcentaje de familias multigeneracionales. [b]Hay muchos factores en la sociedad ecuatoriana que explican esta situación: separaciones, divorcios, madres solteras o porque uno de los padres trabaja en otra ciudad. [c]También resulta por influencia de cuestiones culturales. [d]Existe la tendencia de la «gran familia», en donde padres, abuelos y hasta bisabuelos están juntos, viviendo en una misma casa o trabajando en una misma empresa familiar. [e]La solidaridad familiar y comunitaria es una herencia cultural indígena y latina. [f]En la cultura indígena existen muchas actividades y celebraciones comunitarias, e incluso los vecinos tienen responsabilidades comunes: Ayudan a cuidar la casa y, a veces, hasta cuidar a los hijos.

1. _____ Multigenerational families reflect indigenous traditions.
2. _____ Single mothers may form part of a multigenerational family.
3. _____ Multigenerational families tend to be more stable units.
4. _____ In indigenous cultures, neighbors may care for a family's children.
5. _____ There are many multigenerational families in Ecuador.
6. _____ Multigenerational families benefit from many government programs.

Entrevista 2

A. Sonido y significado

Paso 1: Sonido. The sentences in this activity are based on ideas from the interview with Gabriela Arteta Jácome. First, read each sentence silently and make sure you understand its meaning. Then, listen as the speaker pronounces each sentence in phrases. Repeat the phrase in the interval provided until you can say it smoothly. **¡OJO!** You can pause the audio program if you need more time to practice each sentence.

Gabriela Arteta Jácome
Guayaquil, Ecuador

1. Mis padres están divorciados. Yo vivo con mi madre y mi padrastro.
2. Tengo dos hermanos naturales y tres hermanastros, los hijos de mi padrastro.
3. Nuestra familia es unida, a pesar de que no somos de la misma sangre (*same blood*).
4. Pasamos muchos ratos agradables (*pleasant moments*). Vamos a la playa, salimos a pasear y comemos juntos.
5. Para nosotros, la comunicación es un aspecto primordial. Nosotros no nos separamos. (*We're hardly ever apart.*)

Paso 2: Significado. Indicate which of the following sentences is *not* true, based on the information in **Paso 1.**

a. ☐ El padre y la madre de Gabriela viven juntos.
b. ☐ Hay cinco hijos en la casa de Gabriela.
c. ☐ En la familia de Gabriela pasan mucho tiempo juntos.

B. Respuestas lógicas. First read the questions and divided responses from the interview with Gabriela. Then, listen to the interview and match the first and last part of her responses.

PREGUNTAS Y RESPUESTAS PARTE 1

1. ¿Cómo es tu familia?

   «Mis padres están divorciados. Yo vivo con mi madre y mi padrastro. _____.»

2. ¿Es una familia unida?

   «Nuestra familia es muy unida. A pesar de que no somos de la misma sangre, _____.»

3. ¿Pasan ustedes mucho tiempo juntos?

   «Pasamos muchos ratos agradables. Si no nos vamos a la playa y caminamos, _____.»

4. ¿Qué aspecto de la vida familiar te importa más?

   La familia para nosotros es muy importante. La comunicación es un aspecto primordial. _____.

RESPUESTAS PARTE 2

a. siempre tenemos mucha comunicación y siempre somos muy unidos
b. Tengo dos hermanos naturales y tres hermanastros, los hijos de mi padrastro
c. Nosotros conversamos mucho. Sentimos que a pesar de la distancia, nosotros no nos separamos
d. salimos a pasear, comemos juntos, hablamos mucho. Tenemos ratos muy agradables

C. ¿Entendiste? Answer the following questions in complete sentences, based on the interview with Gabriela.

1. ¿Quiénes viven en la casa de Gabriela?

   ______

2. ¿Cómo es la familia de Gabriela?

   ______

3. ¿Cómo pasan el tiempo juntos?

   ______

4. ¿Qué aspecto de la vida es muy importante para la familia de Gabriela?

   ______

❖ **D. Preguntas para ti.** You will hear three questions. Write down your personal answers.

1. ______
2. ______
3. ______

Forma y función

3.3 Regular -er and -ir Verbs

Clínica de gramática

Here are the present tense forms of the regular verbs **beber** (*to drink*) and **escribir** (*to write*).

beber: STEM **beb-**			
(yo)	beb**o**	(nosotros/as)	beb**emos**
(tú)	beb**es**	(vosotros/as)	beb**éis**
(usted, él/ella)	beb**e**	(ustedes, ellos/as)	beb**en**

escribir: STEM **escrib-**			
(yo)	escrib**o**	(nosotros/as)	escrib**imos**
(tú)	escrib**es**	(vosotros/as)	escrib**ís**
(usted, él/ella)	escrib**e**	(ustedes, ellos/as)	escrib**en**

Verbos. Complete the following table with the correct forms of the verbs indicated.

	yo	él	nosotros	ustedes
1. comer				
2. beber	*bebo*			
3. escribir			*escribimos*	
4. vivir				
5. leer		*lee*		
6. discutir				*discuten*

A. La vida de Ana. Listen to Ana's monologue. Then, indicate whether the following statements are true **(cierto)** or false **(falso).** You will hear the answers on the audio program.

	CIERTO	FALSO
1. Ana vive en una casa muy grande.	□	□
2. Ana y su novio tienen dos clases juntos.	□	□
3. Después de clase, los dos dan un paseo.	□	□
4. Ana y su novio hacen ejercicio.	□	□
5. Por la noche, Ana lee el libro de español.	□	□

B. Mi familia. Use the following information to write complete sentences about the adults in Carlos's family.

MODELO mi padre / vivir / con nosotros →
Mi padre vive con nosotros.

1. mi esposa y yo / leer el periódico / todas las mañanas

   ____

2. yo / beber vino / con la cena

   ____

3. mis hijos / vivir / en un apartamento en Quito

   ____

4. mi hija y mi hermano / discutir / la política cuando hablan

   ____

5. mi hijo / escribir cartas / a su novia

   ____

C. En Ecuador. Complete the following paragraph with verbs from the list. **¡OJO!** Make sure you use the correct form of each verb.

beber, comer, discutir, escribir, leer, vivir

«Mi familia y yo ______________[1] en Ecuador, cerca de Quito. Yo ______________[2] mucho en la biblioteca porque soy estudiante de literatura. En mi familia, todos nosotros ______________[3] juntos todos los días a las 2:00 de la tarde. Los domingos, nosotros ______________[4] vino con la comida (*meal*). Cuando mis tíos nos visitan, mi madre y el hermano de mi padre siempre ______________[5] la política. Mi madre es periodista (*journalist*) y ______________[6] artículos sobre la política de Ecuador.»

3.4 Irregular Verbs **dar, hacer, salir, ver**

Clínica de gramática

These verbs have irregularities only in the **yo** form; otherwise their forms follow the pattern for regular **-ar, -er,** and **-ir** verbs.

dar (*to give*)		**hacer** (*to do; to make*)		**salir** (*to leave; to go out*)		**ver** (*to see*)	
doy	damos	**hago**	hacemos	**salgo**	salimos	**veo**	vemos
das	dais	haces	hacéis	sales	salís	ves	veis
da	dan	hace	hacen	sale	salen	ve	ven

Verbos. Complete the following table with the correct forms of the verbs indicated.

	dar	**hacer**	**salir**	**ver**
1. yo				
2. ustedes				
3. vosotros	*dais*			
4. ellos				
5. usted		*hace*		
6. nosotras				
7. ella				
8. tú				*ves*
9. él			*sale*	

A. La clase de español. Your friend Lisa called you and left a message on your answering machine regarding her Spanish class. Listen to the message, then choose the best answer, based on Lisa's message. You will hear the answers on the audio program.

1. Todos los días Lisa hace _____.
   a. un examen b. una prueba c. una presentación
2. En la clase los estudiantes ven _____.
   a. una presentación b. a su familia c. películas
3. Los estudiantes salen a _____.
   a. practicar español b. tomar un café c. comer en un restaurante
4. La profesora da _____.
   a. mucha tarea b. muchos refrescos c. muchos paseos
5. Los estudiantes hacen _____.
   a. crucigramas en español b. sólo un proyecto c. una presentación

B. ¿Cuándo lo haces? Write sentences to tell when you do the following activities.

MODELO ver televisión →
Veo la televisión los viernes y sábados.

1. dar un paseo ___________________________
2. ver películas ___________________________
3. hacer la tarea ___________________________
4. salir a bailar ___________________________

C. Unos amigos. Complete the conversation between Rolo, Pilar, and Andrés with the correct form of each verb in parentheses.

PILAR: Rolo, ¿(ver: tú) ______________[1] a ese (*that*) chico? Es Andrés, ¿no?

ROLO: Sí, (ver: yo) ______________[2] a ese chico. Es Andrés. ¡Andrés! ¿Adónde (ir: tú) ______________[3]?

ANDRÉS: ¡Eh, Rolo! Yo (ir) ______________[4] al gimnasio.

ROLO: ¿Qué (hacer: tú) ______________[5] en el gimnasio?

ANDRÉS: (Hacer: Yo) ______________[6] ejercicio (*I exercise*) con Ana. ¿Y ustedes? ¿Qué (hacer) ______________[7] aquí?

PILAR: Rolo y yo (dar) ______________[8] un paseo todas las tardes a esta hora.

❖ **D. Una semana típica.** Write a brief paragraph to describe your schedule in a typical week. When possible, contrast your schedule with that of a friend. Use verbs from the following list.

beber, comer, dar, discutir, escribir, hacer, leer, salir, ver, vivir

MODELO Salgo de la residencia a las 7:00, pero mi amiga sale a las 8:00.

____

____

____

____

____

____

____

____

____

❖ Análisis cultural

Keeping in mind the information that you have learned in this chapter, study the following quote and answer the questions.

> "The size of the average family has dropped at a startling rate over the last forty years. In the 1950s, the average Latin American woman had six children. Now that figure has almost halved. The causes of such a rapid fall in childbearing include the more widespread availability of contraception, the spread in girls' education, and the rate of urbanization. In the shanty towns, large families can be a liability: women have to go out to work as maids or in the markets and since they have left their families in the countryside, there is often no one at home to look after the children."
>
> Source: *Faces of Latin America*

1. What variations in family size and structure have you learned about in this chapter? Do these variations seem to correspond to age or place of residence?

____

____

2. Why do you think the spread of girls' education and rate of urbanization have affected family size?

____

____

3. Have similar changes occurred in your country or in other countries with which you are familiar? Think of your own family history for possible answers.

____

____

❖ PORTAFOLIO CULTURAL

Redacción: Una carta a Ecuador

You are going to be an exchange student in Ecuador. Write a letter to your host family describing yourself, your family, and your leisure activities. Ask questions about their family and what they do in their leisure time.

A. Antes de escribir

Paso 1. Look at a map of Ecuador and decide which of the primary areas (coast, highlands, rain forests) interests you the most. Are you interested in staying in a large city, small town, or a small community?

Paso 2. Describe yourself. Write complete sentences to describe 1) your age, 2) your physical appearance (hair, eyes, and so on), and 3) your personality.

Paso 3. Write at least five sentences to describe your family. Describe the members, their personalities, and the kind of family you are. Also write about the activities you enjoy as a family.

Paso 4. Write two to three questions to your host family in Ecuador. Also, write a question that asks what activities they like to do.

B. ¡A escribir! Now you are ready to write your letter. Imagine that the program coordinators at your university have given you the following template to help you compose this important letter. This template contains the formalities, greetings, and language of a formal letter. Using the template, complete the letter with the information you developed in the **pasos** of the **A. Antes de escribir.** Describe your family, yourself, what you like to do, and so on, and ask about your host family in Ecuador. When you address the head of your host family remember to address him or her formally.

Estimado señor (Estimada señora) _______________:

Con mucha alegría hago preparativos para participar en el programa en Ecuador. Con la presente, presento unos detalles personales que ustedes necesitan. También tengo unas preguntas sobre su familia y las actividades que ustedes hacen.

Mi familia es...

¿Y su familia en Ecuador?...

Yo soy...

(Con mi familia) Me gusta...

Espero con mucho entusiasmo mi viaje a Ecuador. Sin más por el momento, quedo

Atentamente,

C. ¡A corregir! Before you hand in your work, check the following aspects of your letter.

☐ Subject/verb agreement
☐ Possessive adjectives (form and agreement)
☐ Adjective/noun agreement

WWW Exploración

Choose and complete *one* of the following research activities. Then, based on your instructor's directions, present your results to the class and/or create a short report to include in your portfolio.

1. Visit the website of the government of Ecuador. Using information found there or by following links, locate information about government programs that benefit the family. What kinds of programs are available? Maternity leaves? Monetary support for large families? Health care benefits for young children? Compare the social benefits in Ecuador with those in your country. Which system is more comprehensive?
2. The reading in this chapter discusses the evolving structure of the family in Ecuador. Follow up on this theme, using printed and electronic resources. What additional changes are taking place in terms of family size, divorce rate, single-parent families, and women in the workplace?
3. Interview a Spanish-speaking person on your campus or in your community. Ask this person the questions that you heard in this chapter's interviews or create questions of your own. Then compare this person's family with the families of Cynthia and Gabriela. How are these families alike/different in terms of size? Family structure? Cohesion?
4. Find more information in your library or on the Internet about Ecuador. Here are some ideas and key words to get you started:
   - **las Islas Galápagos**
   - Ecuador's indigenous peoples: the Quechua, Otavaleños, Salasacas, Saraguros, Huaorani, Zaparo, Cofan, Shuar, Achuar
   - the Afro-Ecuadorian population and culture
   - Conflicts over Ecuador's petroleum industry and environmental concerns

CAPÍTULO

4

Repaso y anticipación

A. La intrusa (*Something that doesn't belong*)

Paso 1. Indicate which word or phrase does not belong in the following series.

1.	☐ visitar a los tíos	☐ visitar a los primos	☐ visitar a los gemelos	☐ visitar a los sobrinos
2.	☐ leer novelas	☐ echar una siesta	☐ dar un paseo	☐ descansar
3.	☐ perros y gatos	☐ cuadernos y lápices	☐ libros y novelas	☐ cartas y revistas
4.	☐ vino	☐ paseo	☐ refresco	☐ cerveza
5.	☐ entrar	☐ salir	☐ vivir	☐ regresar

Paso 2. Now match the following areas of the house with the series from **Paso 1.** (You will learn the names of these rooms later in this chapter.)

a. 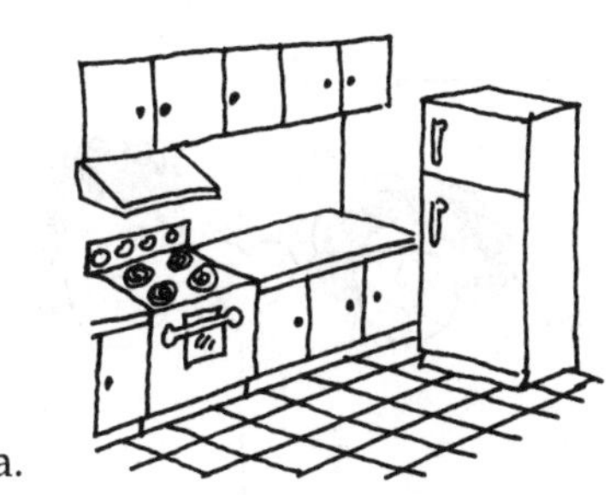

b. 

c. 

d. 

e. 

1. _____ 2. _____ 3. _____ 4. _____ 5. _____

❖ **Paso 3.** Write five sentences about yourself and/or your family using one of the word(s) from each series in **Paso 1.**

MODELOS Mi hermana habla por teléfono toda la tarde.
Yo escucho música por la mañana.

1. ______________________________

2. ______________________________

3. ______________________________

4. ______________________________

5. ______________________________

B. La familia de Manuel

Paso 1. Indicate each family member's relationship to Manuel by writing the corresponding letter(s) in the space provided.

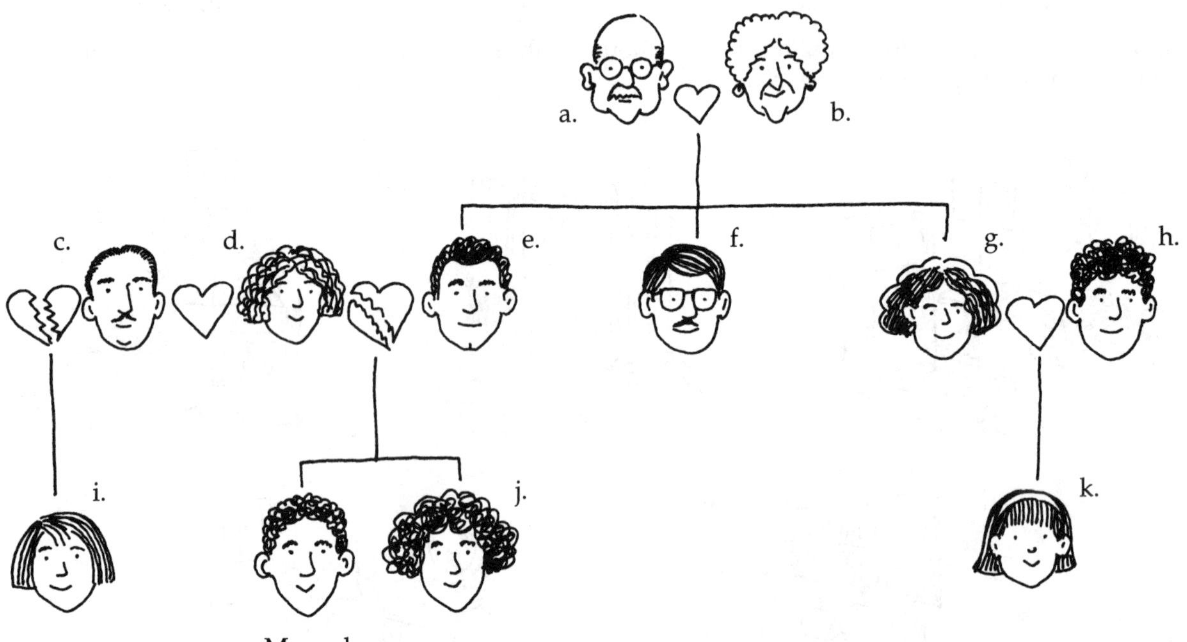

1. _____ hermana
2. _____ hermanastro
3. _____ madre
4. _____ padrastro
5. _____ abuela
6. _____ tío
7. _____ prima
8. _____ abuelo
9. _____ tía
10. _____ padre

❖ **Paso 2.** Now describe your family using the verb **vivir** to talk about family members you live with and the verb **tener** to describe your extended family. Write at least five sentences.

MODELO Vivo con mi padre y mis dos hermanos. No vivo con mi madre. Tengo ocho tíos y catorce primos. No tengo abuelos.

____

____

____

____

____

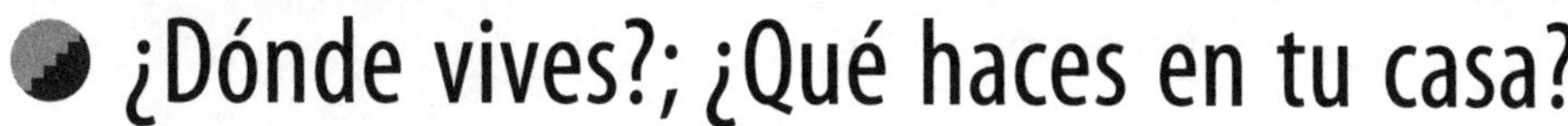

PARTE 1

¿Dónde vives?; ¿Qué haces en tu casa?

A. Casas diferentes

Paso 1. Below and on the following page are drawings of two types of residences in Barcelona. Write the name of each numbered room in the corresponding blank. **¡OJO!** Remember to include the definite article **(el/la).**

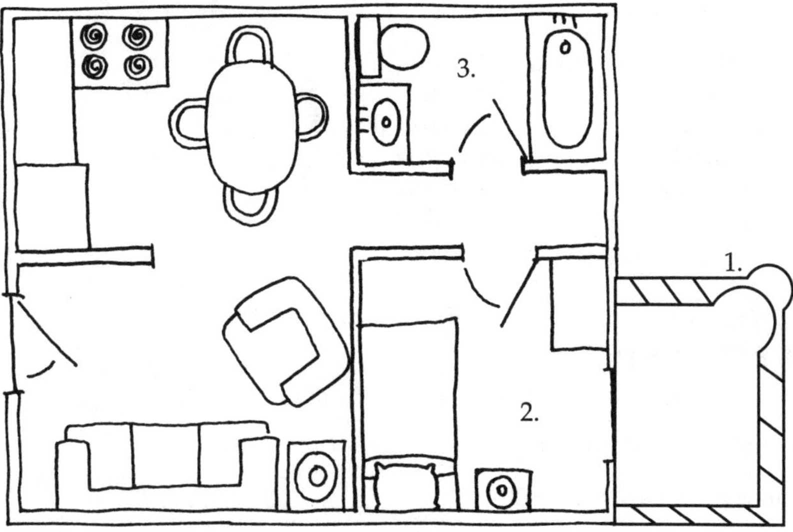

Un piso

1. _______________
2. _______________
3. _______________

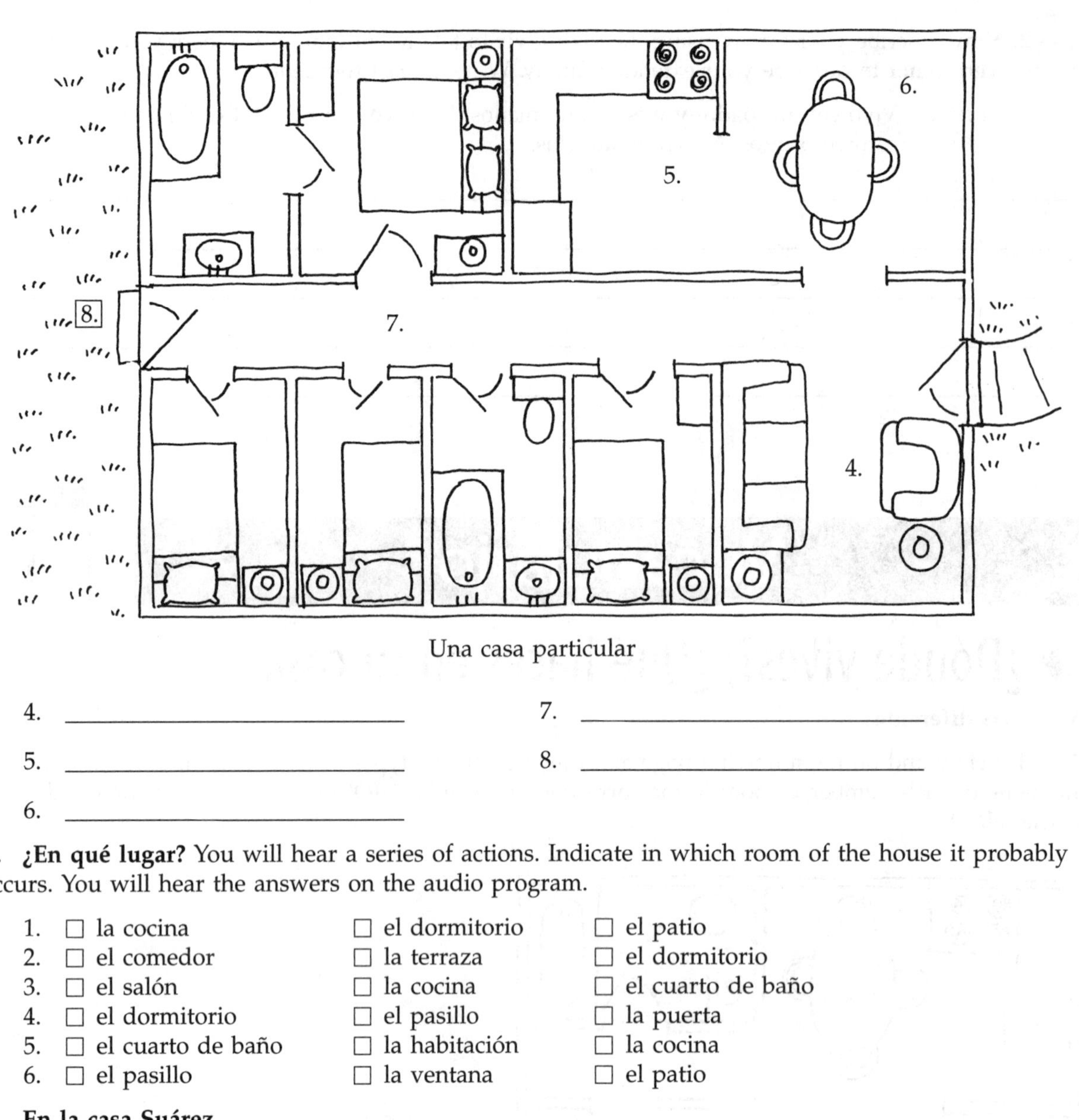

Una casa particular

4. ______________________________ 7. ______________________________

5. ______________________________ 8. ______________________________

6. ______________________________

B. ¿En qué lugar? You will hear a series of actions. Indicate in which room of the house it probably occurs. You will hear the answers on the audio program.

1. ☐ la cocina ☐ el dormitorio ☐ el patio
2. ☐ el comedor ☐ la terraza ☐ el dormitorio
3. ☐ el salón ☐ la cocina ☐ el cuarto de baño
4. ☐ el dormitorio ☐ el pasillo ☐ la puerta
5. ☐ el cuarto de baño ☐ la habitación ☐ la cocina
6. ☐ el pasillo ☐ la ventana ☐ el patio

C. En la casa Suárez

Paso 1. Read what members of the Suárez family are doing at different times of the day, then match each activity with the corresponding part of the house from the list.

la cocina, el comedor, el dormitorio, el jardín, el salón

MODELO Leonora echa una siesta. → el dormitorio

1. Los señores Suárez almuerzan con amigos a las 2:00. ______________________________
2. Lorenzo y Guillermo practican el béisbol por la tarde. ______________________________
3. El abuelo mira la televisión a las 7:30. ______________________________
4. La señora Suárez prepara sándwiches para sus hijos a las 8:00. ______________________________

❖ **Paso 2.** Now, list two activities that you might do in each of the following areas of your home.

MODELO la cocina → preparar la comida, desayunar

1. el salón ________________
2. el dormitorio ________________
3. el patio ________________
4. el jardín ________________
5. el comedor ________________

D. En la casa

Paso 1. Complete the following word puzzle with the correct words from the list. The letters in the gray vertical row will spell an expression related to the puzzle words.

cocina, comedor, garaje, jardín, pasillo, patio, piscina, puerta, residencial, salón, terraza, urbanización, vecinos, ventana

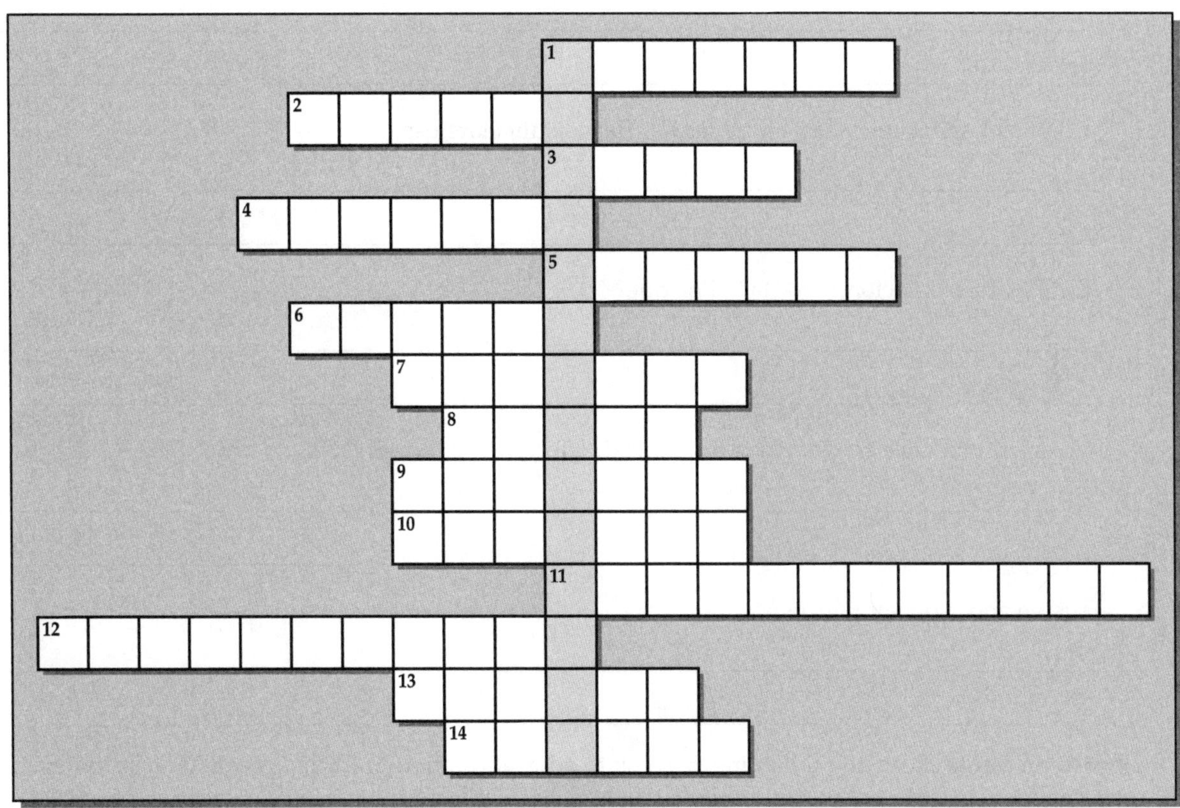

1. Comemos en este cuarto.
2. Entramos por esta parte de la casa.
3. Miramos la televisión o visitamos con familia y amigos en este cuarto.
4. Miramos el jardín por esta parte de la casa.
5. Llegamos de un cuarto a otro cuarto por esta parte de la casa.
6. Preparamos la comida en este cuarto.
7. Esta parte de la casa está afuera (*outside*), pero no es el patio ni (*nor*) el jardín.
8. Comemos en el comedor, o aquí afuera.
9. Son las personas que viven al lado de mi casa.
10. Generalmente, está detras de la casa. Aquí la familia nada (*swims*).

11. Es un barrio.
12. Describe una calle que tiene muchas casas y que no tiene tiendas (*stores*).
13. Nuestro coche está aquí.
14. Es la parte alrededor de (*around*) la casa.

Paso 2. Now, on a separate sheet of paper, create your own word puzzle using words from the **¿Dónde vives?** and **¿Qué haces en tu casa?** vocabulary sections of the textbook. Remember to include vertical and/or horizontal clues in Spanish.

E. ¿Dónde viven? Listen to the following descriptions and indicate whether each person probably lives in **un piso** or **una casa particular.** You will hear the answers on the audio program.

	UN PISO	UNA CASA PARTICULAR
1. Mabel vive en...	☐	☐
2. Juan José vive en...	☐	☐
3. Paco vive en...	☐	☐

❖ **F. Preguntas personales.** Answer the following questions.

1. ¿En qué tipo de casa vives? ¿Te gusta? ¿Por qué sí o por qué no?

   ____

   ____

2. ¿Cuántas habitaciones hay en tu casa? ¿Tienes suficiente espacio?

   ____

   ____

3. ¿Cuál es tu habitación favorita? ¿Por qué?

   ____

   ____

4. ¿Vives en una calle transitada o residencial? ¿Te gusta tu barrio?

   ____

   ____

5. ¿Tus vecinos son simpáticos?

   ____

   ____

G. Un piso en venta. Read the following real estate ad and the note from la señora Murcia to her real estate agent as she describes her family's needs. Then, indicate the reason(s) why this property would be unsuitable.

Piso en venta Precio: 249.420 €

Piso de 5 habitaciones y 1 baño en el centro de Madrid. Muy bien comunicado, autobuses en la puerta. Cerca de muchas empresas y atracciones culturales. Características: 2 dormitorios, cocina amueblada,[a] agua caliente individual, 1 baño, 2 armarios empotrados,[b] calefacción.

Mi marido y yo buscamos un nuevo piso. Nos gusta cocinar e ir al cine y al teatro. Tenemos tres hijos. Tienen 5, 8 y 10 años. Les gusta nadar y jugar al fútbol. Mi marido es escritor.[c] Necesita mucha tranquilidad para concentrarse.

[a]*furnished* [b]*built-in* [c]*writer*

¿Por qué no es bueno este piso para la señora Murcia?

a. ☐ No hay suficientes dormitorios.
b. ☐ El piso está lejos de los teatros.
c. ☐ Probablemente hay mucho ruido (*noise*) en el barrio.
d. ☐ El piso no tiene acceso al transporte público.

Entrevista 1

A. Sonido y significado

Paso 1: Sonido. The sentences in this activity are based on ideas from the interview with María Benjumeda León. First, read each sentence silently and make sure you understand its meaning. Then, listen as the speaker pronounces each sentence in phrases. Repeat the phrase in the interval provided until you can say it smoothly.

María Benjumeda León
Cádiz, España

1. Vivo en Arcos de la Frontera, que es un pueblo precioso.
2. Mi casa es muy grande. Compartimos un patio muy bonito con los vecinos y hay muchas macetas (*flower pots*) y plantas.
3. Tenemos una entrada (*foyer*) con un espejo (*mirror*). También hay un salón, cuatro dormitorios y una cocina pequeña.
4. Somos cuatro hermanos, mis padres y mi abuela.
5. Los vecinos son vecinos de toda la vida. Son muy simpáticos.

Paso 2: Significado. Indicate which of the following phrases is *not* true, based on the sentences in **Paso 1.**

a. ☐ María tiene una familia grande.
b. ☐ Su familia tiene una casa grande.
c. ☐ Su madre también se llama María.

B. Respuestas lógicas. First, read the questions and divided responses from the interview with María. Then, listen to the interview and match the first and last part of her responses.

PREGUNTAS Y RESPUESTAS PARTE 1

1. ¿Dónde vives?

   «Vivo en Arcos de la Frontera, que es un pueblo precioso _____.»

2. ¿Cómo es tu casa?

   «Mi casa es muy grande. Vivimos en una casa de vecinos... _____.»

3. ¿Y el interior?

   «¿El interior? Pues, tenemos una entrada muy grande, con un espejo, muy típico de las casas andaluzas. Y la cómoda, ... _____.»

4. ¿Cuántas personas viven en tu casa?

   «Pues, somos cuatro hermanos: —las personas que no están casadas suelen (*tend to*) vivir con los padres— _____.»

5. ¿Cómo son los vecinos?

   «Los vecinos son vecinos de toda la vida, es como una familia, _____.»

RESPUESTAS PARTE 2

a. y compartimos un patio muy bonito, también muy grande. Y hay muchas macetas y muchas plantas
b. mis padres, mi abuela, que es viuda (*widow*), y mi perro
c. y que está encima de una colina (*hill*) y rodeado (*surrounded*) de viñas (*vineyards*) y de olivos (*olive trees*)
d. Hay un salón que da a (*opens onto*) la calle, cuatro dormitorios, una cocina pequeña y un comedor pegado (*connected*) a la cocina, y todo eso da al patio
e. son muy simpáticos. Y bueno, compartimos el patio, la amistad, y hay mucho respeto, cada uno en su casa

C. ¿Entendiste? Answer the following questions in complete sentences, based on the interview with María.

1. ¿Cómo se llama el pueblo donde vive María?

   ____

2. ¿Cuántas personas viven en su casa?

   ____

3. ¿Cuántas habitaciones hay en la casa de María?

   ____

4. ¿Qué comparte la familia de María con los vecinos?

   ____

❖ **D. Preguntas para ti.** You will hear three questions. Write down your personal answers.

1. ____
2. ____
3. ____

Forma y función

4.1 Demonstrative Adjectives

Clínica de gramática

To point out (or demonstrate) where things are in relation to the speaker and listener, Spanish uses demonstrative adjectives.

Demonstrative Adjectives: Singular

	THIS	THAT	THAT (OVER THERE)
Masculine	**este** edificio	**ese** edificio	**aquel** edificio
Feminine	**esta** casa	**esa** casa	**aquella** casa

Demonstrative Adjectives: Plural

	THESE	THOSE	THOSE (OVER THERE)
masculine	**estos** edificios	**esos** edificios	**aquellos** edificios
feminine	**estas** casas	**esas** casas	**aquellas** casas

To refer to a general idea or group of things with unspecified gender, use the neuter forms **esto, eso,** and **aquello.**

Los demostrativos. Complete the following table with the correct forms of the demonstrative adjectives.

	este	ese	aquel
1. piso			
2. calle		*esa calle*	
3. jardines			*aquellos jardines*
4. alfombras	*estas alfombras*		

A. ¿Dónde están? Listen to each of the following sentences and check the corresponding adverb: **aquí, ahí,** or **allá.** You will hear the answers on the audio program.

	AQUÍ (ESTE/A)	AHÍ (ESE/A)	ALLÁ (AQUEL[LA])
1.	☐	☐	☐
2.	☐	☐	☐
3.	☐	☐	☐
4.	☐	☐	☐
5.	☐	☐	☐
6.	☐	☐	☐
7.	☐	☐	☐
8.	☐	☐	☐

B. Nuestro barrio. Complete each sentence with the appropriate demonstrative adjective, based on the adverb in the sentence. **¡OJO!** Watch out for gender and number agreement.

MODELO ______________ barrio aquí es muy grande. → Este

1. ______________ jardín ahí es típico de nuestro barrio.
2. ______________ casa allá es nueva.
3. ______________ calle aquí es muy transitada.
4. ______________ pisos allá no son parte del barrio.
5. Hay flores (*flowers*) muy bonitas en ______________ terrazas ahí.
6. ______________ familias aquí son buenos vecinos.
7. Todo el barrio comparte ______________ piscina ahí.
8. Muchas familias del barrio van a ______________ parque allá.

C. ¿Te gusta? Answer the following questions, based on the cues in parentheses. Use the correct demonstrative pronoun. **¡OJO!** Don't forget to use the accent mark.

MODELO ¿Te gusta el piso? (ahí no, allá sí) →
No me gusta ése, pero me gusta aquél.

1. ¿Te gusta la casa? (aquí no, ahí sí)

   ____

2. ¿Te gustan los barrios? (ahí sí, aquí no)

   ____

3. ¿Te gusta el condominio? (allá sí, ahí no)

   ____

4. ¿Te gustan las terrazas (allá no, aquí sí)

   ____

D. Tomás y su madre. Tomás is preparing to go to the university. Complete the bits of conversations between Tomás and his mother with the appropriate demonstrative adjectives and pronouns. **¡OJO!** Remember to use the neuter pronouns **(esto, eso, aquello)** when referring to a general idea. Watch out for gender and number agreement. Use an accent for pronouns that replace a specific noun.

MODELO —Tomás, ¿te gusta <u>esta</u> mesa aquí?
—No mamá, no me gusta <u>ésa</u> ahí. Me gusta <u>aquélla</u> allá. →

MAMÁ: Tomás, ¿te gustan _______________[1] pios ahí?

TOMÁS: No, _______________[2] ahí están lejos de la universidad. Me gustan _______________[3] residencias aquí cerca de la universidad.

MAMÁ: ¿Qué es _______________[4] ahí?

TOMÁS: Es el gimnasio. Hay dos gimnasios. _______________[5] allí también tiene piscina. _______________[6] ahí es más grande, pero no tiene piscina.

MAMÁ: ¿Qué es _______________[7] aquí?

TOMÁS: _______________[8] papeles ahí son formularios que necesito rellenar (*fill out*).

4.2 Stem-Changing Verbs (e → ie, o → ue)

Clínica de gramática

Review the patterns of stem changes in the present tense.

pensar (e → ie)		**soler (o → ue)**	
pienso	pensamos	suelo	solemos
piensas	pensáis	sueles	soléis
piensa	piensan	suele	suelen

Cambios de raíz. Complete the following tables with the correct forms of the stem-changing verbs indicated.

1. **cerrar**		2. **almorzar**	

3. **poder**		4. **preferir**	

5. **querer**		6. **volver**	

A. ¿Dónde están?

Paso 1. Listen to the following statements and indicate which place they most likely refer to. You will hear the answers on the audio program.

1. ☐ la entrada ☐ el cuarto de baño ☐ el dormitorio
2. ☐ la cocina ☐ el patio ☐ el dormitorio
3. ☐ la cocina ☐ el cuarto de baño ☐ el salón
4. ☐ el pasillo ☐ el comedor ☐ la ventana
5. ☐ el comedor ☐ el cuarto de baño ☐ el jardín
6. ☐ el dormitorio ☐ la cocina ☐ el patio

Paso 2. Listen to the statements from **Paso 1** again and write the *infinitive* of the stem-changing verb you hear.

1. ____________________ 4. ____________________
2. ____________________ 5. ____________________
3. ____________________ 6. ____________________

B. Los sábados. Complete the following monologue with the correct form of the verbs in parentheses.

En mi casa, nosotros (tener) ________________[1] una rutina durante la semana. Pero los sábados, la rutina (poder) ________________[2] cambiar (*change*) mucho. Muchos sábados yo (dormir) ________________[3] hasta las 11:00 ó 12:00 de la mañana y luego paso mucho del día en mi dormitorio. Mis hermanos (soler) ________________[4] salir con amigos o ir al parque por varias (*several*) horas. Allí, mis hermanos y sus amigos (jugar) ________________[5] al fútbol o al basquetbol. Mis padres (preferir) ________________[6] pasar el día en casa, donde descansan o trabajan. A las 2:00, mis hermanos siempre (volver) ________________[7] a casa y todos nosotros (almorzar) ________________[8] juntos.

C. Preguntas

Paso 1. You want to know more about Spanish customs. Conjugate the verbs in parentheses to form complete questions.

1. ¿Cómo ________________ (soler) ser las casas en Andalucía?
2. ¿Qué deporte ________________ (preferir) los españoles?
3. ¿Qué bebida ________________ (querer) beber con la comida el español típico?
4. ¿Dónde ________________ (poder [yo]) ver jardines bonitos?
5. ¿A qué hora ________________ (almorzar) los españoles?

Paso 2. A Spanish pen pal wrote the following answers to the preceding questions. Complete each sentence with the correct form of the verb in parentheses. Then match the answers logically to the preceding questions.

a. ____ Muchas de las casas ________________ (ser) blancas y bonitas.
b. ____ Nosotros ________________ (poder) ver plantas y flores en los patios de los pueblos.
c. ____ Muchos españoles ________________ (preferir) el fútbol.
d. ____ Muchos españoles ________________ (soler) beber vino tinto.
e. ____ Nosotros ________________ (almorzar) a las 2:00 de la tarde.

❖ **Paso 3.** Write five original questions you could ask to elicit more information about Spanish customs and daily life. **¡OJO!** Remember to use the inverted question mark **(¿)** and to write an accent on the interrogative words (e.g., **¿dónde?**).

1. ____
2. ____
3. ____
4. ____
5. ____

❖ **D. Un día típico en España.** Imagine that you are in Spain. Write what you do in the morning, afternoon, and evening using verbs from the list. Write at least five sentences, and be sure to include the time of day.

almorzar, cerrar, comer, dormir, entender, merendar, pensar, preferir, soler, soñar con, volver

____

____

____

____

____

Pronunciación y ortografía

ll and y; z

Study the explanations in your textbook before doing these activities.

A. Repetición. Repeat the following words, paying careful attention to the sounds of **ll** and **y.** Be sure to use the strong Spanish [y] pronunciation of these letters.

1. millón
2. tortilla
3. apellido
4. allí
5. toalla (*towel*)
6. me llamo
7. desayunar
8. mayoría (*majority*)
9. playa
10. yo
11. leyendo (*reading*)
12. ayuda (*help*)

B. Dictado. Listen to each of the following sentences and write it in the spaces provided. **¡OJO!** Each sentence contains at least one instance of the letter **ll.** You will hear the sentences two times.

1. ______________________________
2. ______________________________
3. ______________________________
4. ______________________________
5. ______________________________

C. El norte (*north*) y el sur (*south*). You have learned that in parts of Spain, the **c** before **e** or **i** and the **z** are pronounced like the English *th.* Read the following words out loud, pronouncing these letters like the English *th.* Then listen to the two speakers and imitate their pronunciation. The first uses the pronunciation common in northern Spain **(th);** the second uses the pronunciation common in parts of southern Spain and Latin America **(s).**

1. cenar
2. tradicional
3. luz
4. urbanización
5. vecino
6. maceta
7. terraza
8. cerca
9. Andalucía

D. Ortografía. Change the following words from singular to plural.

MODELO andaluz → andaluces

1. lápiz ________________
2. luz ________________
3. cruz (*cross*) ________________
4. voz (*voice*) ________________
5. eficaz (*efficient*) ________________

Vocabulario

¿Qué hay en tu habitación?

A. Busca la intrusa. Indicate which household item does not belong. Then, add another word that belongs to the series.

1. ☐ la ventana ☐ la secadora ☐ la cama ____________
2. ☐ el lavabo ☐ el retrete ☐ el escritorio ____________
3. ☐ la cómoda ☐ la mesilla de noche ☐ la ducha ____________
4. ☐ el horno ☐ la estantería ☐ el armario ____________
5. ☐ la alfombra ☐ la bañera ☐ el cuadro ____________
6. ☐ el sillón ☐ el lavaplatos ☐ el horno ____________

B. Mi dormitorio. Listen to Isabel describe her apartment. Check the items that she mentions she has in her apartment. **¡OJO!** Don't check items that she specifically says she does not have. You will hear the answers on the audio program.

☐ la alfombra	☐ la cómoda	☐ el lavabo	☐ la mesilla de noche
☐ el armario	☐ el escritorio	☐ la lavadora	☐ la silla
☐ la cama	☐ la estantería	☐ la mesa	☐ el sillón

C. La mudanza (*move*)

Paso 1. Imagine that you are moving and the furniture movers have arrived with your things. Listen to each question, and select the most logical room for the item. You will hear the answers on the audio program.

	EN LA COCINA	EN EL COMEDOR	EN EL DORMITORIO	EN EL SALÓN
1.	☐	☐	☐	☐
2.	☐	☐	☐	☐
3.	☐	☐	☐	☐
4.	☐	☐	☐	☐
5.	☐	☐	☐	☐

Paso 2. Now, listen to the following questions from a friend about your new house and choose the best answer(s). You will hear the answers on the audio program.

1. ☐ una ducha ☐ un lavabo ☐ un retrete ☐ un horno
2. ☐ en la bañera ☐ en la chimenea ☐ en el salón ☐ en la alfombra
3. ☐ en el baño ☐ en el armario ☐ en el salón ☐ en la cama
4. ☐ en el lavabo ☐ en la mesilla ☐ en el armario ☐ en la nevera
5. ☐ una mesilla ☐ una cómoda ☐ un retrete ☐ una alfombra

❖ **D. En mi apartamento.** Choose at least three pieces of furniture from the list to decorate each room of your new place.

la alfombra, la cama, el cartel, la cómoda, el cuadro, el escritorio, la estantería, el horno, la lámpara, el lavaplatos, la mesa, la mesilla de noche, la nevera, la silla, el sillón, el sofá

MODELO el dormitorio →
En el dormitorio, voy a poner (*to put*) una cama,...

1. el salón

 ___

2. el comedor

 ___

3. la cocina

 ___

4. el dormitorio

 ___

❖ **E. Preguntas personales.** Answer the following questions.

1. Para ti, ¿cuáles son los electrodomésticos más útiles? ¿Por qué?

 ___

2. ¿Prefieres el horno eléctrico o el de gas?

 ___

3. Para ti, ¿es la secadora un electrodoméstico necesario o un lujo?

 ___

4. ¿Duermes con la ventana abierta o cerrada? ¿Por qué?

 ___

5. ¿Qué mueble o electrodoméstico no tienes pero necesitas en tu casa?

 ___

Entrevista 2

A. Sonido y significado

Paso 1: Sonido. The sentences in this activity are based on ideas from the interview with Elena de la Cruz Niggeman. First, read each sentence silently and make sure you understand its meaning. Then, listen as the speaker pronounces each sentence in phrases. Repeat the phrase in the interval provided until you can say it smoothly.

Elena de la Cruz Niggeman
Madrid, España

1. Yo vivo en un piso, un octavo piso (*eighth-floor apartment*).
2. En las ciudades de España, las casas particulares son un lujo.
3. Mi casa tiene tres dormitorios. En uno duermen mis padres, en otro duerme mi hermano y en otro duermo yo.
4. Tenemos un salón, una sala de estar (*family room*), una cocina, tres baños y un cuarto de servicio (*utility room*).

Paso 2: Significado. Indicate which of the following sentences is *not* true, based on the sentences in **Paso 1.**

a. ☐ Elena y su familia comparten un patio con los vecinos.
b. ☐ Es un lujo tener una casa particular en España.
c. ☐ La casa de Elena es muy grande.

B. Respuestas lógicas. First, read the questions and divided responses from the interview with Elena. Then, listen to the interview and match the first and last part of her responses.

PREGUNTAS Y RESPUESTAS PARTE 1

1. ¿Cómo es tu casa?

   «Mi casa es un piso. En España, al contrario de los Estados Unidos, _____.»

2. ¿Dónde está tu casa?

   «Mi casa está en un barrio de Madrid _____.»

3. ¿Es grande?

   «Sí, muy grande. Tiene tres dormitorios: En uno duermen mis padres, en otro duerme mi hermano _____.»

4. ¿Qué sueles hacer en cada habitación?

   «Paso la mayor parte del tiempo en mi cuarto, ahí estudio, escucho música, duermo. En el cuarto de estar pasamos mucho tiempo la familia juntos, _____.»

5. ¿Te gusta tu casa?

   «Sí, me encanta. Por fuera es fea, no te dice nada, _____.»

RESPUESTAS PARTE 2

a. que se llama 'El Parque de las Avenidas', y vivo en un octavo piso
b. vemos la televisión, charlamos. En el salón, bueno, al salón no vamos mucho, sólo cuando tenemos visita (*guests*). En la cocina cocinamos, y en el comedor comemos
c. las casas particulares son un lujo en las ciudades. Y yo vivo en un piso
d. pero por dentro es muy acogedora
e. y en otro duermo yo. Tenemos un salón, una sala de estar, una cocina, tres baños y un cuarto de servicio

C. ¿Entendiste? Match the activities mentioned by Elena to the place where she and her family do each one. Then listen to the interview again to check your answers.

1. Charlamos _____.
2. Cocinamos _____.
3. Comemos _____.
4. Duermo _____.
5. Escucho música _____.
6. Estudio _____.
7. Pasamos tiempo juntos _____.
8. Tenemos visitas _____.
9. Vemos la televisión _____.

a. en el dormitorio
b. en el salón
c. en el cuarto de estar
d. en la cocina
e. en el comedor

❖ **D. Preguntas para ti.** You will hear three questions. Write down your personal answers.

1. ______________________________
2. ______________________________
3. ______________________________

❖ **E. Para ir más allá.** Compare your house to that of either María or Elena. How are they similar? Different? Which do you prefer? Why?

MODELO Al igual que la casa de Elena, mi casa es grande y tiene tres dormitorios. A diferencia de su casa, mi casa es una casa particular, no es un piso.

____
____
____
____
____
____
____
____
____
____
____
____
____
____
____

Forma y función

4.3 The Present Progressive

Clínica de gramática

Review the following model of how to form the present pregressive.

estar + **-ando/-iendo**
habl**ar** → (yo) **estoy** habl**ando**
beb**er** → (tú) **estás** beb**iendo**
viv**ir** → (ellos) **están** viv**iendo**

¡OJO! Review also the irregular forms, like **durmiendo (dormir)** and **leyendo (leer).**

El progresivo. Now complete the following table with the progressive forms of the verbs indicated.

	yo	tú	nosotros/as	ellos/as
1. tomar	*estoy tomando*			
2. dormir				
3. leer				
4. comer			*estamos comiendo*	
5. jugar				
6. compartir				

A. ¿Dónde están?

Paso 1. Listen to each statement, then indicate where the activity is most logically taking place.

1. _____
2. _____
3. _____
4. _____
5. _____
6. _____

a. en el comedor
b. en la clase
c. en la cama
d. en la cafetería
e. en la biblioteca
f. en el jardín

Paso 2. Listen to each sentence from **Paso 1** again, and write down the infinitive of the present participle you hear. (The second column is for **Paso 3.**)

	INFINITIVO	SUJETO
1.	________________	________________
2.	________________	________________
3.	________________	________________
4.	________________	________________
5.	________________	________________
6.	________________	________________

Paso 3. Listen once again, and write down the subject pronoun that corresponds to each sentence.

B. ¿Qué están haciendo? Use the information provided to explain what these people are doing. Use the present progressive.

1. Javier / dormir / la siesta

   ____

2. Marta y Juan / tomar / un café

   ____

3. yo / almorzar / en la cafetería

   ____

4. los niños / jugar / al fútbol

   ____

5. el chef / preparar / la comida

   ____

6. vosotros / estudiar / gramática

   ____

❖ **C. ¿Qué estás haciendo?** Imagine that you have a cellular phone and at several points in the day a nosey friend calls and asks, **¿Qué estás haciendo?** The calls come in at the following times. What would you answer on a typical day?

MODELO Son las 5:00 de la mañana. → ¡Estoy durmiendo!

1. Son las 8:00 de la mañana. ________________________________
2. Son las 10:30 de la mañana. ________________________________
3. Es mediodía. ________________________________

4. Es la 1:30 de la tarde. ______
5. Son las 4:00 de la tarde. ______
6. Son las 7:30 de la tarde. ______
7. Son las 9:00 de la noche. ______
8. Son las 11:30 de la noche. ______

4.4 Affirmative Commands

Clínica de gramática

Review the following table to see how affirmative commands are formed. Here are some points to remember.

- Most affirmative **tú** commands look like the **usted/él/ella** form of the verb.
- Most affirmative **usted** and **ustedes** commands seem to have the "opposite" vowel in their ending.
- Additional spelling changes are made in the **usted** and **ustedes** commands of some verbs to maintain the original sound of the verb stem.
- **Vosotros/as** affirmative commands simply replace the **-r** of the infinitive with **-d.** They never undergo any of the stem or spelling changes of the other commands.
- There are a few verbs with irregular commands that you will learn in later chapters. For now however, you need only learn the affirmative commands for **hacer, salir,** and **tener.**

Infinitivo	***tú***	***usted***	***vosotros/as***	***ustedes***
contestar	contest**a**	contest**e**	contesta**d**	contest**en**
comer	com**e**	com**a**	come**d**	com**an**
escribir	escrib**e**	escrib**a**	escribi**d**	escrib**an**
bus**car**	bus**ca**	bus**que**	busca**d**	bus**quen**
pa**gar**	pa**ga**	pa**gue**	paga**d**	pa**guen**
empe**zar**	emp**ieza**	emp**iece**	empeza**d**	emp**iecen**
esco**ger**	esco**ge**	esco**ja**	escoge**d**	esco**jan**
hacer	**haz**	hag**a**	hace**d**	hag**an**
salir	**sal**	salg**a**	sali**d**	salg**an**
tener	**ten**	teng**a**	tene**d**	teng**an**

Los mandatos afirmativos. Now complete the following table with the affirmative commands of the verbs indicated.

	tú	**usted**	**vosotros/as**	**ustedes**
1. lavar				
2. barrer		*barra*		
3. jugar				*jueguen*
4. cerrar				
5. pensar				
6. soñar	*sueña*			
7. estudiar				
8. leer			*leed*	

A. En clase

Paso 1. Listen to the following commands you might hear in a classroom. Write down the infinitive form of each command you hear. (The second column is for **Paso 2.**)

	INFINITIVO	SUJETO
1.	________________	________________
2.	________________	________________
3.	________________	________________
4.	________________	________________
5.	________________	________________
6.	________________	________________

Paso 2. Now listen to each command from **Paso 1** again, and write down the corresponding subject pronoun: **tú, usted,** or **ustedes,** depending on the person(s) being addressed.

B. Mandatos lógicos. Select the most logical phrase to complete each command.

1. Sal ______________________.

   ☐ el periódico ☐ del cuarto de baño ☐ la tarea

2. Miren ______________________.

   ☐ la pizarra ☐ por la puerta principal ☐ del cuarto de baño

3. Duerme ______________________.

   ☐ el periódico ☐ ocho horas por la noche ☐ por la puerta principal

4. Vuelvan ______________________.

   ☐ a casa a las 10:00 ☐ del cuarto de baño ☐ la tarea

5. Lee ______________________.

   ☐ la pronunciación ☐ por la puerta principal ☐ el periódico

6. Practiquen ______________________.

   ☐ a casa a las 10:00 ☐ la pronunciación ☐ la pizarra

7. Coman ______________________.

   ☐ ocho horas por la noche ☐ en el comedor ☐ la pronunciación

8. Entren ______________________.

   ☐ ocho horas por la noche ☐ por la puerta principal ☐ del cuarto de baño

❖ Análisis cultural

The following quotes about homes and socializing in Spain will add to your knowledge about Spanish culture. Read the following passage and answer the questions that follow the quotes.

"Homes are very private affairs in Spain. Unlike 'townhouses' found in other parts of the world, which usually have a small front garden and a bit of a back yard, providing perfect opportunities for neighbors to exchange friendly chatter over their fences, a townhouse in Spain will have neither. A glance through the large and heavy front doors will usually be rewarded by the sight of attractive inner courtyards, full of greenery and pots of flowers and occasionally a fountain tinkling away. The home is the domain of the Spanish housewife, who, whether working or not, diligently cares for home and family.

"However, don't be surprised to find Spaniards gathering on the pavement in front of their houses to exchange the latest 'news' whilst enjoying the evening breeze in summer or the last rays of sunshine in winter. Foreigners are often puzzled by the Spanish preference for 'street socializing' rather than 'at home socializing.' This, however, encourages neighbors and local residents to get to know one another more intimately."

Source: *Culture Shock! Spain*

1. Where do you socialize? At home or elsewhere? Why do you choose this place? Do you notice any difference between your parents' generation and yours in this respect?

____

____

2. What can a passerby observe of your (parents') house from the street? Can you observe street life from your (parents') house?

____

____

____

3. Compare your (parents') house to the description of the Spanish house. Is your (parents') house more open or more closed to the street? Explain.

____

____

____

❖ PORTAFOLIO CULTURAL

Redacción: Intercambio de casas

You are going to Spain to study for a year at a language institute in Sevilla, and you'd like to offer your house to a Spanish student in exchange for a place to stay in Spain. You have advertised your lodging in a student newspaper at the Universidad de Sevilla, and you now have to write a more detailed e-mail message to an interested student in which you describe your house and its amenities. Also, you must ask questions about the house/apartment where you will live in Sevilla. Complete the following **pasos** on a separate sheet of paper before you write the final draft of your message.

A. Antes de escribir

Paso 1. Think of six adjectives that describe your room, apartment, or house. Give details to support your choice of words. You should describe your residence both physically and aesthetically.

MODELO grande (tres dormitorios y dos cuartos de baño)
conveniente (cerca de la universidad)
acogedor (colores cálidos [*warm*])

Paso 2. Is your place typical for its setting? (Is it a typical university dorm room, apartment, or house?) Why or why not?

MODELOS Mi cuarto es típico porque mi cuarto tiene…
Como todos los cuartos, mi cuarto es…
Mi apartamento (no) es parecido al apartamento típico porque…

Paso 3. Now list some questions you have about your counterpart's accommodations in Spain.

B. ¡A escribir! Compose the e-mail message using the information you listed in **Antes de escribir.** Describe your residence, pointing out how it might be different from the typical room, apartment, or house in Spain, then ask about counterpart's residence. Remember to begin by greeting your counterpart **(Hola, _____)** and to conclude with a typical closing **(Saludos,)** before your name.

C. **¡A corregir!** Before turning in your e-mail message, check the following points.

- ☐ Use of **tener, ser, estar,** and **hay**
- ☐ Spelling of stem-changing verbs
- ☐ Agreement, spelling, and accents of demonstrative adjectives and pronouns
- ☐ Punctuation and accents for questions
- ☐ Adjective/noun agreement

WWW Exploración

Choose and complete *one* of the following research activities. Then, based on your instructor's directions, present your results to the class and/or create a short report to include in your portfolio.

1. Study the two ads for housing in different parts of Spain. Given their style and other information contained in the ads, where do you think they might be located? In a city or in the country? In the mountains or by the beach? In a cold climate or a hot climate? Look at a map of Spain and identify two probable locations for each of these houses.

Urbanización Tosalet

Villa 290 m^2, Parcela 1.340 m^2

5 dormitorios, 3 baños, 2 duchas, sala, comedor, cocina, piscina 5x10, jardín, calefacción central, parking, 3 terrazas descubiertas, 1 terraza cubierta, jardín.

Referencia: APSC0055

Tipo: Apartamento

Situación: Montaña, Urbanización.

Precio: 93.157 Euros

Ático con vistas al mar, situada en Calahonda. Consta de 2 dormitorios, 2 baños, cocina equipada, salón comedor con chimenea, terraza, parking común. Situado en un agradable complejo con jardín y piscina en comunidad.

2. Interview two Spanish-speaking persons on campus or in your community. Ask them to name five household possessions that best express their personality or identity. Then, ask them which parts of their houses they consider private and which public. Compare their answers. Can you draw inferences about their values, levels of education, and social class?
3. Using print and electronic resources, investigate the demographics of two regions of Spain. Are the regions growing or losing population? Is the average population getting younger or older? Can you explain these trends, based on job opportunities, immigration, geographic location?
4. Find more information in your library or on the Internet about Spain. Here are some ideas and key words to get you started:

   - **las autonomías** (the autonomous regions of Spain)
   - **la Guerra Civil española** (1936–1939)
   - **la dictadura de Franco** (1939–1975)
   - the official languages (**castellano, catalán, gallego, euskera,** and others)
   - ETA and the Basque separatist movement
   - the Moorish influence in Spanish history, art, and architecture
   - Spanish festivals: **Semana Santa, las Fallas, las corridas de toros,** and so on
   - **el AVE** (the Spanish bullet train)
   - **tapas** and other Spanish foods

CAPÍTULO

5

Repaso y anticipación

A. En casa

Paso 1. Complete each sentence with the appropriate room.

la cocina, el comedor, el cuarto de baño, el dormitorio, el salón

1. Preparamos la comida en ____________________.
2. Almuerzas con la familia en ____________________.
3. Los niños echan una siesta en ____________________.
4. Descansamos y conversamos con amigos en ____________________.
5. La tía Anita está en la ducha en ____________________.

Paso 2. Now listen to each statement and check the appropriate area of the house. You will hear the answers on the audio program.

	LA COCINA	EL JARDÍN	EL PASILLO	LA PUERTA	EL SALÓN
1.	☐	☐	☐	☐	☐
2.	☐	☐	☐	☐	☐
3.	☐	☐	☐	☐	☐
4.	☐	☐	☐	☐	☐
5.	☐	☐	☐	☐	☐

❖ **Paso 3.** Now describe things you do in at least five areas of your home. Choose areas from the list.

la cocina, el comedor, el cuarto de baño, el dormitorio, el jardín, el pasillo, el patio, el salón, la terraza

____

____

____

____

____

____

B. Los muebles

Paso 1. Match each piece of furniture or appliance with an activity.

1. _____ el sofá
2. _____ la cama
3. _____ el horno
4. _____ las sillas y la mesa
5. _____ el escritorio

a. almorzar
b. estudiar
c. echar una siesta
d. preparar la comida
e. dormir por la noche

❖ **Paso 2.** Now, write down at least one piece of furniture or appliance that you associate with the following rooms.

1. el comedor: ___________________________
2. la cocina: ___________________________
3. el cuarto de baño: ___________________________
4. el salón: ___________________________
5. el dormitorio: ___________________________

C. Asociaciones lógicas

Paso 1. Read over the following vocabulary that describes food stores and the kinds of food they sell. Match each store with an item.

1. _____ carnicería
2. _____ frutería
3. _____ panadería
4. _____ pescadería
5. _____ verdulería

a. pescado
b. pan
c. carne
d. verduras
e. frutas

Paso 2. What suffix does each store have in common? What do you think it means?

____

D. Las comidas. You will learn words for many food items in this chapter. Try to label the following drawings with the corresponding food name from the list. Base your guesses on spelling and sound similarities with English.

el azúcar, la ensalada, el jamón, el limón, la papa, la piña, la sal, la sopa, el tomate

1. ___________________ 2. ___________________ 3. ___________________

4. ____________________

5. ____________________

6. ____________________

7. ____________________

8. ____________________

9. ____________________

E. Orígenes culinarios.

Paso 1. Match each dish with its origin.

1. _____ la pizza
2. _____ el sushi
3. _____ el café
4. _____ el chow mein
5. _____ los *croissants*
6. _____ las enchiladas

a. chino
b. italiano
c. francés
d. japonés
e. mexicano
f. colombiano

Paso 2. Now write complete sentences using the information in **Paso 1.** Be sure to use the correct form of the verb **ser** and make the adjectives agree. The first one is done for you.

1. La pizza es italiana.
2. ____
3. ____
4. ____
5. ____
6. ____

PARTE 1

Vocabulario

En el mercado; ¿Cómo es la comida? ¿Cómo está el plato?

A. ¿Qué categoría? Check the category to which each food item belongs.

	CARNE	FRUTA	POSTRE	PESCADO	VERDURA
1. pollo	☐	☐	☐	☐	☐
2. aguacate	☐	☐	☐	☐	☐
3. jamón	☐	☐	☐	☐	☐
4. pastel	☐	☐	☐	☐	☐
5. salmón	☐	☐	☐	☐	☐
6. cebolla	☐	☐	☐	☐	☐
7. cereza (*cherry*)	☐	☐	☐	☐	☐
8. flan	☐	☐	☐	☐	☐

B. Gustos muy particulares. Imagine that you are preparing a meal for four friends. One is an athlete; another is a vegetarian who does not drink alcohol; the third doesn't like Mexican food. Fortunately, the fourth friend eats everything. What foods could you prepare? Compose two menus.

	MENÚ I	MENÚ II
entrada	______________	______________
plato principal	______________	______________
verduras	______________	______________
postre	______________	______________
bebida	______________	______________

C. ¿Qué es? Listen to each comment or exchange, then check the corresponding category. You will hear the answers on the audio program.

1. ☐ una fruta ☐ un pastel
2. ☐ unas bebidas ☐ unas verduras
3. ☐ un plato principal ☐ una entrada
4. ☐ unas frutas ☐ unos pescados
5. ☐ una bebida ☐ una entrada

D. Descripciones. Complete each sentence with the correct form of the most logical adjective.

agrio, amargo, crudo (*raw*), fresco, frito, maduro, picante, tierno, viejo

MODELO Prefiero comer verduras ______________ porque cuando cocinas las verduras, pierdes (*you lose*) vitaminas. →
crudas

1. No me gusta este pan. Está ______________ y seco.
2. La limonada está muy ______________. Necesita más azúcar.
3. ¡El café es horrible! Es muy fuerte (*strong*) y ______________.

4. Los plátanos están muy ______________________. Casi (*Almost*) están negros.
5. No me gustan los jalapeños ni la salsa mexicana. No puedo comer comida ______________________.
6. El bistec está muy rico. Es muy ______________________. Casi no necesito cuchillo (*knife*).
7. Prefiero ir al mercado. Las verduras y las frutas son más ______________________ allí.
8. Eduardo no come comidas ______________________ porque está a dieta.

❖ **E. ¿Qué comes?** Write a brief description about the foods you like and dislike. Also, tell what you eat or drink nearly every day.

MODELO Me gustan los mariscos y… No me gustan los tomates… Casi todos los días como…

____

____

____

____

____

❖ **F. ¿Qué opinas?** Give your opinion on the following nutrition questions.

1. ¿Es mejor cocinar con mantequilla o con aceite de oliva?

   ____
2. ¿Cuántas frutas debes comer cada día?

   ____
3. ¿Es mejor el café o el té? ¿Cuántas tazas tomas por día?

   ____
4. ¿El queso es bueno para la salud o tiene demasiado colesterol?

   ____
5. ¿Consideras que un sándwich es un almuerzo saludable?

   ____
6. ¿Son buenos para la salud los platos picantes?

   ____
7. ¿Hay que evitar completamente las comidas fritas, o está bien comerlas de vez en cuando (*occasionally*)?

   ____

Entrevista 1

A. Sonido y significado

Paso 1: Sonido. The sentences in this activity are based on the interview with Karina de Frías Otero. First, read each sentence silently and make sure you understand its meaning. Then, listen as the speaker pronounces each sentence in phrases. Repeat the phrase in the interval provided until you can say it smoothly.

Karina de Frías Otero
Santo Domingo, República Dominicana

1. En Santo Domingo, vamos a los supermercados a hacer nuestras compras.
2. Ahí compramos vegetales y frutas y productos enlatados (*canned*) y congelados (*frozen*).
3. En los pueblos, como en Baní, donde vive mi abuela, las personas van al mercado para comprar sus vegetales y frutas frescas.
4. En los mercados regularmente las frutas son más frescas. Las personas que las cultivan (*grow them*) son las mismas que las venden.
5. La cocina dominicana es una gran mezcla de culturas. Nosotros estamos muy influenciados por los españoles, los ingleses y los franceses.

Paso 2: Significado. Indicate which of the following sentences is *not* true, based on the sentences in **Paso 1.**

a. ☐ En la capital muchas personas van a los supermercados.
b. ☐ En los pueblos, las frutas más frescas se encuentran en los supermercados.
c. ☐ La cocina dominicana tiene muchas influencias diferentes.

B. Respuestas lógicas. First, read the questions and divided responses from the interview with Karina. Then, listen to the interview and match the first and last part of her responses.

PREGUNTAS Y RESPUESTAS PARTE 1

1. ¿Adónde vas para hacer la compra?

   «En Santo Domingo, vamos a los supermercados. Ahí es que vamos a hacer nuestras compras de vegetales, _____.»

2. ¿Es así en todo el país?

   «En los pueblos, como en Baní, donde vive mi abuela, en las afueras, sí, las personas van al mercado para comprar sus vegetales y frutas frescas. _____.»

3. ¿Cuáles son algunas de las ventajas de los mercados?

   «En los mercados regularmente las frutas son más frescas, _____.»

4. ¿Qué frutas y vegetales se ven en estos mercados?

   «¿Frutas? Se encuentran: los guineos, los mangos, la chinola, la piña, los cocos de agua, que son muy populares, las naranjas también, que les llamamos chinas. _____.»

5. ¿Cómo es la cocina dominicana?

   «La cocina dominicana es una gran mezcla de culturas. Nosotros pues estamos muy influenciados por los españoles, _____.»

6. ¿Hay un plato nacional?

   «El plato nacional, es el arroz con habichuelas. Las habichuelas pueden ser blancas, negras o rojas. _____.»

RESPUESTAS PARTE 2

a. Como vegetales: la batata, el ñame, la papa, el plátano,... los molondrones. Y básicamente éstos son los más importantes
b. Si vas a comer este plato solamente debes pedir 'la bandera nacional', y esto es lo que tendrás, un plato de arroz con habichuelas
c. y frutas también, y productos enlatados y congelados
d. igualmente los vegetales. Las mismas personas que las venden son las mismas personas que las cultivan
e. los ingleses y los franceses. Y eso es lo que se ve en nuestra cultura, nuestra comida y toda esta gran mezcla de sabores de diferentes países
f. Y luego van al supermercado ya para congelados y enlatados

C. ¿Entendiste? Answer the following questions in complete sentences, based on the interview with Karina.

1. En la capital, ¿dónde hacen la compra muchas personas?

   ____

2. ¿Dónde compra mucha gente en los pueblos?

   ____

3. ¿Por qué prefiere Karina el mercado?

   ____

4. ¿Qué ingredientes contiene el plato nacional dominicano?

   ____

❖ **D. Preguntas para ti.** You will hear three questions. Write down your personal answers.

1. ____
2. ____
3. ____

Forma y función

5.1 Speaking Impersonally: **se** + Verb

Clínica de gramática

A very common way to express what people do in general is by using **se** + *verb*. The verb is in the third-person singular or plural form, depending on the number of nouns you are referring to.

se + *singular verb* + *singular noun*

Se vend**e** un piso.

se + *plural verb* + *plural noun*

Se vend**en** varios pisos.

¿Cómo se preparan los *nachos*? The following statements are some steps for making *nachos,* a common North American snack. Choose the correct form of the verb in parentheses. **¡OJO!** Pay special attention to the verb endings (third-person singular or plural).

1. Se (compra/compran) las tortillas fritas (*chips*) y otros ingredientes.
2. Se (coloca/colocan) las tortillas fritas en un plato.
3. Se (distribuye/distribuyen) el queso rallado (*grated*) sobre las tortillas fritas.
4. Se (cubre/cubren) con salsa picante.

A. En el mercado. Listen to the speaker describe a day at the market. Indicate whether each statement refers to people in general or to a specific person or group of people. You will hear the answers on the audio program.

MODELOS (*you hear*) Como manzanas. →
(*you mark*) específico
(*you hear*) Aquí se come bien. →
(*you mark*) general

	ESPECÍFICO	GENERAL
1.	☐	☐
2.	☐	☐
3.	☐	☐
4.	☐	☐
5.	☐	☐
6.	☐	☐
7.	☐	☐
8.	☐	☐

B. Un folleto. Imagine that you are preparing a brochure with information for tourists visiting Venezuela. Use the following information to form sentences to include in the brochure. **¡OJO!** Use **se** + *verb* in your sentences.

MODELO comprar: muchas frutas en los mercados venezolanos →
Se compran muchas frutas en los mercados venezolanos.

1. encontrar: caraotas (frijoles negros) en todas las comidas

____

2. comer: muchos mariscos y pescados

____

3. ir de compras: con gusto porque las tiendas son muy lindas

____

4. almorzar: a las 2:00 en punto

____

5. beber: vino con el almuerzo, igual que en Europa

____

C. ¡A cocinar! Read how Chef Bruno makes **flan al caramelo,** a popular custard dessert eaten everywhere in Spain and Latin America. Then rewrite the steps using the "*se* **impersonal**" so that it resembles a typical recipe.

Flan al caramelo

Ingredientes

1 taza y 3 cucharadas de azúcar
1 litro de leche
6 huevos

Preparación

1. Se _______________ (hacer) el caramelo con 3 cucharadas de azúcar.
2. Se _______________ (batir [*to beat*]) los huevos, la leche y el azúcar.
3. Se _______________ (echar [*to pour*]) la mezcla en un molde.
4. Se _______________ (meter [*to insert*]) el flan en el horno por 30 minutos.
5. Se _______________ (sacar) el flan del horno y se _______________ (dejar) enfriar.

❖ **D. Mi receta.** Now it's your turn. Write down in Spanish the recipe for your favorite dish. Make a list of ingredients, and don't forget to use **se** + *verb.*

Nombre del plato: _______________________

Ingredientes

Preparación

1. ______________________________
2. ______________________________
3. ______________________________
4. ______________________________
5. ______________________________

5.2 **Por** and **para**

Clínica de gramática

There are two prepositions in Spanish that can be translated as *for* in English: **por** and **para.** However, the two are not interchangeable, so take note of the basic reasons for using each one.

por	**para**
• *through space or through time* • *length or duration of time* • *fixed expressions*	• *purpose or goal* • *recipient or destination*

Los planes. Complete each sentence with **por** or **para,** as appropriate.

1. Vamos a Maracaibo ____________ una semana.
2. Vamos a quedarnos (*stay*) en un hotel ____________ tres días.
3. ____________ ir al centro, se toma el autobús.
4. Tenemos que esperar el autobús ____________ veinte minutos.
5. Busco un regalo ____________ mi hermana.
6. Pensamos regresar ____________ la tarde.

A. Los usos

Paso 1. Indicate the reason for using **por** or **para** in the following sentences.

1. Esta tarde salgo para Caracas.

   ☐ *purpose or goal* ☐ *recipient* ☐ *destination*
2. Voy a Caracas para comprar frutas y verduras.

   ☐ *purpose or goal* ☐ *recipient* ☐ *destination*
3. Pienso estar en la ciudad por cuatro horas.

   ☐ *through space* ☐ *through time* ☐ *length or duration of time* ☐ *fixed expression*

4. Voy a dar paseos por las calles porque son muy bonitas.

☐ *through space* ☐ *through time* ☐ *length or duration of time* ☐ *fixed expression*

5. Las manzanas son para mi hija, las naranjas son para mi esposa.

☐ *purpose or goal* ☐ *recipient* ☐ *destination*

6. Puedo llevar por lo menos dos bolsas (*bags*) de verduras y frutas.

☐ *through space* ☐ *through time* ☐ *length or duration of time* ☐ *fixed expression*

Paso 2. Now complete each sentence with **por** or **para.** Then write down the reason why.

MODELO Alicia va al mercado ________ comprar lechuga y tomates. →
para, *purpose or goal*

	REASON
1. Se usan huevos y leche ________ hacer flan.	________________
2. Voy a cocinar ________ unas horas.	________________
3. Damos un paseo ________ el parque todos los días.	________________
4. Estas verduras son ________ mi abuela.	________________
5. Necesitamos ir ________ esa calle para llegar al mercado.	________________
6. Salen ________ el mercado ahora. ¿Vas?	________________

B. Mi rutina de entresemana (*on weekdays*). Complete the following paragraph with **por** and **para.**

________[1] la mañana, doy un paseo ________[2] nuestro barrio. Camino[a] ________[3] una hora, ________[4] lo menos tres mañanas a la semana. Cuando vuelvo a casa, preparo el desayuno ________[5] mi familia. Mis hijos salen ________[6] la escuela a las 7:30. Mi esposa va a su oficina a las 8:00. Yo trabajo en casa, ________[7] eso, llego a mi oficina sin[b] problemas. Entro en mi oficina a las 9:00 y pongo[c] música clásica ________[8] concentrarme.[d]

[a]*I walk* [b]*without* [c]*I put on* [d]*concentrate*

C. Expresiones fijas (*fixed*). Rewrite each pair of sentences as one sentence using an expression from the list.

por ejemplo, por eso, por favor, por lo menos

MODELO Comemos muchas frutas en Venezuela. Hay lechosas y mangos. →
Comemos muchas frutas en Venezuela, por ejemplo, lechosas y mangos.

1. La comida venezolana es rica. Las arepas y las hallacas son comidas venezolanas.

____

2. No me gusta la carne. No como hamburguesas.

____

3. Es importante comer muchas frutas. Una manzana por día es bueno.

____

4. Me gusta mucha sal en mi ensalada. ¿Puedes pasarme la sal?

____

Pronunciación y ortografía

Special Letter Combinations

Read and study the explanations in your text before completing these activities.

A. La pronunciación. Repeat the following words, paying special attention to the sounds of **c, qu, g, gu,** and **j.**

1. reja (*grillwork on window*)
2. aquí
3. bajo
4. enseguida (*right away*)
5. escoger (*to choose*)
6. ginebra (*gin*)
7. girar (*to spin*)
8. jardín
9. agua (*water*)
10. joya (*jewel*)
11. queja (*complaint*)
12. querer

B. Cognados. Listen and repeat each cognate. Then listen again and write the English equivalent from the list.

agent, correct, direct, general, genius, geology, pajama, protect

1. ________________________
2. ________________________
3. ________________________
4. ________________________
5. ________________________
6. ________________________
7. ________________________
8. ________________________

PARTE 2

Vocabulario

Las comidas del día; En el restaurante

A. Comparaciones. Compare the following food and drink items based on the words in parentheses. **¡OJO!** Watch adjective/noun agreement.

MODELO las frutas del mercado / las frutas del supermercado (fresco) →
Las frutas del mercado son más frescas que (tan frescas como) las frutas del supermercado.

1. el limón / las uvas (agrio)

____

2. la langosta / el pollo (caro)

____

3. el té / el café (amargo)

____

4. el pastel de chocolate / la manzana (dulce)

____

5. los jalapeños / los pimientos verdes (picante)

______

6. las piñas / las naranjas (delicioso)

______

7. el ajo / la cebolla (esencial)

______

8. el desayuno / el almuerzo (importante)

______

❖ **B. Comparaciones.** Compare the following pairs of food items. You can use adjectives from the list or others that you know.

agrio, barato, caro, dulce, grande, pequeño

MODELO las espinacas / la lechuga →
Las espinacas son más verdes que la lechuga.

1. el melón / el plátano

______

2. el pescado / los camarones

______

3. el jamón / el bistec

______

4. el limón / la naranja

______

5. las zanahorias / el maíz

______

❖ **C. Las comidas.** Answer the following questions about your meals and meals in your country.

1. ¿A qué hora desayunas? En general, ¿a qué hora se desayuna en tu región?

______

______

2. ¿Cuándo se abren los restaurantes para el almuerzo? ¿A qué hora almuerzas tú?

______

______

3. ¿Con quién almuerzas los domingos? Generalmente, ¿con quién se almuerza los domingos?

______

______

4. ¿Con quién cenas en restaurantes elegantes? ¿Hasta (*Until*) qué hora se puede cenar en un restaurante elegante?

____

____

D. Crucigrama. Read the definitions and complete the crossword puzzle with the defined words from the list.

algo, cocina, comprar, cuenta, desea, entrada, freír, lata, merendar, nada, pedir, plato, primer, principal, servir, taza, un poco de, vaso

HORIZONTAL

1. Prepara comida.
5. Podemos guardar (*save*) los productos que están en esto por mucho tiempo.
6. Es común preparar el pollo y las papas de esta manera.
7. Es lo opuesto (*the opposite*) de «mucho de».
9. Este plato suele incluir (*include*) carne y verduras.
14. Es sinónimo de «quiere».
15. Es comer algo ligero (*light*) entre las comidas principales.
16. Servimos el té y el café en esto.
17. Es la cosa en que se sirve la comida.

VERTICAL

2. Es conseguir algo con dinero (*money*).
3. Es lo opuesto de «nada».
4. Es el trabajo que hacen los meseros para sus clientes.
8. Es la comida que comemos al principio (*beginning*) de la comida.
9. Es el plato que comemos antes del plato principal pero después de la entrada.
10. Es la cosa que pedimos después de una comida en un restaurante.
11. Es explicar al mesero lo que deseas comer.
12. Es lo opuesto de «algo».
13. Servimos agua y refrescos en esto.

E. Todo lo contrario. Rewrite the following affirmative statements to make them negative. **¡OJO!** Remember to use **no** before the verb if a negative word follows.

MODELO Tengo algunas recetas venezolanas. →
No tengo ninguna receta venezolana.

1. Este plato tiene algo de queso.

   ____

2. Este restaurante sirve algunos platos vegetarianos.

   ____

3. Hay algo en este menú para los niños.

   ____

4. Esta salsa tiene algún ingrediente exótico.

   ____

5. Me gustaría probar (*try*) algunas frutas tropicales.

   ____

F. En el restaurante. Choose the correct verbs to complete the following conversation.

MESERO: Buenas tardes. ¿Qué (desean / traen)[1]?
SEÑOR: Buenas tardes. ¿Hay platos especiales? ¿Qué nos (pide / recomienda)[2]?
MESERO: Tenemos un bistec muy tierno. ¿Qué les (traigo / recomiendo)[3] de plato principal?
SEÑOR: (Me gustaría / Se debe)[4] pedir el bistec.
SEÑORA: A mí también.
(*después de la comida*)
SEÑOR: ¿Nos (trae / sirve)[5] la cuenta, por favor?
MESERO: Cómo no, señores.

❖ **G. En el restaurante.** Use the following expressions to put together an exchange between a waiter and client. You will need to add phrases and sentences of your own. Make the exchange at least eight lines long.

¿Qué desea de... ?　　Me gustaría...
¿Y de... ?　　¿Me trae... , por favor?
¿Qué recomienda usted?

de entrada / de primer plato / de plato principal / de postre / de beber

____
____
____
____
____
____
____
____
____
____

Entrevista 2

A. Sonido y significado

Paso 1: Sonido. The sentences in this activity are based on ideas from the interview with Patricia Nevil Gallego. First, read each sentence silently and make sure you understand its meaning. Then, listen as the speaker pronounces each sentence in phrases. Repeat the phrase in the interval provided until you can say it smoothly.

Patricia Nevil Gallego
Caracas, Venezuela

1. Mi plato favorito es **el pabellón criollo.** Está compuesto de (*composed of*) arroz blanco, tajadas (*fried bananas*), caraotas, que son frijoles negros, y la carne desmechada (*shredded beef*).
2. La comida más importante es **la arepa.** Está hecha de harina de maíz (*corn flour*). Las arepas se ponen en el horno o se hacen fritas también. Se comen con queso o con caraotas.
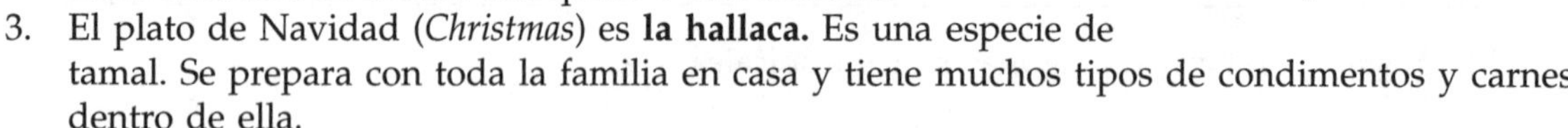
3. El plato de Navidad (*Christmas*) es **la hallaca.** Es una especie de tamal. Se prepara con toda la familia en casa y tiene muchos tipos de condimentos y carnes dentro de ella.
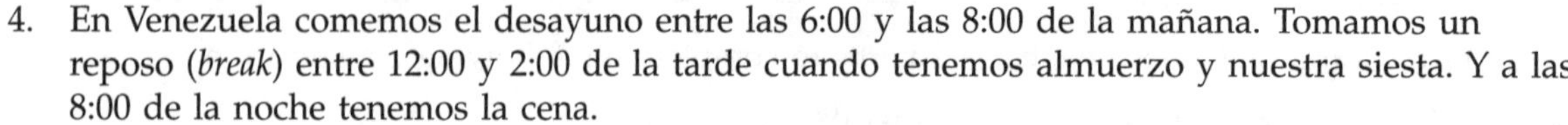
4. En Venezuela comemos el desayuno entre las 6:00 y las 8:00 de la mañana. Tomamos un reposo (*break*) entre 12:00 y 2:00 de la tarde cuando tenemos almuerzo y nuestra siesta. Y a las 8:00 de la noche tenemos la cena.

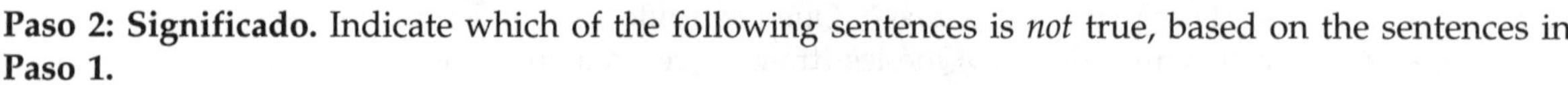

Paso 2: Significado. Indicate which of the following sentences is *not* true, based on the sentences in **Paso 1.**

a. ☐ La arepa se come con otras comidas.
b. ☐ Los venezolanos tienen tres comidas al día.
c. ☐ El pabellón criollo es un plato vegetariano.

B. Respuestas lógicas. First, read the questions and divided responses from the interview with Patricia. Then, listen to the interview and match the first and last part of her responses.

PREGUNTAS Y RESPUESTAS PARTE 1

1. ¿Cuál es tu plato favorito?

   «Mi plato favorito es **el pabellón criollo.** Está compuesto de arroz blanco, tajadas, caraotas, _____.»

2. ¿Qué comidas típicas se comen en tu país?

   «Bueno, la más importante es **la arepa.** Éste es un plato que se come todos los días. Está hecho de harina de maíz, viene precocida y se prepara con agua tibia. _____.»

3. ¿Hay otros platos importantes?

   «Sí, el plato de Navidad, que es **la hallaca.** Es como una especie de tamal. Se prepara con toda la familia en casa, toma muchísimo tiempo para hacer. Está también hecha de una masa de maíz y _____.»

4. ¿A qué hora son las comidas en Venezuela?

«Pues en Venezuela comemos entre las 6:00 y las 8:00 de la mañana el desayuno, ya que todos comenzamos nuestros quehaceres a las 9:00. Después, tenemos un reposo entre 12:00 y 2:00 de la tarde _____.»

RESPUESTAS PARTE 2

a. que es cuando tenemos almuerzo y nuestra siesta. Y después volvemos a casa a las 6:00 de la noche y como hasta las 8:00 de la noche tenemos la cena
b. tiene muchos tipos de condimentos y carnes dentro de ella. Se envuelve también en una hoja de banana y se cocina lentamente. Es muy sabrosa
c. Se hace una mezcla, se hacen los pancitos, se ponen en el horno o se hacen fritos también, y éstos se pueden comer con queso, caraota o huevo,... lo que tú quieras
d. que son los frijoles negros, y la carne desmechada

C. ¿Entendiste? Answer the following questions in complete sentences, based on the interview with Patricia.

1. ¿Qué ingredientes contiene el pabellón criollo?

____

2. ¿Cuál es el ingrediente principal de la arepa?

____

3. ¿En qué ocasión se preparan las hallacas, típicamente?

____

4. ¿Entre qué horas tienen el almuerzo los venezolanos?

____

❖ **D. Preguntas para ti.** You will hear three questions. Write down your personal answers.

1. ______________________________
2. ______________________________
3. ______________________________

Forma y función

5.3 Stem-Changing Verbs (**e** → **i**)

Clínica de gramática

Certain **-ir** verbs change their last stem vowel from **e** to **i** when that vowel is stressed. Here is the conjugation of the verb **pedir** with the stressed vowel underlined and the stem vowel in boldface.

pedir			
(yo)	pido	(nosotros/as)	pedimos
(tú)	pides	(vosotros/as)	pedís
(usted, él/ella)	pide	(ustedes, ellos/as)	piden

Cambios de raíz. Complete the following table with the correct forms of the verbs indicated.

	yo	nosotros/as	tú	ellos/as	vosotros/as
1. servir			*sirves*		
2. freír				*fríen*	
3. decir					*decís*
4. conseguir					
5. medir					

A. Un restaurante familiar. Complete the sentence with the correct form of the verb in parentheses.

1. Mis hermanos y yo generalmente ________________________ (conseguir) un buen trabajo todos los veranos porque mi familia tiene un restaurante.
2. José, mi hermano mayor, ________________________ (servir) el vino, y yo el agua.
3. Yo siempre les ________________________ (decir) «gracias» a los clientes.
4. La especialidad del restaurante es el pollo frito. Mis padres ________________________ (freír) el pollo con frutas. ¡Es riquísimo!
5. Si vas a nuestro restaurante y ________________________ (pedir) el pollo frito, debes pedir la salsa de la casa también. ¡Es única!

B. En la cafetería. Unscramble the words and conjugate the verbs to form sentences that explain what students eat in the cafeteria and what they think about the food.

1. pedir / hamburguesas / en la cafetería / nosotros

   ____

2. papas fritas / servir / ellos / con las hamburguesas

   ____

3. freír / el cocinero (*cook*) / por quince minutos / las papas

   ____

4. el cocinero / medir bien / no / frecuentemente / los ingredientes

   ____

5. decir / muchos estudiantes / «No me gusta la comida de la cafetería.»

   ____

C. Quejas en el restaurante

Paso 1. Complete each sentence with the correct form of the most logical verb from the list. (The check boxes are for **Paso 2.**)

conseguir, decir, freír, medir, pedir, servir

		C	M
1.	El chef ______________ todo con aceite viejo.	☐	☐
2.	Mucha gente no ______________ claramente (*clearly*) lo qué desea comer.	☐	☐
3.	Esos señores siempre ______________ mucho pan con la comida.	☐	☐
4.	No se ______________ bebidas alcohólicas en este restaurante.	☐	☐
5.	Este restaurante es muy popular. No se ______________ una mesa después de la 1:00.	☐	☐
6.	Los chefs de este restaurante no ______________ bien los ingredientes.	☐	☐

Paso 2. Now go back to the sentences in **Paso 1** and check whether the complaint was most logically registered by a client (C) or a waiter (M). If both might have made the complaint, check both boxes.

❖ **D. Tu restaurante favorito.** Answer the following questions about your favorite restaurant in complete sentences.

1. ¿Qué tipo de comida se sirve en tu restaurante favorito?

   ____

2. ¿Qué pides en ese restaurante?

   ____

3. ¿Siempre consigues una mesa fácilmente en ese restaurante? ¿Qué haces si no puedes conseguir una mesa?

____

4. ¿Qué dicen los meseros de ese restaurante cuando llegas?

____

5.4 Direct Object Pronouns

Clínica de gramática

Direct object pronouns **(pronombres de complemento directo)** can replace direct object nouns in a sentence. Here are the direct object pronouns in Spanish.

Los pronombres de complemento directo

me	me	**nos**	us
te	you (*fam. s.*)	**os**	you (*fam. pl.*)
lo/la	him, her, it (*m., f.*), you (*form. s. m., f.*)	**los/las**	them (*m., f.*), you (*form. pl.*)

Object pronouns are placed *before* conjugated verbs and attached *after* infinitives and the **-ndo** form.

—¿Haces **la tarea** todos los días?

—Sí, **la** hago siempre. ¿A qué hora vas a hacer**la** esta noche?

Las preferencias gastronómicas. Explain what you do with the following foods by writing the correct direct object pronoun: **lo/la/los/las.**

MODELO ¿Las verduras? _________ como todos los días. → Las

1. ¿La pizza? _________ puedo comer a todas horas.
2. ¿Los refrescos? _________ sirvo con muchas comidas.
3. ¿Las papas? _________ frío en un sartén (*frying pan*) con aceite.
4. ¿El bistec? _________ recomiendo mucho. ¡Es muy sabroso!
5. ¿La salsa? _________ prefiero con la carne.
6. ¿Las hallacas? _________ hago en casa con mi familia.

A. Las comidas. Underline the direct object pronoun in the following sentences. Then write the noun or subject pronoun (*referent*) to which it refers.

MODELOS Para la cena, voy a preparar pollo frito. Mis hijos lo comen con mucho gusto. →
lo; pollo frito
Mis amigos me llaman los sábados para salir. →
me; yo

		REFERENT
1.	Pedro siempre pide vino con las comidas, pero Gloria lo detesta.	___
2.	Mis padres me invitan a comer todos los domingos.	___
3.	Las verduras son importantes para la dieta. Las como todos los días.	___
4.	El mesero trae la cuenta y nosotros la pagamos.	___
5.	Muchos restaurantes sirven platos exóticos ahora. ¿Los comes tú?	___
6.	Esta sopa de pollo tiene mucho ajo. No la voy a pedir más.	___
7.	¿Te conocen en este restaurante?	___
8.	Siempre os vemos en este restaurante.	___
9.	Este plato normalmente tiene papas, pero hoy no las tiene.	___
10.	Los tamales de mi abuela son exquisitos. Los como todos los días.	___

B. ¿Qué haces? Listen to the speaker give you a situation. Check the correct response to each situation, based on the direct object.

MODELO (*you hear*) El mesero trae pan a tu mesa.
(*you see*) La como. / Lo como.
(*you mark*) Lo como.

1. ☐ La gasto. ☐ Lo gasto.
2. ☐ Las llamo. ☐ Los llamo.
3. ☐ Las hago. ☐ Los hago.
4. ☐ La leo. ☐ Lo leo.
5. ☐ La pido. ☐ Lo pido.
6. ☐ La pago. ☐ Lo pago.

C. Una cena. Imagine that your Spanish class is having a potluck dinner and your instructor asks you who is bringing what. Answer each question using the direct object pronoun and the answer in parentheses.

MODELO ¿Quién tiene las tazas de plástico? (Felipe) →
Felipe las tiene.

1. ¿Quién hace las arepas? (yo)
   ___
2. ¿Quién compra las bebidas? (nosotros)
   ___
3. ¿Quién trae la música? (Raúl)
   ___
4. ¿Quién va a cocinar el pastel? (usted)
   ___
5. ¿Quién prepara el arroz con pollo? (Carmen)
   ___

6. ¿Quién llama a los invitados? (Esteban y Lidia)

____

7. ¿Quién hace el guacamole? (ustedes)

____

8. ¿Quién cocina la carne? (Paloma)

____

9. ¿Quién trae las ensaladas? (yo)

____

10. ¿Quién va a comprar los platos de papel? (Marisol)

____

❖ **D. Mis comidas y bebidas favoritas.** List five of your favorite dishes or drinks. Then write a sentence about each one using a verb from the list and a direct object pronoun to refer to the item.

beber, comer, freír, hacer, pedir, preferir, preparar, servir

MODELO el jugo de naranja; Lo bebo por la mañana.

	LA COMIDA / BEBIDA	LA ORACIÓN
1.	____________	____________________
2.	____________	____________________
3.	____________	____________________
4.	____________	____________________
5.	____________	____________________

❖ Análisis cultural

The following quotes come from a handbook for tourists who visit the Dominican Republic. Keep in mind the information you have already learned about meals in Spanish-speaking countries as you read this passage, then answer the questions that follow the quotes.

"After lunch, Dominicans usually stretch out for their afternoon **siesta,** which lasts a couple of hours, before they're ready to face the world again. In small towns, and in many larger ones as well, businesses close for several hours to accommodate the Dominican tradition of a large lunch and a short nap in the middle of the day. You'll see that government offices quite often post hours that show them open during the middle of the afternoon, but I defy you to find many civil servants on the job during that time."

"Most Dominicans try to eat **almuerzo** at home if possible, but increasing numbers of workers must take some type of lunch with them and don't have time for a **siesta.** More and more, the modern workaday world is gaining on the old, Spanish traditions. And more and more businesses in Santo Domingo and Santiago are foregoing the siesta period altogether."

Source: *Dominican Republic Handbook*

1. What is the role of the afternoon **siesta** in the Caribbean?

____

____

2. What are the benefits of taking a nap after lunch? What are the disadvantages?

____

____

3. What changes in the traditional Dominican meal habits are taking place? Why?

____

____

4. Would you classify these changes in the Dominican routine as positive or negative? Explain.

____

____

❖ PORTAFOLIO CULTURAL

Redacción: Una reseña (*review*)

Imagine that you are writing a review for a Venezuelan magazine of a local restaurant that you know well.

A. Antes de escribir

Paso 1. On a separate sheet of paper, choose the restaurant you want to review and write a few sentences describing its location, its size (big or small), and how often you eat there.

Paso 2. Choose some of the adjectives you would use to describe the restaurant from the following list. Look up words you do not know and add other adjectives that you would like to use.

bueno	mediocre	malo
delicioso	así, así	repugnante
excelente	ni fu ni fa	asqueroso
exquisito	insípido	aburrido
fantástico	regular	horrible

Paso 3. Now jot down some notes related to the following categories that might be useful in your review.

origen étnico	horario
platos especiales (ingredientes, preparaciones, etcétera)	servicio
ambiente	precios

B. ¡A escribir! Using the information you collected in **Antes de escribir,** organize your review into four principal paragraphs.

1. Name and locate the restaurant, describe the cuisine in general, price range, and atmosphere.
2. Describe at least two dishes in some detail (ingredients, preparation, presentation).
3. Give a recommendation (positive, negative, ambivalent) and support the recommendation with a reason.

4. Based on what you have learned about Caribbean cuisine, state whether this restaurant would be popular or not from the Caribbean point of view. Explain why or why not.

   VOCABULARIO ÚTIL

   Sería popular   *It would be popular*

C. **¡A corregir!** Before you turn in your review, check the following points.

☐ Spelling of stem-changing verbs
☐ Adjective/noun agreement
☐ Use of direct objects and synonyms to avoid repetition

WWW Exploración

Choose and complete *one* of the following research activites. Then, based on your instructor's directions, present your results to the class and/or create a short report to include in your portfolio.

1. Create a menu that you might find in a typical Venezuelan or Dominican restaurant. Write a brief description of each dish. Be sure to include prices in the local currencies.
2. Investigate changes in traditional Venezuelan and Dominican eating habits. To what extent have these habits been influenced by North American culture? What is the role of fast food in these countries?
3. Have dinner at a restaurant that serves the cuisine of a Spanish-speaking country. Write a review of that restaurant, and compare the food to traditional Caribbean food.
4. Find more information in your library or on the Internet about the Dominican Republic or Venezuela. Here are some ideas and key words to get you started:

   La República Dominicana

   - Dominican music: **merengue, bachata,** and so on
   - U.S. intervention in Dominican history (1916, 1965)
   - Santo Domingo (the oldest European settlement in the Americas [1496])
   - the original inhabitants of **La Española:** the Taíno and the Arawak
   - the dictatorship of Rafael Trujillo (1930–1961)
   - the Jewish community of Sosúa
   - **Parques Nacionales: Los Haïtises,** Armando Bermúdez and José del Carmen Ramírez, **Jaragua, la Isla Cabritos**

   Venezuela

   - President Hugo Chávez, and the coup of 2002
   - Venezuela and OPEC
   - **los ranchos,** the sprawling slums of modern Caracas
   - **el Río Orinoco** (the third-longest river in South America)
   - **Salto Ángel** (the world's highest waterfall)
   - **Colonia Tovar**
   - the original inhabitants: Cariban, Arawak, and Chibcha
   - Simón Bolívar, **el libertador**

Nombre ________________ Fecha ________________ Clase ________________

CAPÍTULO 6

Repaso y anticipación

A. El trabajo y el tiempo libre

Paso 1. ¿Con qué asocias las siguientes actividades, con el trabajo o con el tiempo libre? Marca cada actividad lógicamente.

		EL TRABAJO	EL TIEMPO LIBRE
1.	mirar la televisión	☐	☐
2.	servir comida y bebidas	☐	☐
3.	escribir programas para la computadora	☐	☐
4.	hablar por teléfono con los clientes	☐	☐
5.	cocinar en un restaurante	☐	☐
6.	pedir comida y bebidas	☐	☐
7.	cocinar hamburguesas en el jardín	☐	☐
8.	escuchar música	☐	☐
9.	escuchar al profesor	☐	☐
10.	bailar	☐	☐
11.	hablar por teléfono con los parientes	☐	☐
12.	escribir cartas	☐	☐
13.	enseñar	☐	☐
14.	jugar al tenis	☐	☐

Paso 2. Ahora, escribe seis oraciones, tres para explicar qué haces en tu tiempo libre y tres para explicar qué haces para el trabajo o para tus estudios. Si deseas, puedes usar actividades del **Paso 1.**

____

____

____

____

____

____

B. Muchos años de salud

Paso 1. ¿Qué hacen las personas que viven más de cien años? Indica los alimentos que probablemente son una parte importante de su dieta **(sí)** y las que generalmente evitan (*avoid*) **(no).**

		SÍ	NO
1.	ensaladas verdes	☐	☐
2.	manzanas	☐	☐
3.	papas fritas	☐	☐
4.	mariscos	☐	☐
5.	mantequilla	☐	☐
6.	frijoles	☐	☐

7. azúcar ☐ ☐
8. sal ☐ ☐
9. pasteles ☐ ☐
10. verduras ☐ ☐

Paso 2. Ahora, indica las actividades que son importantes para mantener (*maintain*) la salud física (*health*) y vivir cien años.

☐ caminar una milla (*mile*) o más al día
☐ cenar en restaurantes elegantes
☐ hacer la compra
☐ hacer ejercicio con regularidad
☐ dormir hasta tarde
☐ mirar la televisión
☐ hablar por teléfono
☐ beber cerveza
☐ desayunar bien
☐ echar una siesta al día

❖ **Paso 3.** Usa las ideas de los **Pasos 1** y **2** para describir con cuatro o cinco oraciones la rutina de una persona que vive muchos años. Si deseas, puedes usar otros verbos y comidas.

MODELO Siempre duerme ocho horas cada noche. Por la mañana…

____

____

____

____

____

____

C. El estrés y la relajación

Paso 1. Completa las siguientes descripciones con la forma correcta de cada verbo entre paréntesis.

Felisa Saracibar

Yo (tener) ________________[1] mucho estrés en mi vida. Mi esposo y yo (trabajar) ________________[2] en una oficina grande. Yo (salir) ________________[3] para el trabajo a las siete y media de la mañana y mi esposo (llevar) ________________[4] a nuestros hijos a la escuela. Muchas noches yo no (volver) ________________[5] a casa hasta las ocho o nueve de la noche. Yo (soler) ________________[6] cocinar la cena pero a veces mi esposo (preferir) ________________[7] comprar hamburguesas o pollo frito después del trabajo. Yo les (servir) ________________[8] la cena a mis hijos primero porque ellos (tener) ________________[9] que hacer su tarea antes de acostarse. Casi nunca (poder: nosotros) ________________[10] cenar juntos, porque no hay tiempo.

Víctor Vilas

Yo siempre (estar) ______________[11] cansado. (Dormir: Yo) ______________[12] de seis a ocho horas por noche pero no (tener) ______________[13] energía. Mi esposa (decir) ______________[14] que el problema (ser)______________[15] mi dieta. Durante el día yo (trabajar) ______________[16] mucho. Nunca (desayunar: yo) ______________[17] porque no hay tiempo y (almorzar) ______________[18] muy poco. Muchos días sólo (comer: yo) ______________[19] chocolate y un refresco. Pero, por la noche, (cenar: yo) ______________[20] bien.

Paso 2. Ahora, escribe una recomendación para Felisa y otra para Víctor, basándote en los problemas que tienen.

MODELO Señora, usted necesita trabajar menos y…

Felisa: ____

____

Víctor: ____

____

Vocabulario

La hora exacta y aproximada; La rutina diaria; El estrés y la relajación

A. ¿Qué hora es?

Paso 1. Empareja (*match*) la hora que escuchas con el reloj correspondiente. Vas a escuchar las respuestas en el programa auditivo.

a. 

b. 

c. 

d.

e. 

f. 

1. ____ 2. ____ 3. ____ 4. ____ 5. ____ 6. ____

Paso 2. Ahora, escribe la hora correcta con oraciones completas.

MODELO → Son las tres y veinte.

1. ______________________________

2. ______________________________

3. ______________________________

4. ______________________________

5. ______________________________

B. Las obligaciones. Completa cada idea con la palabra o la frase más lógica. Escribe la letra de la palabra o frase en el espacio en blanco.

a. a eso de	c. a tiempo	e. hasta	g. tarde
b. a mediodía	d. desde	f. llegar temprano	h. ¿Tienes la hora?

1. ¡Ay, necesito llegar a la oficina ya! No sé qué hora es. _____
2. Si quieres hablar con la profesora antes de clase, debes _____.
3. Yo no almuerzo _____. Prefiero almorzar _____ la una porque hay menos gente.
4. Ese estudiante nunca llega _____. Siempre llega de cinco a diez minutos _____.
5. Enseño _____ las ocho _____ mediodía.

C. Asociaciones

Paso 1. Empareja cada actividad a continuación con la parte correspondiente de la casa.

1. _____ cepillarse los dientes
2. _____ vestirse
3. _____ levantarse
4. _____ bañarse
5. _____ ducharse

a. la cama
b. la ducha
c. el lavabo
d. la cómoda
e. la bañera

Paso 2. Ahora, completa el horario con las actividades de la lista que explican lo que Ángela va a hacer mañana. Ordena las actividades cronológicamente.

cepillarse los dientes, despertarse, ducharse, levantarse, maquillarse (*to put on make up*), vestirse

MODELO A las seis Angela va a _______________. → despertarse

1. A las seis y cuarto Ángela va a _______________.
2. A las seis y media Ángela va a _______________.
3. A las ocho Ángela va a _______________.
4. A las ocho y diez Ángela va a _______________.
5. A las ocho y veinte Ángela va a _______________.

❖ **Paso 3.** Explica qué vas a hacer esta noche antes de acostarte. Escribe por lo menos cinco oraciones.

MODELO A las siete, voy a…

____

____

____

____

____

____

D. Una vida sin estrés. Completa cada recomendación con la palabra o frase correspondiente de la lista.

café, copa, divertirte, hacer ejercicio, insomnio, sufres, tomar una siesta

1. Cuando ______________________________ de mucho estrés, no es bueno tomar una ______________________________ para relajarte.
2. Si tienes una oficina privada, debes ______________________________ por diez o quince minutos a eso de las dos.
3. Si sufres de ______________________________, es mejor no tomar ______________________________ por la tarde.
4. Debes ______________________________ durante tu tiempo libre.
5. Para mantener la salud física, debes ______________________________ tres o cuatro veces por semana.

E. ¿Qué debe hacer? Lee cada situación y explica qué debe hacer cada persona. Usa palabras del vocabulario.

MODELO Son las siete y media. Ana tiene clase a las ocho pero está en la cama todavía. →
Debe levantarse y vestirse rápido (*quickly*).
o No debe quedarse en la cama después de despertarse.
o Debe despertarse más temprano.

1. Por la mañana Pedro no puede despertarse y siempre llega tarde a clase.

____

____

2. Felipe se despierta a las nueve, pero está muy mal.

____

____

3. Laura tiene clase a las siete y media de la mañana. Le gusta dormir hasta tarde y muchos días sale sin desayunar.

____

____

4. Catalina sufre de insomnio todas las noches, pero no quiere tomar medicinas.

____

____

5. Alejandra es estudiante y sufre de mucha ansiedad. Estudia y trabaja todo el tiempo. No tiene tiempo libre.

____

____

Entrevista 1

A. Sonido y significado

Paso 1: Sonido. Las siguientes oraciones se basan en la entrevista con Güido Rivera Melgar. Primero, lee cada oración y comprueba su significado. Después, escucha mientras el narrador pronuncia cada oración frase por frase. Repite cada frase en las pausas hasta que puedas decir toda la oración con fluidez.

Güido Rivera Melgar
Santa Cruz, Bolivia

1. Me levanto muy temprano, a eso de las 7:00 de la mañana.
2. Almorzamos con la familia, luego tomo una siesta de una media hora.
3. En los horarios informales, casi no se viene a la hora (*on time*). Pero para las reuniones oficiales, como ir al médico, hay que (*one must*) estar a la hora.
4. Para relajarme, hago ejercicio en la mañana. Es importante hacer ejercicio para mantener la salud.
5. Hay varias causas del estrés. La gente no planifica, no piensa qué es lo que va a hacer. Otro motivo es la incertidumbre (*uncertainty*).

Paso 2: Significado. Indica cuál de las siguientes oraciones *no* es cierta, según las oraciones del **Paso 1.**

a. ☐ Güido pasa mucho tiempo con la familia y los amigos.
b. ☐ Güido es una persona perezosa.
c. ☐ Mucha gente no llega a tiempo para las fiestas.

B. Respuestas lógicas.

B. Respuestas lógicas. Primero, lee las preguntas y respuestas divididas de la entrevista con Güido. Luego, escucha la entrevista y empareja la primera y segunda partes de sus respuestas.

PREGUNTAS Y RESPUESTAS PARTE 1

1. ¿Cómo es un día típico para usted?

   «Me levanto muy temprano, a eso de las 7:00 de la mañana, hago un poco de ejercicios, luego tomo mi desayuno. A las 8:00 más o menos voy a mi trabajo, donde estoy hasta el mediodía. Luego regreso a la casa donde almorzamos con la familia, luego tomo una siesta de una media hora. _____.»

2. ¿Se respetan los horarios en Bolivia?

   «Generalmente se respetan los formales. Los informales, como decir las fiestas, casi no se viene a la hora y se espera que la persona venga retrasada entre quince y veinte minutos, no más. _____.»

3. ¿Qué hace para relajarse?

   «Generalmente hago ejercicio en la mañana, me levanto muy temprano. Otros días lo hago en la tarde, después de, de almuerzo. _____.»

4. ¿Qué cosas le causan estrés?

   «Son varias, ¿no? Uno es en el trabajo, la improvisación, la gente no planifica, no piensa qué es lo que va a hacer. Lo hace en el momento que se da. Entonces, _____.»

RESPUESTAS PARTE 2

a. Pero las reuniones oficiales como ir al dentista, al médico, hay que estar a la hora
b. uno no puede hacer planes. El otro motivo es la incertidumbre. Uno no se sabe si va a haber trabajo mañana o no, entonces eso causa que uno se preocupe y por tanto tiene estrés
c. Es importante hacer ejercicio para mantener la buena salud y así también le ayuda a uno a solucionar sus problemas psicológicos que uno tiene
d. A las 2:00 de la tarde regreso al trabajo. Luego estoy en el trabajo hasta las 6:00 de la tarde. A eso de las 8:00 tomamos una cena, pequeña cena. Luego salgo con mis amigos y me vengo a la casa a eso de las 12:00, a veces, y me acuesto a descansar

C. ¿Entendiste? Contesta las siguientes preguntas con oraciones completas, según la entrevista con Güido.

1. ¿Qué actividades hace Güido en un día típico?

   ____

   ____

2. ¿Con qué retraso es aceptable llegar a una fiesta en Bolivia?

   ____

3. Según Güido, ¿para qué tipos de problemas es bueno el ejercicio?

   ____

4. ¿Cuáles son las causas principales del estrés para los bolivianos?

   ____

❖ **D. Preguntas para ti.** Vas a escuchar tres preguntas. Escribe tus respuestas personales.

1. ____
2. ____
3. ____

Forma y función

6.1 Reflexive Pronouns

Clínica de gramática

A reflexive verb construction consists of a verb and a *reflexive pronoun.* Here are the forms of the reflexive verb **levantarse** (*to get up*).

levantarse	
(yo) **me** levanto	(nosotros/as) **nos** levantamos
(tú) **te** levantas	(vosotros/as) **os** levantáis
(usted, él/ella) **se** levanta	(ustedes, ellos/as) **se** levantan

Los lunes por la mañana. Completa las siguientes oraciones con la forma apropiada de los verbos entre paréntesis. ¡OJO! Cuidado con los pronombres reflexivos.

1. Yo ____________________ (despertarse) a las 5:30 en punto.
2. Vosotros ____________________ (levantarse) a las 6:00.
3. Tú ____________________ (ducharse) a las 8:00.
4. Nosotros ____________________ (vestirse) a las 8:30.
5. Él ____________________ (bañarse) después de hacer ejercicio.
6. Ella ____________________ (cepillarse) los dientes después de desayunar.
7. Ellos ____________________ (acostarse) temprano en la noche.

A. ¿Quién es? Escucha las siguientes oraciones y luego indica a quién se refieren. Vas a escuchar las respuestas en el programa auditivo.

1. ☐ él ☐ ustedes
2. ☐ tú ☐ nosotros
3. ☐ tú ☐ ella
4. ☐ usted ☐ yo
5. ☐ vosotros ☐ ellas

B. Y después... Indica lo que lógicamente haces después de cada actividad.

1. Me ducho y después _____.

   ☐ me baño ☐ me pongo la bata ☐ me duermo

2. Ando en bicicleta y después _____.

   ☐ me ducho ☐ me levanto ☐ me acuesto

3. Me afeito y después _____.

   ☐ me visto ☐ me acuesto ☐ me despierto

4. Me pongo el pijama y después _____.

   ☐ me baño ☐ me despierto ☐ me cepillo los dientes

5. Me cepillo los dientes y después _____.

   ☐ me despierto ☐ me acuesto ☐ me levanto

C. Las tres amigas. Completa la siguiente historia con la forma apropiada de los verbos entre paréntesis.

Claudia, Pepa y yo tenemos un apartamento cerca de la universidad. Las tres somos muy distintas y tenemos costumbres bien diferentes. Yo, por ejemplo, ____________________[1] (levantarse) muy temprano para ir a correr. Después de correr, ____________________[2] (ducharse) rápidamente y ____________________[3] (vestirse) para poder estudiar una hora antes de ir a clase. Pepa y Claudia, en cambio, ____________________[4] (acostarse) muy tarde porque les gusta estudiar por la noche. Entonces ____________________[5] (quedarse) en cama hasta las 9:30 de la mañana. Claudia ____________________[6] (bañarse) por la noche y Pepa lo hace por la mañana, por eso nunca tenemos problemas con el baño. Las tres, sin embargo, tenemos una costumbre en común: Los fines de semana cambiamos de imagen totalmente. ____________________[7] (maquillarse), ____________________[8] (ponerse) nuestra mejor ropa y ____________________[9] (reunirse) con otros amigos para tomar una copa en la plaza. Tenemos costumbres distintas, pero nos llevamos muy bien y somos muy buenas amigas.

❖ **D. Mi rutina diaria**

Paso 1. Usa números para ordenar cronológicamente las siguientes actividades según tu rutina diaria. No incluyas las actividades que no haces.

_____ acostarse	_____ ducharse / bañarse
_____ afeitarse	_____ estudiar
_____ almorzar	_____ ir a clase
_____ cenar	_____ levantarse
_____ cepillarse los dientes	_____ maquillarse
_____ desayunar	_____ reunirse con amigos
_____ despertarse	_____ vestirse

Paso 2. Ahora, basándote en las actividades del **Paso 1,** describe un día típico para ti. Si deseas, puedes incluir otras actividades. Usa palabras como **primero** y **luego** para expresar tus ideas.

MODELO Generalmente me despierto a las 6:00. Luego,…

____

____

____

____

____

____

6.2 **Saber** and **conocer**

Clínica de gramática

Spanish has two verbs that can be translated into English as *to know:* **saber** (*to know facts and information*) and **conocer** (*to know* [*be familiar with*] *a person, place, or thing*). Note that only the **yo** forms are irregular in the present tense.

saber		conocer	
sé	sabemos	**conozco**	conocemos
sabes	sabéis	conoces	conocéis
sabe	saben	conoce	conocen

Saber es poder. Indica si las siguientes oraciones incompletas se refieren a cosas que *sabes* o *conoces.*

	SÉ	CONOZCO
1. _____ el nombre de mi profesor(a) de español.	☐	☐
2. _____ una buena librería en esta ciudad.	☐	☐
3. _____ Bolivia.	☐	☐
4. _____ hablar quechua.	☐	☐
5. _____ a un artista boliviano.	☐	☐
6. _____ un restaurante barato cerca de la universidad.	☐	☐
7. _____ cocinar.	☐	☐

A. En la calle. Completa las siguientes preguntas y respuestas con la forma correcta de **saber** o **conocer.**

1. —¿_______________ tú al amigo de María Elena?

   —Sí, lo _______________, pero no _______________ de dónde es.
2. —¿_______________ ustedes el restaurante El Sol?

   —Sí, nosotros lo _______________, pero no _______________ dónde está.
3. —¿_______________ usted a qué hora abre la cafetería El Diamante?

   —Sí, abre a las 8:00 de la mañana, pero no _______________ a qué hora cierra.
4. —¿_______________ tú quién está en la oficina?

   —_______________ que un estudiante está en la oficina, pero no lo _______________.

B. Para divertirnos. Completa el siguiente monólogo con la forma correcta de **saber** o **conocer.**

Esta tarde, después del trabajo, mis amigos y yo vamos a reunirnos en casa de Pedro para escuchar música y relajarnos. Yo no _______________[1] dónde vive Pedro, pero Alejandro _______________[2] a la familia de Pedro bien y _______________[3] llegar a su casa. La familia de Pedro es interesante. Yo no _______________[4] a todos los miembros de su familia, pero _______________[5] que Pedro tiene una abuela de origen inca. Su abuela _______________[6] hablar quechua y español y _______________[7] muchas de las historias de la tradición oral. Alejandro no _______________[8] si la abuela va a estar en casa de Pedro esta noche, pero espero que sí (*I hope so*).

C. Mis experiencias en La Paz. Las siguientes oraciones describen las experiencias de Kim en Bolivia durante su programa de intercambio. Completa cada oración con la forma apropiada de **saber** o **conocer.**

1. Mis primos bolivianos _______________ conducir, pero no _______________ la ciudad.
2. Mi mamá boliviana _______________ hablar un poco de quechua, además de español.
3. Tú no _______________ a mi amiga boliviana. ¡Es una maravilla!

4. Nadie en mi país ________________ mi número de teléfono aquí en La Paz.
5. Muy pocos norteamericanos ________________ los tratamientos naturales que usan los aimaras.

D. Preguntas

Paso 1. Escribe preguntas, usando la siguiente información y la forma correcta de **saber** o **conocer.**

MODELO tú: el número de teléfono del profesor →
¿Sabes el número de teléfono del profesor?

1. ustedes: alguna persona famosa

 ____

2. tú: hablar otra lengua

 ____

3. usted: cuántos años tiene la profesora

 ____

4. tú: la cultura indígena de Bolivia

 ____

5. ustedes: bien la ciudad donde viven

 ____

Paso 2. Ahora, escribe una respuesta lógica para cada pregunta del **Paso 1.** Usa el complemento del pronombre directo si es necesario.

MODELO ¿Sabes el número de teléfono del profesor? →
Sí, lo sé. / No, no lo sé.

1. ____
2. ____
3. ____
4. ____
5. ____

Pronunciación y ortografía

Written Accents (II)

Antes de completar estas actividades, revisa las reglas que aprendiste en esta sección del **Capítulo 2** del texto. Luego, lee la información de esta sección del **Capítulo 6.**

A. Diptongos

Paso 1. Escucha y repite los siguientes pares de palabras. Las palabras están divididas en sílabas.

1. seria (se-ria)	sería (se-rí-a)
2. reunir (reu-nir)	reúno (re-ú-no)
3. esquió (es-quió)	esquío (es-quí-o)
4. aula (au-la)	aún (a-ún)

Paso 2. Ahora, escucha las siguientes palabras con dos vocales fuertes **(a, e, o).** Nunca hay dos vocales fuertes en una sílaba.

1. teatro (te-a-tro)
2. peor (pe-or)
3. ahora (a-ho-ra)
4. poema (po-e-ma)

B. Dictado. Escucha y escribe las siguientes palabras. **¡OJO!** Escribe los acentos necesarios. Vas a escuchar cada palabra dos veces.

1. ______
2. ______
3. ______
4. ______
5. ______
6. ______
7. ______
8. ______

C. Redacción. Las siguientes oraciones no tienen los acentos escritos necesarios. Escucha cada oración y luego escribe los acentos que faltan (*are missing*). Vas a escuchar cada oración dos veces.

1. Si tu no tienes tu libro, puedes usar mi libro.
2. No se como vamos a llegar hasta La Paz.
3. Es dificil eliminar el estres de la vida.
4. ¿Adonde vas para relajarte cuando estas cansado?
5. Solo falta un dia mas para el sabado.

Vocabulario

PARTE 2

El clima; ¿Cómo te afecta el clima?

A. ¿Qué estación es? Escucha las siguientes descripciones e indica la estación o el lugar y mes correspondientes. Vas a escuchar las respuestas en el programa auditivo.

1. ☐ Es un día típico de diciembre en Alaska.
   ☐ Es un día típico de septiembre en La Paz.
2. ☐ Es un día típico de julio en Louisiana.
   ☐ Es un día típico de agosto en Bolivia.
3. ☐ También hace mucho sol.
   ☐ Va a ser un invierno difícil.

4. ☐ Es el primer día de otoño.
   ☐ Está nublado esta tarde.
5. ☐ Hace mucho sol y calor.
   ☐ Nieva y hace frío.

❖ **B. El pronóstico del tiempo.** Describe el clima típico para las siguientes fechas en tu región.

MODELO el 12 de marzo →
Hoy va a hacer fresco y un poco de sol. Por la tarde va a llover.

1. el 2 de febrero
   ____
2. el 22 de agosto
   ____
3. el 10 de octubre
   ____
4. el 12 de abril
   ____

❖ **C. Estoy…** Escribe oraciones para explicar cuándo te sientes de las siguientes maneras.

MODELO aburrido/a → Estoy aburrido cuando estoy en la clase de biología.

1. aburrido/a
   ____
2. enojado/a
   ____
3. cansado/a
   ____
4. triste
   ____
5. contento/a
   ____

D. En el consultorio (*doctor's office*). Empareja cada dibujo con la oración correspondiente.

a. Tengo la garganta inflamada.
b. Abre la boca y di: «aaaaa».
c. Me duele la cabeza.
d. Tengo fiebre.
e. Saca la lengua.

1. _____
2. _____

3. ____

4. ____

5. ____

❖ **E. ¿Qué haces?** Contesta las siguientes preguntas con oraciones completas en español.

1. ¿Qué haces cuando estás aburrido/a?
____
2. ¿Qué haces cuando tienes dolor de cabeza?
____
3. ¿Qué haces cuando hace mal tiempo los sábados?
____
4. ¿Qué haces cuando tienes fiebre?
____
5. ¿Qué haces cuando te duele la garganta?
____

Entrevista 2

A. Sonido y significado

Paso 1: Sonido. Las siguientes oraciones se basan en la entrevista con Mirtha Olmos Carballo. Primero, lee cada oración y comprueba su significado. Después, escucha mientras la narradora pronuncia cada oración frase por frase. Repite cada frase en las pausas hasta que puedas decir toda la oración con fluidez.

1. El clima de La Paz es bien frío. Estamos rodeados de montañas, a más o menos 4.000 metros de altura (*altitude*).
2. El clima te afecta mucho, porque hay muchos resfriados.
3. La mayoría de la genta se cuida por sí misma (*by themselves*). No va necesariamente al médico.

Mirtha Olmos Carballo
La Paz, Bolivia

4. Muchas personas usan remedios caseros (*home remedies*), como la sopa de pollo o té con limón. Eso te cura.
5. **El soroche** es el mal de altura. Lo sufren los turistas, pero a nosotros no nos afecta.

Paso 2: Significado. Indica cuál de las siguientes oraciones *no* es cierta, según las oraciones del **Paso 1.**

a. ☐ El clima de La Paz es tropical.
b. ☐ Mirtha no suele ir al médico; prefiere usar remedios caseros.
c. ☐ El soroche no es un problema para los que viven allí.

B. Respuestas lógicas. Primero, lee las preguntas y respuestas divididas de la entrevista con Mirtha. Luego, escucha la entrevista y empareja la primera y segunda partes de sus respuestas.

PREGUNTAS Y RESPUESTAS PARTE 1

1. ¿Cómo es el clima de La Paz?

   «El clima en La Paz es bien frío. Estamos rodeados de montañas. _____.»

2. ¿Cómo te afecta el clima?

   «Hay muchos resfriados. A veces sales con una ropa ligera porque el sol está bien fuerte. _____.»

3. ¿Cómo se curan los resfriados?

   «Bueno, la mayoría de la gente se cuida por sí misma. No va necesariamente al médico. _____.»

4. ¿Y tomas medicinas?

   «A veces voy a la farmacia y el farmacéutico me receta _____.»

5. ¿Se usan remedios naturales?

   «Bueno, generalmente en el campo. La gente campesina utiliza remedios naturales. _____.»

6. ¿Qué es **el soroche?**

   «**El soroche** es el mal de altura. Lo sufren los turistas, pero a nosotros no nos afecta. _____.»

RESPUESTAS PARTE 2

a. En la ciudad, no mucho, pero de vez en cuando, sí
b. Puedes usar remedios caseros como la sopa con pollo o té con limón. Y eso te cura
c. Casi más o menos como a 4.000 metros de altura. Es bastante frío
d. remedios para la gripe. Depende de los síntomas
e. Y eso consiste en que te falta el aire cuando caminas o que a veces te duele la cabeza. Así que tienes que tener cuidado antes de reanudar tus actividades cuando vayas a La Paz
f. De pronto viene un viento fuerte también y mucho frío, y te resfrías. Así que tienes que tener mucho cuidado

C. ¿Entendiste? Contesta las siguientes preguntas con oraciones completas, según la entrevista con Mirtha.

1. ¿Cómo es el clima de La Paz?

   ____

2. ¿Qué tipos de remedios prefiere la gente allí?

   ____

3. ¿Dónde se usan más los remedios naturales?

   ____

4. ¿Cuáles son los síntomas del soroche?

______

❖ **D. Preguntas para ti.** Vas a escuchar tres preguntas. Escribe tus respuestas personales.

1. ______
2. ______
3. ______

❖ **E. ¿Qué opinas?**

Paso 1. Los remedios naturales también son populares en los Estados Unidos y el Canadá, pero las personas que los usan no son necesariamente indígenas. ¿Qué tipos de personas prefieren usar hierbas naturales? ¿Por qué? ¿Qué opinas tú de los remedios naturales? ¿Son eficaces? ¿Deben ser controlados por el gobierno?

______

Paso 2. Describe el clima de La Paz y luego compáralo con el clima de tu región. ¿Cuál es más saludable (*healthy*) en tu opinión? ¿Por qué?

______

Forma y función

6.3 Uses of **ser** and **estar** (Summary)

Clínica de gramática

Spanish has two verbs that can be translated into English as *to be:* **estar** and **ser.** Here is a summary of the most frequent uses of each verb.

estar	**ser**
a. to talk about health	a. to indicate the time and location of events
b. to express location of people and objects	b. to express origin, composition, or possession
c. to express actions currently in progress	c. to tell time
d. to describe a change from the normal state of being	d. to express definition, occupation, or nationality
	e. to describe the normal state of being

***¿Ser* o no *ser*?** Subraya (*Underline*) la forma del verbo (**ser** o **estar**) que se debe usar para expresar las siguientes ideas.

1. Mis amigos son / están en la biblioteca.
2. El piano es / está de madera.
3. Soy / Estoy muy bien, gracias. ¿Y usted?
4. La reunión es / está a las 6:00.
5. Mi abuela es / está enferma y tiene que ir al hospital.
6. El hospital es / está en la Avenida Simón Bolívar.
7. Los estudiantes son / están frustrados hoy porque tienen un examen.
8. *Entrevistas* es / está un libro para aprender español.

A. *¿Ser* o *estar?* Escucha las siguientes oraciones e indica la respuesta correspondiente. **¡OJO!** Recuerda los usos de **ser** y **estar.** Vas a escuchar las respuestas en el programa auditivo.

1.	☐ Son de Bolivia.	☐ Están en Bolivia.
2.	☐ Susana está nerviosa.	☐ Susana es una persona nerviosa.
3.	☐ Es una persona enferma.	☐ Está enferma.
4.	☐ Está en el hospital.	☐ Es en el hospital.
5.	☐ Son las 3:00.	☐ Es a las 3:00.

B. ¿Por qué? Indica por qué se usa **ser** o **estar.** Escribe la letra de la función en el espacio en blanco correspondiente.

1. _____ Son las 3:00, la hora de mi siesta.
2. _____ Estoy haciendo ejercicio para tener más energía.
3. _____ El hospital está en la Avenida Simón Bolívar.
4. _____ Esta medicina es de hierbas.
5. _____ Ese médico es de Sucre.
6. _____ La reunión es en casa de Ana.
7. _____ El hospital es muy grande.
8. _____ Esta medicina es de Roberto.
9. _____ Mi perro está muy enfermo.

a. la hora/fecha
b. posesión
c. lugar de una cosa/persona
d. lugar de un evento
e. composición
f. origen
g. estado/condición
h. característica
i. el progresivo

C. Estudiantes de intercambio. Completa las siguientes declaraciones sobre un programa de intercambio con la forma correcta de **ser** o **estar.**

1. Lisa Rice de Oregon: «Nosotros _______________ en Bolivia para aprender el idioma y conocer las costumbres de este país. _______________ aprendiendo mucho.»
2. Peter Kleps de Mississippi: «La diversidad de la gente boliviana _______________ muy interesante para mí.»
3. Jocelyn Bumstead de New Jersey: «Lo siento. Hoy yo _______________ enferma porque tengo soroche, mal de altura. Pero me gusta mucho el programa.»
4. Gil Chapoton del Canadá: «Yo _______________ del Canadá. Creo que los estudiantes _______________ muy contentos aquí en Bolivia. La gente _______________ maravillosa.»
5. Rachel García y Rosa Martín de California: «Nosotras nunca _______________ aburridas. Tenemos muchas actividades y conferencias después de clase. Hay una conferencia esta tarde. _______________ en el Museo Nacional.»

❖ **D. Reacciones.** Explica cómo estás en las siguientes situaciones.

MODELO después de despertarte →
Después de despertarme, estoy cansado.

1. antes de un examen final de español

____

2. antes de recibir las notas finales

____

3. antes de un viaje

____

4. después de correr cuatro millas

____

5. después de una comida grande

____

6. después de ver una película violenta

____

❖ Análisis cultural

En esta cita, el escritor Paul Theroux describe su estancia en La Paz. Su descripción puede ayudarte a comprender cómo se sienten algunos turistas en Bolivia.

> "It drizzled constantly: cold rain, ice slivers, hail. But most people were dressed for the weather. They wore thick overcoats and heavy sweaters, wool hats, and even mittens and gloves. The Indians had a bulky rounded look, and some wore earflaps under their derby hats. I saw the sun once. It appeared one morning between a break in the mist that hung over the canyon, and it was powerfully bright without being warm, simply a blinding flash that was soon eclipsed by more mist. The weather report in the daily paper was usually the same—cloudy, fog, some rain, no change—like a certain season in northern Maine, except that here I was never able to elude my feeling of the bends or my nausea. I was tired but could not sleep; I had no appetite; one drink and I was staggering. And it is hard to be a stranger in a cold city: the people stay indoors, the streets are empty after the stores close, no one lounges in the parks, and the purposefulness—or what looks like it—in a cold climate is always a reproach to an idle traveler."
>
> Source: *The Old Patagonian Express by Paul Theroux*

1. En tu opinión, ¿en qué estación del año está este escritor en La Paz? ¿Por qué piensas así?

____

____

2. ¿Crees que el autor esté bien preparado para el clima de la ciudad? Explica.

____

____

3. ¿Qué síntomas tiene el autor? ¿Qué enfermedad puede tener?

____

____

4. ¿Qué efecto tiene el clima en la vida de las personas? ¿Cómo contribuye a la impresión que el autor tiene de la ciudad?

____

____

5. ¿Crees que el autor se sienta (*feels*) como miembro de la cultura del país o que se sienta excluido? Explica.

____

____

6. En general, ¿crees que el autor esté a gusto en La Paz? ¿Por qué sí o por qué no?

____

____

❖ PORTAFOLIO CULTURAL

Redacción: Consejos

Vas a escribir un artículo sobre la calidad de vida en tu región con consejos (*advice*) para las personas que quieren vivir allí. Sigue los pasos de **Antes de escribir** para organizar tus ideas.

A. Antes de escribir

Paso 1. En una hoja de papel aparte, evalúa la calidad de vida de tus circunstancias. Usa las siguientes categorías para apuntar las ventajas de vivir en tu región.

- el clima de mi región
- la geografía de mi región
- los horarios sociales de mi región (teatros, conciertos, etcétera)
- la gente que vive en mi región

Paso 2. Haz una lista de los problemas de tu comunidad y de sus posibles soluciones. Incluye los problemas médicos más comúnes.

MODELO Hay mucha basura en las calles después de los partidos de fútbol norteamericano. → organizar un grupo de estudiantes voluntarios para limpiar las calles después de los partidos

B. ¡A escribir! Escribe un artículo de tres párrafos con la siguiente estructura.

1. Ventajas de vivir en mi comunidad
2. Problemas de mi comunidad
3. Soluciones
4. Tu conclusión: ¿Es bueno vivir en tu región?

C. ¡A corregir! Antes de entregar tu artículo, revisa los siguientes puntos.

☐ Los pronombres y verbos reflexivos
☐ La concordancia (*agreement*) de los adjetivos y sustantivos (*nouns*)
☐ Las formas verbales

Exploración

Escoge y completa *una* de las siguientes actividades. Luego, presenta tus resultados a la clase o crea una versión escrita para incluir en tu portafolio, según las indicaciones de tu profesor(a).

1. La curandería es una práctica curativa tradicional en algunas áreas del mundo hispanohablante. Usa recursos de la biblioteca y del Internet para contestar las siguientes preguntas. ¿Dónde se originó la curandería? ¿Dónde se practica? ¿Qué es un curandero o una curandera? ¿Qué importancia tiene en el proceso curativo? ¿Cuáles son algunos de los ritos de la curandería? En tu opinión, ¿es la curandería una práctica curativa válida? Explica.
2. Entrevista a varios hispanohablantes de tu universidad o comunidad sobre las medicinas, los médicos y la curación. ¿Qué métodos prefieren ellos? ¿Y sus familias? ¿Hay diferencias entre sus preferencias y las de sus padres o de sus hijos? ¿Prefieren prácticas tradicionales o modernas? ¿Por qué? ¿Han cambiado sus preferencias después de vivir en este país?
3. ¿Hay una enfermedad que predomine en tu ciudad o región? ¿Por qué? ¿Qué remedios se usan para curarla? ¿Puedes identificar áreas del mundo hispanohablante donde sufren de esa enfermedad también? ¿Cómo la curan en esos lugares? Usa guías turísticas y otros recursos para investigar el tema.

4. Busca más información sobre Bolivia en el Internet o en tu biblioteca. Puedes usar las siguientes ideas y palabras clave para empezar tu investigación:
    - los paisajes extraordinarios: el lago Titicaca, la selva amazónica, el gran salar de Uyuni
    - las dos capitales bolivianas: La Paz y Sucre
    - los usos históricos de la coca en Bolivia
    - la ciudad colonial de Potosí
    - las lenguas indígenas de Bolivia: el quechua, el aimara
    - el camino del Takesi
    - los problemas sociales y económicos: la Guerra del Agua

CAPÍTULO

7

Repaso y anticipación

A. El clima y la ropa. Escucha los siguientes comentarios sobre el tiempo y escribe la letra del dibujo correspondiente. Vas a escuchar las respuestas en el programa auditivo.

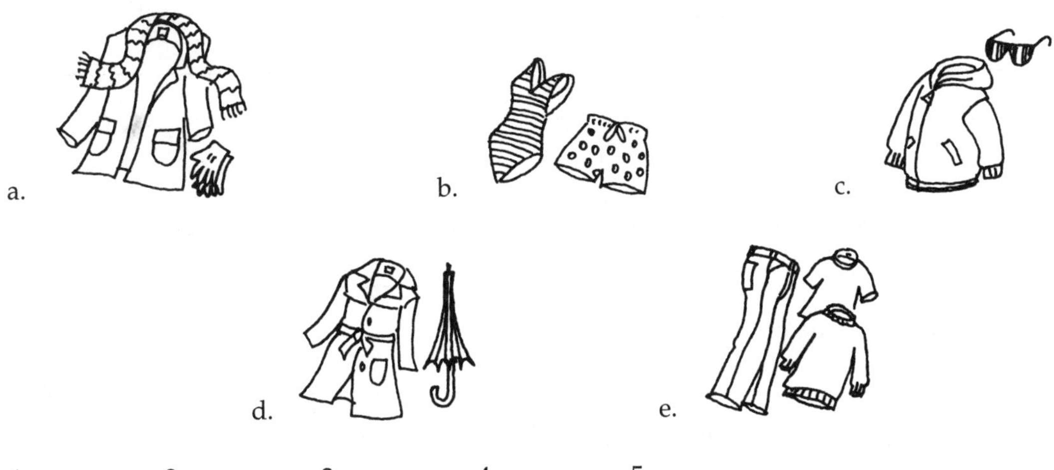

1. _____ 2. _____ 3. _____ 4. _____ 5. _____

B. Asociaciones

Paso 1. Empareja cada actividad con el dibujo correspondiente.

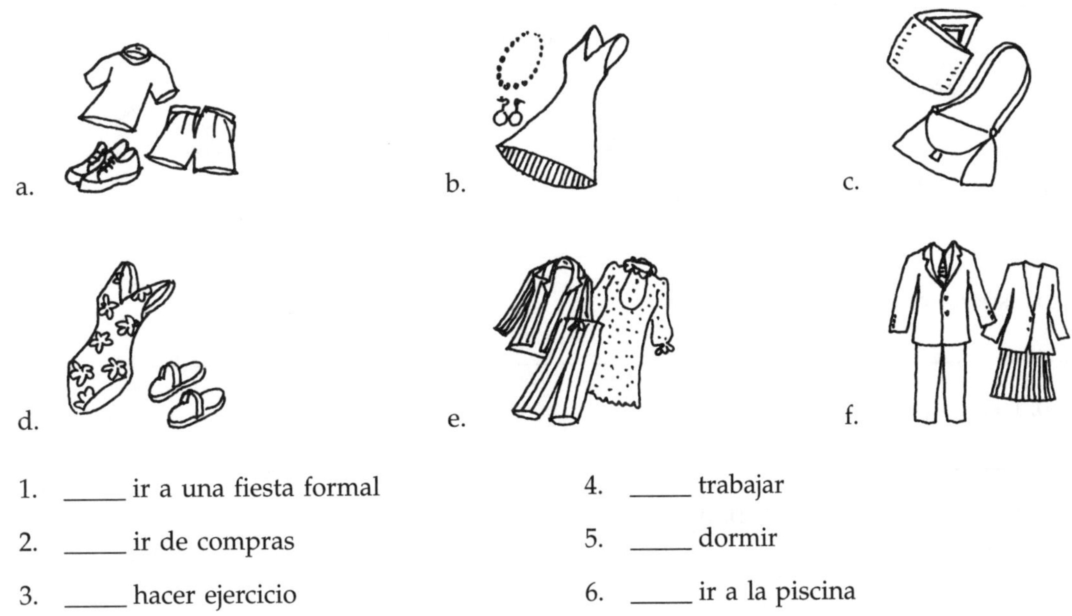

1. _____ ir a una fiesta formal
2. _____ ir de compras
3. _____ hacer ejercicio
4. _____ trabajar
5. _____ dormir
6. _____ ir a la piscina

❖ **Paso 2.** Ahora, escoge tres de las actividades del **Paso 1** y explica cuándo te gusta hacerlas.

MODELO dormir → Me gusta dormir hasta tarde los sábados.

1. ______________________________
2. ______________________________
3. ______________________________

❖ **C. Un día de compras.** Imagina que vas a pasar el sábado con un amigo o una amiga. Contesta las siguientes preguntas.

1. ¿A qué hora te despiertas?

____

2. ¿Qué haces después de levantarte?

____

3. ¿Con quién vas a ir de compras?

____

4. ¿Dónde desayunas y almuerzas cuando vas de compras, en casa o en un restaurante?

____

5. ¿Adónde prefieren ir de compras tu amigo/a y tú?

____

6. ¿Qué hacen después? ¿Van al cine? ¿Qué otras actividades hacen?

____

D. Unos turistas en México. Karen y Tom son turistas. ¿Qué están haciendo en los siguientes momentos?

MODELO 10:15, visitar la catedral →
Son las diez y cuarto y están visitando la catedral.

1. 10:45, hablar con otros turistas en el parque

____

2. 2:00, comer en un restaurante típico

____

3. 3:15, esperar el postre

____

4. 3:50, leer un periódico de México

____

5. 4:30, tomar un autobús a las ruinas aztecas

____

6. 5:00, ver unas pirámides

____

7. 7:45, escuchar música en el parque

____

8. 12:00, dormir en un hotel elegante

____

PARTE 1

Vocabulario

En el almacén; En la tienda

A. Descripciones. Escucha las siguientes descripciones e indica si probablemente describen a un hombre, a una mujer o a cualquiera de los dos (*either one*). Vas a escuchar las respuestas en el programa auditivo.

	UN HOMBRE	UNA MUJER	CUALQUIERA DE LOS DOS
1.	☐	☐	☐
2.	☐	☐	☐
3.	☐	☐	☐
4.	☐	☐	☐
5.	☐	☐	☐

B. Combinaciones. Empareja las siguientes prendas de ropa (*articles of clothing*).

1. _____ un vestido gris
2. _____ un traje pardo
3. _____ unos vaqueros
4. _____ una blusa blanca
5. _____ una bolsa roja de cuero

a. un suéter morado de algodón
b. una falda verde
c. unos zapatos rojos
d. unas medias de nailon negras
e. una corbata de seda

C. ¿Adónde van? Escucha a las siguientes personas e indica adónde van según lo que llevan o se ponen. Vas a escuchar las respuestas en el programa auditivo.

1. ☐ a una fiesta elegante ☐ al centro comercial
2. ☐ a la universidad ☐ a la ópera
3. ☐ a una reunión importante ☐ a un café para tomar una copa
4. ☐ al cine ☐ a la playa
5. ☐ al trabajo ☐ al supermercado

❖ **D. ¿Qué haces?** Escribe una oración para explicar lógicamente lo que haces en las siguientes situaciones. Usa palabras de la lista.

cambiar, devolver, mostrarle, probar, regatear

MODELO Compro una camisa. La camisa me queda grande. →
Cambio la camisa por otra.

1. Soy dependienta en una tienda de ropa. Un cliente quiere ver los vestidos formales.

____

2. Un pariente me regala unos pantalones que no me gustan. Los pantalones son de una tienda que conozco.

3. En el mercado, veo una bolsa que me gusta pero es cara.

❖ **E. Tus prendas personales.** Describe las siguientes prendas de ropa con oraciones completas.

1. tu conjunto (*outfit*) preferido

2. tus prendas más duraderas (*sturdy, long-lasting*)

3. tus prendas más caras o más elegantes

4. las prendas que provocan más cumplidos (*compliments*)

Entrevista 1

A. Sonido y significado

Paso 1: Sonido. Las siguientes oraciones se basan en la entrevista con Minerva Rubio Andalón. Primero, lee cada oración y comprueba su significado. Después, escucha mientras la narradora pronuncia cada oración frase por frase. Repite cada frase en las pausas hasta que puedas decir toda la oración con fluidez.

Minerva Rubio Andalón
México, D.F., México

1. Ayer fui (*I went*) a hacer una de las cosas que más me gusta hacer: ir de compras.
2. En el centro comercial, las cosas son un poco más caras, por eso fui a mi lugar favorito: el tianguis.
3. El tianguis es un mercado sobre ruedas (*on wheels*): el día domingo está en mi colonia (*neighborhood*), el martes en la colonia siguiente; se mueve de un lado a otro.
4. En el tianguis puedes encontrar fruta. Puedes encontrar pescado, pollo, carne, todo lo que tú necesitas en un mismo lugar. Por eso es mi favorito.
5. Pude (*I managed to*) encontrar un regalo muy bonito para mi hija, ahora que hace calor. Encontré (*I found*) unos huaraches (*sandals*). Fue (*It was*) un regalo perfecto porque los necesitaba (*she needed them*).

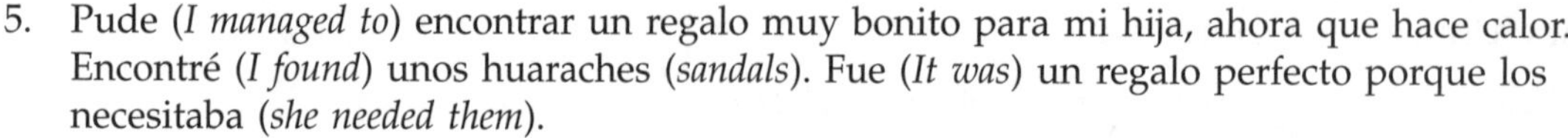

6. A mi sobrina le regalé (*I gave*) una muñeca que habla, y a mi sobrino un carro a control remoto. Y todo eso, lo encontré en el tianguis.

Paso 2: Significado. Indica cuál de las siguientes oraciones *no* es cierta, según las oraciones del **Paso 1.**

a. ☐ A Minerva le gusta ir de compras en el tianguis.
b. ☐ Las cosas son más baratas en el tianguis que en el centro comercial.
c. ☐ Los artículos del tianguis no son buenos para regalos.

B. Respuestas lógicas. Primero, lee las preguntas y respuestas divididas de la entrevista con Minerva. Luego, escucha la entrevista y empareja la primera y segunda partes de sus respuestas.

PREGUNTAS Y RESPUESTAS PARTE 1

1. ¿Qué hiciste (*did you do*) ayer?

   «Bueno, ayer fui a hacer una de las cosas que me gusta hacer más: ir de compras. _____.»

2. ¿Adónde fuiste (*did you go*)?

   «Primero fui a un centro comercial, pero en el centro comercial las cosas son un poco más caras. Mi lugar favorito es el tianguis. _____.»

3. ¿Qué es el tianguis?

   «El tianguis es un mercado sobre ruedas. Le llamamos mercado sobre ruedas porque el día domingo es el día que está en mi colonia. _____.»

4. ¿Por qué te gusta el tianguis?

   «¿Por qué me gusta? Porque tú puedes encontrar desde un pequeño llavero hasta un vestido de fiesta. Ahí puedes encontrar comida. Puedes encontrar fruta. _____.»

5. ¿Qué compraste (*did you buy*) para tu hija?

   «Bueno, en el tianguis pude encontrar un regalo muy bonito para ella, ahora que hace calor. Encontré unos huaraches _____.»

6. ¿Qué le regalaste (*did you give*) a tu familia en Navidades?

   «A mi hermana, le regalé una pulsera; a mi sobrina, le regalé una muñeca que habla; a mi sobrino, un carro a control remoto _____.»

RESPUESTAS PARTE 2

a. y fue un regalo perfecto para ella porque los necesitaba
b. Puedes encontrar pescado, pollo, carne, todo lo que tú necesitas en un mismo lugar. Por eso es mi favorito
c. y a mi otra hermana, un bonito collar. Y todo eso, lo encontré en el tianguis
d. En el tianguis pude encontrar el regalo perfecto para ella y a un precio considerable, un precio que yo puedo pagar
e. El martes es en la colonia siguiente. Y el miércoles puede estar en otra colonia. Se mueve de un lado a otro y tú puedes encontrar cosas muy interesantes
f. Ayer fui a comprar un regalo para mi hija porque va a ser su cumpleaños

C. ¿Entendiste? Contesta las siguientes preguntas con oraciones completas, según la entrevista con Minerva.

1. ¿Adónde fue (*did* [*she*] *go*) de compras Minerva? (Menciona dos lugares.)

   ____

2. ¿Qué es el tianguis?

   ____

3. ¿Por qué le gusta el tianguis a Minerva?

   ____

4. ¿Qué cosas compró (*did she buy*) en el tianguis?

____

❖ **D. Preguntas para ti.** Vas a escuchar tres preguntas. Escribe tus respuestas personales.

1. ____
2. ____
3. ____

Forma y función

7.1 The Preterit

Clínica de gramática

The preterit is one of two past tenses in Spanish. To form the preterit for regular verbs, add the following endings to the verb stem. Note that the endings for **-er** and **-ir** verbs are identical in all persons.

llev-ar		volv-er		viv-ir	
llev**é**	llev**amos**	volv**í**	volv**imos**	viv**í**	viv**imos**
llev**aste**	llev**asteis**	volv**iste**	volv**isteis**	viv**iste**	viv**isteis**
llev**ó**	llev**aron**	volv**ió**	volv**ieron**	viv**ió**	viv**ieron**

¿Qué pasó? Completa las siguientes tablas con las formas del pretérito.

1. **llevar**		2. **beber**	
	llevamos		
		bebió	

3. **recibir**		4. **preparar**	

5. **conocer**		6. **decidir**	

A. De compras. Escucha las siguientes oraciones e indica si describen lo que le pasó a Luisa ayer o lo que le pasa a Luisa hoy. Vas a escuchar las respuestas en el programa auditivo.

MODELOS (*oyes*) Me probé un vestido increíble en el almacén.
(*indicas*) ayer

(*oyes*) Necesito comprar una camisa para mi padre.
(*indicas*) hoy

	AYER	HOY
1.	☐	☐
2.	☐	☐
3.	☐	☐
4.	☐	☐
5.	☐	☐
6.	☐	☐

B. Un viaje a México. Paula viajó a México el año pasado. Completa su descripción con la forma correcta del pretérito de los verbos entre paréntesis.

El año pasado yo (viajar) ______________________[1] con mi hermana a México. Nosotras (quedarse) ______________________[2] en Querétaro por un mes con una familia mexicana muy amable. Mi hermana y yo (salir) ______________________[3] de compras antes de volver a los Estados Unidos para comprar regalos. A mí me (gustar) ______________________[4] mucho los mercados de Mexico. Yo (aprender) ______________________[5] a regatear muy bien y (comprar) ______________________[6] muchas cosas a muy buen precio.

C. La tía Concha. A la tía Concha le gusta ir de compras. Completa la siguiente descripción de un día típico con la forma correcta del pretérito de los verbos entre paréntesis.

La tía Concha (decidir) ______________________[1] ir al centro comercial para comprar unos regalos. (Llamar) ______________________[2] a unas amigas para ir a almorzar antes de hacer las compras. Las amigas (almorzar) ______________________[3] en un restaurante popular del centro comercial, y después todas (salir) ______________________[4] a sus tiendas favoritas. La tía Concha (comprar) ______________________[5] un collar de oro en la joyería. Después, en una tienda (probarse) ______________________[6] unos zapatos de cuero. Unos momentos después, la tía Concha (ver) ______________________[7] a dos de sus amigas en la perfumería y (entrar)

_____________________[8] para mostrarles su collar de plata. Pero según una de las amigas, la tía Concha (pagar) _____________________[9] demasiado[a] por el collar. La tía Concha (regresar) _____________________[10] a la joyería y (devolver) _____________________[11] el collar.

[a]*too much*

D. El fin de semana pasado. Usa la siguiente información para formar oraciones completas. Usa el pretérito de los verbos y añade las palabras que faltan.

1. Tomás y Paco / salir / el centro comercial

   ____

2. Magda / probarse / unas botas de cuero / la tienda

   ____

3. Jorge y yo / comprar / comida / el supermercado

   ____

4. tú / cenar / el restaurante / tu novio

   ____

5. yo / llevar / el perro (*dog*) a la veterinaria

   ____

6. ustedes / cambiar / los pantalones / por otros

   ____

E. Claudia en México. Claudia pasó tres meses en México y les está contando sus experiencias a sus amigas estadounidenses. Completa su descripción con la forma correcta del pretérito de los verbos entre paréntesis.

1. Yo (pasar) _____________________ seis semanas en Cuernavaca y (quedarse) _____________________ con una familia mexicana muy amable.
2. Mis amigos y yo (tomar) _____________________ cuatro clases bastante interesantes en la universidad y allí (conocer) _____________________ a muchos jóvenes mexicanos.
3. Mi papá mexicano me (llevar) _____________________ a visitar muchos lugares históricos y turísticos.
4. También yo (recibir) _____________________ de mi familia muchos regalos de artesanía tradicional y (aprender) _____________________ mucho de las costumbres mexicanas.
5. Mi hermano mayor (salir) _____________________ con nosotros muchas veces a tomar refrescos en los cafés.
6. Mis amigos y yo (volver) _____________________ a los Estados Unidos un poco tristes pero con muchas ganas de ver a nuestra familia de nuevo.

F. Las preguntas. Forma preguntas que requieran la información subrayada en las siguientes respuestas. Usa la forma correcta del pretérito y las palabras interrogativas correspondientes.

MODELO Compré los pantalones <u>en esta tienda</u>. →
¿Dónde compraste los pantalones?

1. <u>Esa dependienta</u> me mostró los vestidos formales.

____

2. Pedro devolvió <u>la corbata</u>.

____

3. Los zapatos de tenis me quedaron <u>muy grandes</u>.

____

4. Jose le regaló <u>un impermeable</u> a Luis.

____

5. Los aretes costaron <u>ciento cincuenta pesos</u>.

____

❖ **G. El sábado pasado.** Escribe cinco oraciones para describir tus actividades del sábado pasado. Usa la forma correcta del pretérito. Puedes usar los verbos de la lista u (*or*) otros que conoces.

cenar, comer, comprar, despertarse, devolver, estudiar, hablar, levantarse, ponerse, preparar, probarse, regresar, salir

____

____

____

____

____

____

7.2 Indirect Objects and Pronouns

Clínica de gramática

Indirect object pronouns tell *to whom* or *for whom* the action of the verb is directed. Here are the indirect object pronouns **(pronombres de complemento indirecto)** in Spanish.

Los pronombres de complemento indirecto

me	to/for me	**nos**	to/for us
te	to/for you (*fam. s.*)	**os**	to/for you (*fam. pl.*)
le	to/for you (*form. s.*), him/her	**les**	to/for you (*form. pl.*)/them

En la tienda. Lee las siguientes oraciones y subraya el pronombre de complemento indirecto. Luego, subraya dos veces el complemento directo.

MODELO Le preguntamos el precio de los vestidos a la dependienta. →
Le preguntamos el precio de los vestidos a la dependienta.

1. Mi amiga me devolvió el suéter.
2. La dependienta les mostró a ustedes unos vestidos.
3. Siempre les enviamos un recibo (*receipt*) a nuestros clientes.
4. Mis padres te compraron un regalo en esta tienda.
5. Yo le abrí la puerta del probador a mi amiga.

A. ¡Qué buen detalle! (*What a thoughtful gesture!*) Angélica siempre piensa en sus amigos y familia cuando está de viaje. Completa las siguientes oraciones con el pronombre de **complemento indirecto** que corresponde a las palabras subrayadas para saber qué hizo Angélica durante su viaje a México.

1. ______________ mandó un correo electrónico diariamente a Pedro y Luis, sus mejores amigos.
2. ______________ escribió una carta muy larga a mí.
3. ______________ ofreció consejos a una estudiante frustrada que tenía (*was having*) problemas.
4. ______________ enseñó algunos modismos mexicanos a nosotros.
5. ______________ regaló un libro fabuloso a sus padres mexicanos.
6. ______________ compró unos aretes de plata a ti.

B. ¿Quién recibió los regalos? Escucha las siguientes oraciones e indica quién recibió el regalo. Vas a escuchar las respuestas en el programa auditivo.

MODELO (*oyes*) Mi papá le compró una cartera a mi hermana.
(*ves*) ella / tú
(*indicas*) ella

1. ☐ yo ☐ tú
2. ☐ él ☐ ustedes
3. ☐ ella ☐ tú
4. ☐ ellos ☐ nosotros
5. ☐ ellas ☐ vosotros
6. ☐ vosotros ☐ ustedes
7. ☐ nosotros ☐ ustedes
8. ☐ yo ☐ usted

C. *¿Le o les?* Completa las siguientes oraciones con el pronombre correcto, **le** o **les.**

1. __________ escribo un recibo a la señora por las cosas que compró.
2. La muchacha __________ compra flores a su mamá para su cumpleaños.
3. El estudiante __________ regala camisetas a sus amigos.
4. __________ explico el precio a los clientes.
5. __________ muestro las faldas a la mujer.
6. __________ traigo otros zapatos al señor alto.

D. Un día en Querétaro. Completa las siguientes oraciones con el pronombre de complemento indirecto correcto.

1. __________ compraste muchos regalos a tus amigos.
2. __________ hablamos a los vendedores (*merchants*) del tianguis.
3. __________ escribí a ti una tarjeta postal (*postcard*) desde Querétaro.

4. Me probé un sombrero en el tianguis y ________ quedó muy bien.
5. El vendedor ________ ofreció un descuento a Inés y a mí.
6. ________ di (*I gave*) mi dinero al vendedor.

E. Nuestra familia. Usa la siguiente información para formar oraciones completas. Usa el pronombre de complemento indirecto correcto y el pretérito del verbo.

MODELO mi abuela / comprar / un libro / a nosotros →
Mi abuela nos compró un libro a nosotros.

1. mi esposo / comprar / chocolates / a los niños

   ____

2. tus padres / regalar / ropa / a nosotros

   ____

3. los niños / mostrar / sus regalos / a mí

   ____

4. yo / comprar / otro reloj / a ti

   ____

5. tú / regalar / un abrigo / a tu madre

   ____

Pronunciación y ortografía

Written Accents (III); Consonant + Vowel Combinations

Lee y estudia la información en el libro de texto antes de hacer estas actividades.

A. Escucha y escribe los verbos. Vas a escuchar cada uno dos veces.

1. ______________ 6. ______________
2. ______________ 7. ______________
3. ______________ 8. ______________
4. ______________ 9. ______________
5. ______________ 10. ______________

B. ¿Presente o pasado? Escucha las siguientes oraciones e indica si están en el presente o en el pasado. Luego, indica el sujeto. Vas a escuchar las respuestas en el programa auditivo. **¡OJO!** Algunas oraciones pueden estar en el presente o en el pasado.

MODELO Habló con la dependienta. → pasado, él

	PRESENTE	PASADO	SUJETO	
1.	☐	☐	☐ ella	☐ yo
2.	☐	☐	☐ él	☐ yo
3.	☐	☐	☐ ellos	☐ nosotros
4.	☐	☐	☐ ella	☐ yo
5.	☐	☐	☐ él	☐ yo
6.	☐	☐	☐ usted	☐ yo
7.	☐	☐	☐ ellas	☐ yo
8.	☐	☐	☐ ella	☐ yo
9.	☐	☐	☐ tú	☐ yo
10.	☐	☐	☐ ustedes	☐ nosotros
11.	☐	☐	☐ él	☐ yo
12.	☐	☐	☐ ella	☐ yo

Vocabulario

En el mercado de artesanías

A. En el mercado. Subraya la mejor opción para completar las siguientes oraciones.

1. Hay muchas cosas (hechas / pagadas) por los indígenas en el mercado.
2. En el mercado, puedes (vender / regatear) para conseguir un buen precio.
3. Las artesanías no suelen (pagar / costar) mucho.
4. Las artesanías de este mercado son de (alto precio / alta calidad).
5. Generalmente, no puedes (mostrar / pagar) con tarjeta de crédito en el mercado.

B. ¿Cuánto cuesta? Explica cuánto cuestan las siguientes cosas según el dibujo. **¡OJO!** En México, $ = pesos.

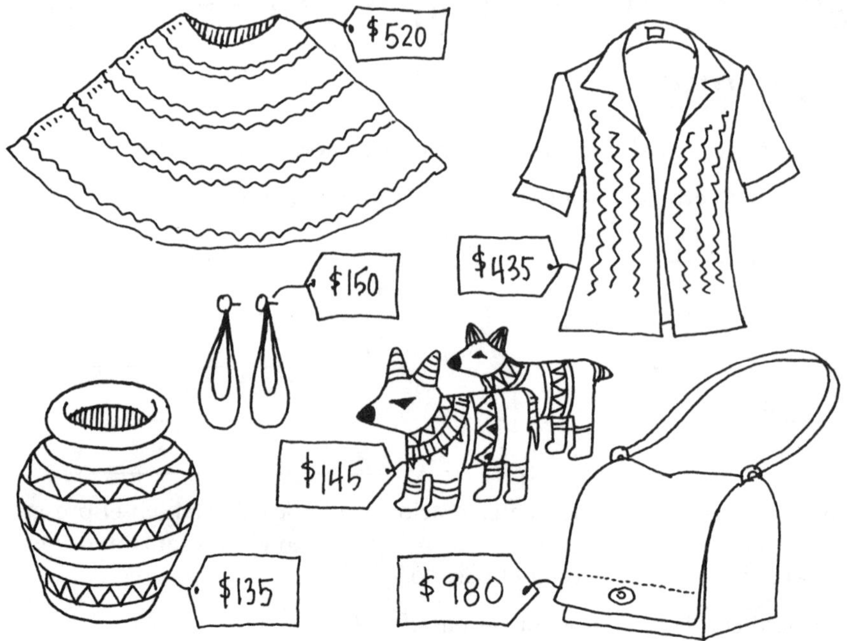

MODELO el recipiente de barro (*clay pot*) →
El recipiente de barro cuesta ciento treinta y cinco pesos.

1. los aretes de plata
______
2. el poncho de lana
______
3. los alebrijes (animalitos de madera)
______
4. la bolsa de cuero
______
5. la guayabera de seda
______

C. El regateo. Lee las siguientes preguntas y luego escucha la conversación entre un vendedor y una turista en el mercado. Entonces, indica la respuesta correcta para cada pregunta según la conversación. Si deseas, puedes escuchar más de una vez.

1. La turista busca _____.
   ☐ el mercado de artesanías ☐ regalos para sus amigos ☐ regalos para su familia
2. La turista no quiere aretes de plata porque _____.
   ☐ no le gusta la plata ☐ compra para hombres ☐ son muy caros
3. La turista no quiere comprar ponchos porque _____.
   ☐ hace calor donde vive ☐ son muy grandes ☐ son feos
4. La turista no quiere comprar camisetas porque _____.
   ☐ prefiere las camisetas del almacén
   ☐ prefiere los regalos hechos a mano
   ☐ no tienen los colores que desea
5. El vendedor le muestra _____ de cuero.
   ☐ botas ☐ carteras ☐ cinturones
6. El vendedor le dice que las carteras cuestan _____ cada una.
   ☐ $500 ☐ $1000 ☐ $1500
7. La turista dice que es caro y le ofrece _____ por tres carteras.
   ☐ $400 ☐ $1000 ☐ $600
8. Al final, la turista compra las tres carteras por _____.
   ☐ $750 ☐ $1400 ☐ $1230

Entrevista 2

A. Sonido y significado

Paso 1: Sonido. Las siguientes oraciones se basan en la entrevista con Martín Delfín Lira. Primero, lee cada oración y comprueba su significado. Después, escucha mientras el narrador pronuncia cada oración frase por frase. Repite cada frase en las pausas hasta que puedas decir toda la oración con fluidez.

Martín Delfín Lira
Zacatecas, México

1. En México hay diferentes tipos de tiendas: el centro comercial, el tianguis y el mercado de artesanías.
2. En el mercado de artesanías, puedes encontrar sarapes, platos pintados, cerámicas, artesanías de plata, como medallas y cosas que la mujer se pone en el pelo.
3. En las zonas turísticas hay muchos centros comerciales, pero en otros estados, no hay muchos.
4. En los centros comerciales de México encuentras lo mismo (*the same thing*) que encuentras en Estados Unidos.
5. Pero en México, uno va al centro comercial para hacer sus compras y no se relaciona con la gente.

Paso 2: Significado. Indica cuál de las siguientes oraciones *no* es cierta, según las oraciones del **Paso 1.**

a. ☐ En México, hay varias opciones para ir de compras.
b. ☐ Los centros comerciales son accesibles en todo el país.
c. ☐ Los centros comerciales mexicanos son similares a los estadounidenses.

B. Respuestas lógicas. Primero, lee las preguntas y respuestas divididas de la entrevista con Martín. Luego, escucha la entrevista y empareja la primera y segunda partes de sus respuestas.

PREGUNTAS Y RESPUESTAS PARTE 1

1. ¿Qué tipos de tiendas hay en México?

   «Depende de lo que necesites: Hay el centro comercial, _____.»

2. ¿Qué cosas se pueden encontrar en los mercados de artesanías?

   «Bueno, especialmente hay una cosa que se llama **sarape,** que los indígenas trabajan muy duro y es muy bonito. Toma de tres a cuatro semanas para hacerlo. _____.»

3. ¿Hay muchos centros comerciales en México?

   «Sí, sí, hay bastantes, especialmente en las zonas turísticas. _____.»

4. ¿Se parecen los centros comerciales de México a los de los Estados Unidos?

   «Sí, se parecen bastante porque encuentras lo mismo que encuentras en Estados Unidos. Pero _____.»

RESPUESTAS PARTE 2

a. En otras estados, la verdad no hay mucho
b. Hay otra cosa que son platos pintados a manos, muy bonitos, y artesanías de plata, que son medallas y unas cosas que la mujer se pone en el pelo para detenérselo
c. hay una diferencia de que en México va uno, hace sus compras y no se relaciona con otra gente
d. el tianguis y el mercado de artesanías

C. ¿Entendiste? Contesta las siguientes preguntas con oraciones completas, según la entrevista con Martín.

1. ¿Qué tipos de tiendas hay en México?

____

2. ¿Qué puedes encontrar en los mercados de artesanías?

____

3. ¿En qué se diferencian los centros comerciales mexicanos de los de los Estados Unidos?

____

❖ **D. Preguntas para ti.** Vas a escuchar tres preguntas. Escribe tus respuestas personales.

1. ____
2. ____
3. ____

Forma y función

7.3 More About the Verb **gustar**

Clínica de gramática

To express likes and dislikes, Spanish speakers often use the verb **gustar** (*to be pleasing*). Here is the complete set of phrases for talking about people's preferences.

Los usos de *gustar* en el presente

(a mí) **me gusta(n)**	(a nosotros/as) **nos gusta(n)**
(a ti) **te gusta(n)**	(a vosotros/as) **os gusta(n)**
(a usted, él/ella) **le gusta(n)**	(a ustedes, ellos/as) **les gusta(n)**

¿Qué te gusta? Indica lo que honestamente te gusta y lo que no te gusta. También escoge la forma correcta del verbo **gustar.**

	SÍ	NO	ME GUSTA	ME GUSTAN
1. las clases a las 8:00 a.m.	☐	☐	☐	☐
2. un suéter de algodón	☐	☐	☐	☐
3. los centros comerciales	☐	☐	☐	☐
4. un anillo de diamantes	☐	☐	☐	☐
5. los veranos	☐	☐	☐	☐
6. los inviernos	☐	☐	☐	☐
7. la ropa informal	☐	☐	☐	☐
8. las películas de amor	☐	☐	☐	☐

A. Los gustos. Escucha las siguientes preguntas e indica el objeto a que se refieren. Vas a escuchar las respuestas en el programa auditivo.

MODELO (*oyes*) ¿Te gustan?
(*lees*) el cinturón / los cinturones
(*indicas*) los cinturones

1. ☐ la chaqueta gris ☐ las chaquetas grises
2. ☐ el mercado al aire libre ☐ los mercados al aire libre
3. ☐ la muñeca de trapo ☐ las muñecas de trapo
4. ☐ la máscara mexicana ☐ las máscaras mexicanas
5. ☐ la cartera de cuero ☐ las carteras de cuero
6. ☐ la pulsera de plata ☐ las pulseras de plata
7. ☐ el centro comercial ☐ los centros comerciales
8. ☐ la bolsa de cuero ☐ las bolsas de cuero

B. Más gustos. Completa las siguientes oraciones con la forma correcta de **gustar.**

1. A nosotros nos ______________________ más los restaurantes mexicanos que los chinos.
2. A mí me ______________________ más la música rock que el jazz.
3. A mis padres les ______________________ llevar ropa formal.
4. A los turistas les ______________________ las artesanías hechas a mano.
5. A mi mejor amiga le ______________________ los alebrijes.
6. A ti te ______________________ más el supermercado que el mercado del barrio.
7. A nosotros nos ______________________ los pantalones vaqueros.
8. A ustedes les ______________________ las camisetas de esta tienda.
9. A Julieta le ______________________ escuchar la música salsa.
10. A vosotros os ______________________ la ciudad de Querétaro.

C. La ropa que nos gusta. Usa la siguiente información para formar oraciones completas con el verbo **gustar.**

MODELO a mi hermano / las corbatas rojas →
A mi hermano le gustan las corbatas rojas.

1. a los profesores **/** la ropa formal

   ____

2. a nosotros **/** las camisetas de algodón

   ____

3. a mí **/** las camisetas de seda

   ____

4. a los estudiantes **/** los pantalones cortos

   ____

5. a mi madre **/** los centros comerciales

   ____

6. a mi padre **/** las zapaterías para hombres

   ____

7. a ti / el sombrero nuevo

____

8. a ustedes / los mercados al aire libre

____

❖ **D. Mi clase de español.** Escribe cinco oraciones para describir lo que te gusta y lo que no te gusta de tu clase de español. Puedes usar palabras de la lista si quieres.

las actividades en clase, el aula, las composiciones, la cultura hispana, los exámenes, hablar en español, el libro, la música, la tarea

MODELO A mí (no) me gusta hablar en español en clase.

1. ____
2. ____
3. ____
4. ____
5. ____

7.4 The Verb **quedar**

Clínica de gramática

The verb **quedar** can be used in a few different ways. Here is a summary of the most common uses.

Usos del verbo *quedar*	
quedar	*to be located:* El teatro **queda** detrás del gimnasio.
quedarle (*like* **gustar**)	*to fit; to look good:* ¿**Te quedan** grandes esos zapatos?
	to have left, have remaining: Sólo **me quedan** 10 dólares.
quedarse (*reflexive*)	*to stay, remain:* **Me quedo** en casa los domingos por la mañana.

¿Lleva pronombre o no? Completa cada oración con un pronombre de complemento indirecto, un pronombre reflexivo o ningún pronombre, según el contexto. **¡OJO!** Llena el espacio en blanco con «0» si no se requiere ningún pronombre.

1. Ella ________ quedó con una familia mexicana por tres semanas.
2. ¡Guau! A ella ________ queda súper ese vestido. A mí no.
3. Disculpe señor, ¿me puede decir dónde ________ queda la biblioteca?
4. ¿No nos puede bajar el precio un poco más, señora? Sólo ________ quedan cien pesos.

A. ***¿Quedar, quedarle* o *quedarse?*** Lee las siguientes oraciones e indica el uso de **quedar.**

1. La plaza La Corregidora queda a dos cuadras de mi casa.
   ☐ *to fit / to look good* ☐ *to have left* ☐ *to stay* ☐ *to be located*
2. Me queda bien esta blusa.
   ☐ *to fit / to look good* ☐ *to have left* ☐ *to stay* ☐ *to be located*

3. Quiero quedarme en Querétaro una semana más.
   ☐ *to fit / to look good* ☐ *to have left* ☐ *to stay* ☐ *to be located*
4. Este vestido no te queda bien.
   ☐ *to fit / to look good* ☐ *to have left* ☐ *to stay* ☐ *to be located*
5. Mi novio prefiere quedarse en casa por la noche.
   ☐ *to fit / to look good* ☐ *to have left* ☐ *to stay* ☐ *to be located*
6. Querétaro queda a tres horas de la Ciudad de México.
   ☐ *to fit / to look good* ☐ *to have left* ☐ *to stay* ☐ *to be located*
7. Solamente me quedan dos dólares para comer algo.
   ☐ *to fit / to look good* ☐ *to have left* ☐ *to stay* ☐ *to be located*
8. Tengo prisa. No me queda tiempo para hablar.
   ☐ *to fit / to look good* ☐ *to have left* ☐ *to stay* ☐ *to be located*

❖ **B. ¿Cómo le queda?**

Paso 1. Piensa en la ropa que tienes. Describe una cosa que te queda bien, otra que te queda pequeña y otra que te queda grande.

MODELO Tengo una camisa roja que me queda bien.
Tengo unos vaqueros viejos que me quedan pequeños.
Tengo unos zapatos de cuero que me quedan grandes.

1. ______________________________
2. ______________________________
3. ______________________________

Paso 2. Ahora, piensa en la ropa de un amigo / una amiga y describe algo que suele llevar que le queda bien, otra cosa que le queda pequeña y otra que le queda grande.

1. ______________________________
2. ______________________________
3. ______________________________

❖ Análisis cultural

Lee la siguiente cita sobre los almacenes (*department stores*) y contesta las preguntas.

"Among the several Mexican department store chains, one of the best is Sanborn's. Along with the usual department store fare, the typical Sanborn's contains a pharmacy with common North American brand medicines, a selection of English-language books and magazines, a cafeteria serving up good Mexican food, and clean restrooms. Woolworth Mexicana is found in several Mexican cities and is a more downscale alternative to Sanborn's.

Purchasing something at a Mexican department store is usually a two-step process. First you present the item(s) to a uniformed attendant, who rings it up at a cash register. Then the cashier hands you a receipt, but not the item, and takes the purchase to another counter, where you must show your receipt to receive your purchase.

Unlike in Mexican markets, where price-haggling is expected, department store . . . prices are fixed."

Source: *Mexico Handbook*

1. ¿En qué se parecen Sanborn's y un almacén de tu país? ¿En qué se diferencian?

____

____

2. ¿Qué servicios les ofrece Sanborn's a los turistas? ¿Ofrecen algo similar los grandes almacenes de tu país?

____

____

3. ¿En qué se diferencia la manera de pagar en Sanborn's del sistema de pagar en los almacenes norteamericanos?

____

____

❖ PORTAFOLIO CULTURAL

Redacción: Una guía de compras

Vas a diseñar una guía de compras de tu ciudad para turistas. En tu guía vas a describir los lugares más interesantes para ir de compras, dónde se consiguen los precios más bajos y cuáles son los productos especiales que se ofrecen en tu ciudad.

A. Antes de escribir

Paso 1. En una hoja de papel aparte, apunta (*jot down*) tus observaciones sobre el ir de compras en tu ciudad. Usa las siguientes categorías para organizar tus ideas:

- los lugares interesantes para ir de compras (centros comerciales, tiendas generales pero pequeñas, tiendas especializadas, etcétera)
- los productos especiales que se ofrecen en estos sitios
- dónde se consiguen los precios más bajos
- los horarios y otra información sobre cada sitio, por ejemplo, la dirección, quiénes suelen comprar allí, si se permite regatear, si se aceptan tarjetas de crédito, si se pueden devolver los artículos, etcétera

Paso 2. Apunta tus impresiones sobre el tema o tus experiencias personales.

Paso 3. Revisa tus apuntes y organiza una composición para escoger un enfoque (*focus*). Puedes usar las observaciones de tus apuntes del **Paso 1** para apoyar (*support*) tu idea principal, por ejemplo, si quieres enfocar en

- un producto típico de tu ciudad, primero habla del producto y después del lugar donde se consigue, el precio, etcétera.
- un tipo de lugar para ir de compras, primero describe el lugar y después los artículos que se venden allí, los precios, etcétera.
- objetos o productos económicos (caros o de lujo), primero describe estos productos y después menciona dónde se venden los precios, etcétera.
- otro aspecto (por ejemplo, en los horarios de las tiendas), primero habla de la importancia de ese aspecto (por ejemplo, las ventajas de una tienda que abre 7 días o 24 horas) y después de las tiendas de este tipo, sus productos, etcétera.

B. ¡A escribir! Ahora escribe dos o tres párrafos sobre el tema. En el primer párrafo, presenta la idea principal. En el segundo párrafo, da más información. Puedes incluir en el tercer párrafo tus impresiones o experiencias personales sobre el ir de compras como actividad en tu ciudad.

C. ¡A corregir! Antes de entregar tu guía, revisa los siguientes puntos.

- ☐ El uso de **se** + *verbo* para expresar ideas de una forma impersonal
- ☐ El uso de los pronombres de complemento indirecto
- ☐ La concordancia entre los sustantivos y los adjetivos

WWW Exploración

Escoge y completa *una* de las siguientes actividades. Luego, presenta tus resultados a la clase o crea una versión escrita para incluir en tu portafolio, según las indicaciones de tu profesor(a).

1. En este capítulo, escuchaste la entrevista con Martín en la que él explica la diferencia entre los mexicanos y los estadounidenses al hacer compras. Según él, para los mexicanos, ir de compras o a un centro comercial no es una manera de reunirse con amigos como lo es en los Estados Unidos. ¿Estás de acuerdo con la idea de que el centro comercial de los Estados Unidos o del Canadá es también un centro social? Entrevista a dos o tres hispanohablantes de tu comunidad para saber qué opinan de los centros comerciales. ¿Tienen la misma opinión que Martín? ¿Van ahora a los centros comerciales para reunirse con amigos? ¿Prefieren las tiendas y los almacenes de tu comunidad o los de su propio país?
2. Busca catálogos y anuncios de países hispanohablantes que dan el precio de productos que usamos todos los días: ropa, coches, etcétera. Hay algunos catálogos hispanos en el Internet. Compara los precios de cinco productos con los precios norteamericanos de los mismos productos. Luego busca información sobre los salarios mensuales en un país hispanohablante y en tu país. Calcula el porcentaje de un salario mensual promedio (*average*) que gastaría (*would spend*) un hispanohablante y el porcentaje que gastaría un norteamericano. Son más o menos caras estas cosas en los países hispanohablantes?
3. Imagina que vas a viajar a México por una semana. Usa información de las bibliotecas, de agencias de viaje o del Internet para hacer dos planes de viaje: uno de lujo con transporte, hoteles, comidas y actividades de primera clase y otro viaje supereconómico. ¿Qué tipo de viaje prefieres y por qué? Luego, escribe un itinerario de viaje para un mexicano que viene a tu ciudad o región.
4. Busca más información sobre México en el Internet o en tu biblioteca. Puedes usar las siguientes ideas y palabras clave para empezar tu investigación:
   - los mercados de artesanía en México
   - las grandes cadenas norteamericanas en México (COSTCO, WalMart, McDonald's, etcétera)
   - las lenguas indígenas de México (maya, náhuatl, etcétera)
   - las crisis ecónomicas (1995, 1998, FOBAPROA, etcétera)
   - el impacto de NAFTA en la economía mexicana / en la vida de los mexicanos
   - el turismo en México (Acapulco, Oaxaca, Cancún, etcétera)
   - la rebelión zapatista y el subcomandante Marcos
   - la Revolución Mexicana y el PRI (Partido Revolucionario Institucional)

CAPÍTULO 8

Repaso y anticipación

❖ **A. La casa**

Paso 1. ¿Qué ideas asocias con las siguientes partes de la casa? Apunta por lo menos una actividad (verbo), un sustantivo y un adjetivo para cada parte de la casa.

MODELO jardín →
descansar, cocinar hamburguesas, flores, plantas, agradable, verde

1. el jardín ______________________
2. el dormitorio ______________________
3. la cocina ______________________
4. el comedor ______________________
5. el patio ______________________
6. el garaje ______________________
7. el cuarto de baño ______________________

Paso 2. ¿En qué partes de la casa prefieres pasar tu tiempo libre? ¿Por qué?

MODELO Prefiero pasar mi tiempo libre en ____________ porque ____________.

____

____

____

____

❖ **B. Las edades y el tiempo libre.** ¿Cambia la edad la forma en que la gente pasa el tiempo libre? Describe cómo los siguientes grupos de personas típicamente pasan su tiempo libre. Puedes usar palabras de la lista a continuación si quieres.

acostarse a la(s)... , bailar, comer helado (en restaurantes, en casa), dar un paseo, discutir la política, echar una siesta, ir de compras (al cine), jugar a... , reunirse con amigos, viajar

MODELO los niños pequeños →

Los niños pequeños típicamente juegan durante el día, pero echan una siesta por la tarde.

1. los adolescentes

____

____

2. los padres de niños pequeños

____

____

3. los abuelos

____

____

4. los estudiantes universitarios jóvenes

____

____

C. ¡Dinero! Completa la siguiente narración con la forma correcta del pretérito de los verbos entre paréntesis.

Ayer yo (decidir) ____________[1] ir al centro. Yo (llamar) ____________[2] a mis amigos Sara y Nacho. Ellos (llegar) ____________[3] a mi casa a las 11:00. Nosotros (salir) ____________[4] a mediodía porque yo (invitar) ____________[5] a los dos a tomar un café antes de ir al centro. Cuando nosotros (llegar) ____________[6] al centro comercial, (bajar [*to get out*]) ____________[7] del carro y de repente Nacho (exclamar) ____________[8] «¡No lo creo!» Él (señalar [*to point*]) ____________[9] con el dedo un papel en el suelo. Lo (tomar) ____________[10] con la mano y (ver) ____________[11] un billete de $1.000. Todos nosotros (gritar [*to shout*]) ____________[12] de alegría y Nacho nos (llevar) ____________[13] a almorzar a un restaurante elegante. Antes de volver a casa, él (comprar) ____________[14] regalos para toda la familia.

❖ **D. ¿Qué haces?** Lee las siguientes situaciones y contesta las preguntas para indicar cómo reaccionarías (*you would react*). Usa el pronombre de complemento directo o indirecto en cada respuesta.

MODELO Estás participando en una competencia de deporte y tu rival tiene un accidente. ¿Qué haces? ¿Ayudas a tu rival? →
Yo (no) lo ayudo.

1. En un restaurante te traen una sopa en la que flotan dos pelos. ¿Qué haces?

____

2. ¿Qué haces con la sopa con los dos pelos? ¿Comes la sopa así? ¿Devuelves la sopa?

____

3. Recibes una carta con tu nombre, ¡pero la carta es para otra persona! ¿Qué haces? ¿Lees toda la carta? ¿Devuelves la carta?

____

4. Estás estudiando porque tienes un examen importante mañana. Unos amigos te llaman por teléfono para salir. ¿Qué haces? ¿Contestas el teléfono o no? ¿Contestas pero les dices que estás ocupado/a?

____

5. Encuentras dinero en la calle. ¿Qué haces? ¿Buscas al dueño (*owner*)? ¿Gastas el dinero?

____

Vocabulario

Los deportes; Los pasatiempos

A. ¿Qué deporte? Escribe los deportes que corresponden a las siguientes descripciones.

1. requiere esfuerzo (*effort*) físico

____

2. se hace en el agua

____

3. se juega en equipos

____

4. se juega con pelotas (*balls*)

____

5. se puede jugar a solas (*alone*)

____

B. Definiciones. Empareja cada definición con la palabra que le corresponde.

1. _____ una persona entusiasta que va a todos los partidos de un equipo
2. _____ lo opuesto de ganar
3. _____ el evento en que compiten dos equipos
4. _____ un deporte en que se monta a caballo
5. _____ un deporte en que se anda en bicicleta
6. _____ deportes de origen asiático
7. _____ un deporte que se juega con raqueta
8. _____ una actividad que se hace sobre el agua o la nieve

a. la equitación
b. las artes marciales
c. el tenis
d. el aficionado
e. perder
f. esquiar
g. el ciclismo
h. el partido

C. ¿Qué hacen? Describe qué hacen las personas en los siguientes dibujos. Puedes usar palabras de la lista si quieres.

acampar, coleccionar estampillas, escalar montañas, jugar al ajedrez, jugar a los naipes, pintar un cuadro, tejer

MODELO  Rosario → Rosario pinta un cuadro.

1. 

Mi familia ______________

____

2. 

Mi padre y mi tío ______

____

3. 

José Alberto y Alejandra

____

4. 

Doña Pilar ____________

____

5. 

Santiago y yo ___________

____

6. 

Mi hermana ____________

____

D. Mi familia. Escucha a María Elena hablar de su familia. Luego, escribe las actividades que corresponden a cada persona. Puedes escuchar más de una vez si quieres.

MODELO el padre → tenis, golf...

1. el padre ______________________
2. la madre ______________________
3. el hermano mayor ______________________
4. la hermana menor ______________________
5. María Elena ______________________

Entrevista 1

A. Sonido y significado

Paso 1: Sonido. Las siguientes oraciones se basan en la entrevista con Mitch Ortega Caraballo. Primero, lee cada oración y comprueba su significado. Después, escucha mientras el narrador pronuncia cada oración frase por frase. Repite cada frase en las pausas hasta que puedas decir toda la oración con fluidez.

Mitch Ortega Caraballo
San Juan, Puerto Rico

1. Mi pasatiempo favorito, además de mi cultura y aprender de mi gente, es mi música. Me encanta ir a la playa, caminar en el bosque, mantenerme en forma (*keep in shape*), pero mi pasatiempo favorito es mi música.
2. Me gusta correr en la playa. Me gusta llevar a mi familia a hacer barbacoas (*barbecues*) y nadar.
3. El jueves en la playa, nadé, corrí y, después de que me tuve en forma, pues hicimos una barbacoa, cenamos y vimos la caída del sol (*sunset*), pero muy bonito.
4. El deporte nacional de Puerto Rico, sin discusión ninguna, es la pelota (*baseball*). Todos los niñitos desde jovencitos quieren ser un ídolo como Roberto Clemente u Orlando Cepeda.
5. En Puerto Rico, jugamos baloncesto, pelota y voleibol. Casi todas las chicas se dedican al voleibol y los hombres a la pelota.
6. El balompié (*soccer*) en Puerto Rico, nunca hemos aprendido (*we've never learned*) a jugarlo, el fútbol americano tampoco. Pero las chicas y los chicos de colegio están empezando a aprender las reglas de este juego ahora.

Paso 2: Significado. Indica cuál de las siguientes oraciones *no* es cierta, según las oraciones del **Paso 1.**

a. ☐ Mitch está muy orgulloso (*proud*) de la cultura de Puerto Rico.
b. ☐ La última vez que Mitch fue a la playa, fue solo.
c. ☐ En Puerto Rico los chicos y las chicas suelen practicar deportes diferentes.

B. Respuestas lógicas. Primero, lee las preguntas y respuestas divididas de la entrevista con Mitch. Luego, escucha la entrevista y empareja la primera y segunda partes de sus respuestas.

PREGUNTAS Y RESPUESTAS PARTE 1

1. ¿Cuál es tu pasatiempo favorito?

   «Mi pasatiempo favorito es, además de mi cultura y aprender de mi gente, es mi música. Me encanta ir a la playa. Me encanta correr a caballo. _____.»

2. ¿Con qué frecuencia vas a la playa y qué te gusta hacer allí?

   «Voy dos, tres veces en semana. Me gusta correr en la playa. _____.»

3. ¿Cómo fue la última vez que fuiste a la playa y qué hiciste?

   «¡*Wow!* ¡Qué bonito, el jueves, un día precioso. Nadé, corrí y, después de que me tuve en forma, _____.»

4. ¿Cuál es el deporte más importante en Puerto Rico?

   «El deporte nacional de Puerto Rico, sin discusión ninguna, es la pelota. Es un deporte que en todos los pueblos, _____.»

5. ¿Hay otros deportes importantes?

   «[En] Puerto Rico, jugamos baloncesto, jugamos pelota y voleibol. Las chicas destacan mucho más en voleibol. _____.»

6. ¿Y el fútbol?

   «El balompié en Puerto Rico nunca hemos aprendido a jugarlo, el fútbol americano tampoco nos ha llegado. Pero _____.»

RESPUESTAS PARTE 2

a. Me gusta llevar a la familia a hacer barbacoas, nadar, mantenerme en forma
b. las chicas y los chicos de colegio están empezando a aprender las reglas de este juego ahora. Posiblemente en el futuro lo juguemos
c. Me encanta caminar en el bosque, pero mi pasatiempo favorito es mi música. Es lo más bonito, creo que, en la unión de nuestra gente
d. todos los niñitos desde jovencitos es lo que quieren hacer, ser un ídolo como Roberto Clemente o [Orlando] Cepeda. Simplemente representar a Puerto Rico, jugando pelota es muy bonito
e. pues hicimos una barbacoa, cenamos, vimos la caída del sol, pero muy bonito
f. Hay ahora, en el presente, jugando pelota, pero casi todas las chicas en Puerto Rico se dedican al voleibol y los hombres a la pelota

C. ¿Entendiste? Contesta las siguientes preguntas con oraciones completas, según la entrevista con Mitch.

1. ¿Qué pasatiempos le gustan a Mitch?

   ____

2. ¿Qué hizo (*did he do*) la última vez que fue a la playa?

   ____

3. ¿Cuál es el deporte más importante de Puerto Rico?

____

4. ¿Qué deportes practican los chicos y las chicas puertorriqueñas?

____

❖ **D. Preguntas para ti.** Vas a escuchar tres preguntas. Escribe tus respuestas personales.

1. ____
2. ____
3. ____

Forma y función

8.1 Irregular Forms of the Preterit

Clínica de gramática

Many Spanish verbs have irregular forms in the preterit. Here are the irregular preterit forms for the verbs **dar** (*to give*), **hacer** (*to do; to make*), **ir** (*to go*), and **ser** (*to be*). Note: **Hizo** is spelled with a **-z-** to maintain the stem sound. **Ir** and **ser** have identical forms, but context will make the meaning clear.

dar		hacer		ir/ser	
di	dimos	hice	hicimos	fui	fuimos
diste	disteis	hiciste	hicisteis	fuiste	fuisteis
dio	dieron	hizo	hicieron	fue	fueron

The preterit of the following verbs is formed by attaching a set of irregular endings to irregular stems. These irregular endings are similar to those for the preterit of **hacer: -e, -iste, -o, -imos, -isteis, -ieron.** Note: Verbs with a stem-final **-j** drop the **-i-** of the **-ieron** ending (e.g., **decir → dijeron**).

Infinitivo	Raíz	Conjugaciones
andar	anduv-	anduve, anduviste, anduvo, anduvimos, anduvisteis, anduvieron
estar	estuv-	estuve, estuviste, estuvo, estuvimos, estuvisteis, estuvieron
tener	tuv-	tuve, tuviste, tuvo, tuvimos, tuvisteis, tuvieron
poder	pud-	pude, pudiste, pudo, pudimos, pudisteis, pudieron
poner	pus-	puse, pusiste, puso, pusimos, pusisteis, pusieron
querer	quis-	quise, quisiste, quiso, quisimos, quisisteis, quisieron
saber	sup-	supe, supiste, supo, supimos, supisteis, supieron
venir (*to come*)	vin-	vine, viniste, vino, vinimos, vinisteis, vinieron
decir	dij-	dije, dijiste, dijo, dijimos, dijisteis, dij**eron**
traer	traj-	traje, trajiste, trajo, trajimos, trajisteis, traj**eron**
reducir	reduj-	reduje, redujiste, redujo, redujimos, redujisteis, reduj**eron**

¿Qué hicieron el fin de semana pasado? Completa las siguientes oraciones con la forma correcta del pretérito de los verbos entre paréntesis para decir qué hicieron estas personas el fin de semana pasado.

El fin de semana pasado...

1. yo ______________________ (andar) en bicicleta.
2. mi hermana ______________________ (ir) al cine con un amiga.
3. Jaime ______________________ (hacer) *camping* con su familia.
4. tú ______________________ (querer) llamarme por teléfono, pero no ______________________ (poder) porque mi teléfono no sirve (*doesn't work*).
5. nosotros ______________________ (dar) una fiesta, los invitados ______________________ (traer) música y comida y todos la pasamos chévere.
6. ¿Por qué no ______________________ (venir) vosotros a la fiesta?

A. ¿Qué verbo es? ¿Reconoces estos verbos? Escribe el infinitivo y el sujeto de las siguientes formas verbales.

	Infinitivo	**Sujeto**
1. pudimos	*poder*	
2. puse		
3. tuvo		
4. viniste		*tú*
5. trajeron		
6. quisisteis		

B. Silvia en Puerto Rico. Silvia y su familia pasaron dos semanas de vacaciones en Puerto Rico. Completa las siguientes oraciones que describen su viaje con los verbos de la lista.

estuvimos, fueron, hicieron, hizo, hubo, llevamos, pudo

1. Nosotros ______________________ en Puerto Rico por dos semanas.
2. Mi padre no habla español, pero ______________________ hablar con los puertorriqueños en inglés.
3. ______________________ mucho calor todos los días.
4. Nosotros ______________________ los trajes de baño para nadar en la playa.
5. En el bar del hotel, ______________________ una fiesta la última noche del viaje.

6. La pasamos tan bien que mis padres ______________________ planes para volver.
7. Los puertorriqueños ______________________ muy amables con nosotros.

C. El verano pasado. La acción del siguiente párrafo ocurrió el verano pasado, pero los verbos están en el presente. Escribe el pretérito de cada verbo subrayado en el espacio en blanco correspondiente. La primera oración sirve de modelo.

El verano pasado vamos a San Juan de Puerto Rico. Tenemos[1] mucha suerte porque mi padre puede[2] encontrar boletos baratos. La agencia nos da[3] un descuento y nos reduce[4] el precio bastante. Es[5] tan barato el viaje que mi abuela viene[6] con nosotros. Hacemos[7] varios deportes acuáticos en la playa. A la vuelta, traemos[8] muchas cosas que compramos[9] en las tiendas de Puerto Rico.

MODELO vamos → fuimos

1. ______________________
2. ______________________
3. ______________________
4. ______________________
5. ______________________
6. ______________________
7. ______________________
8. ______________________
9. ______________________

D. Un domingo por la tarde. Escucha lo que hizo la famila de Ignacio Sánchez el domingo por la tarde e indica la frase que completa las siguientes oraciones.

1. La familia de Ignacio _____.

   ☐ se quedó en casa ☐ fue a un partido de béisbol ☐ vio un partido en la televisión

2. Acompañó a la familia _____.

   ☐ un sobrino ☐ un amigo ☐ una esposa

3. Los padres llevaron _____.

   ☐ comida ☐ helados ☐ chaqueta

4. Ellos vieron el partido _____.

   ☐ de pie ☐ acostados ☐ sentados

5. Los últimos diez minutos del partido fueron _____.

   ☐ malos ☐ desastrosos ☐ buenos

6. Los niños recibieron _____.

   ☐ una pelota ☐ un reloj ☐ un autógrafo

❖ **E. La mejor fiesta de mi vida.** Contesta las siguientes preguntas sobre la mejor fiesta de tu vida. **¡OJO!** Usa el pretérito y escribe oraciones completas.

1. ¿Fuiste solo/a o con alguien?

   ____

2. ¿Te pusiste ropa elegante o informal?

   ____

3. ¿Llevaste comida o bebidas a la fiesta?

____

4. ¿Fue mucha o poca gente a la fiesta?

____

5. ¿Hiciste algo especial después o fuiste a casa inmediatamente?

____

6. ¿Estuviste alegre o triste después de la fiesta?

____

❖ F. **El mejor viaje.** Describe lo que pasó durante el mejor viaje de tu vida. Si quieres, puedes inventar un viaje. Puedes usar verbos de la lista. Escribe por lo menos seis oraciones y usa el pretérito.

andar, dar, decir, estar, haber, hacer, ir, poder, poner, querer, reducir, saber, ser, tener, traer, venir

____

____

____

____

____

____

8.2 Stem-Changing Verbs in the Preterit

Clínica de gramática

The **-ir** verbs that have stem changes in the present tense also undergo a stem change in the preterit: In the third-person forms only, the **-e-** or **-o-** of the stem changes to **-i-** or **-u-**, respectively. The regular preterit endings are then added: **-í, -iste, -ió, -imos, -isteis, -ieron.**

servir (i, i)

PRESENTE		PRETÉRITO	
sirvo	servimos	serví	servimos
sirves	servís	serviste	servisteis
sirve	sirven	sirvió	sirvieron

dormir (ue, u)

PRESENTE		PRETÉRITO	
duermo	dormimos	dormí	dormimos
duermes	dormís	dormiste	dormisteis
duerme	duermen	durmió	durmieron

Práctica. Completa la siguiente tabla con la forma de los verbos en el pretérito. **¡OJO!** No todos los verbos tienen cambio de raíz en el pretérito.

	yo	usted	nosotros/as	ustedes
1. sentir				
2. morir	*morí*			
3. volver				
4. dormir				
5. perder		*perdió*		
6. vestirse				
7. divertirse				
8. pedir				
9. servir				*sirvieron*

A. ¿Quién lo hizo? Esto es lo que ocurrió en el partido de baloncesto de anoche. Completa las siguientes oraciones con uno de los sujetos de la lista para especificar quién hizo cada acción.

yo, tú, él, nosotras, vosotros, ellos

1. ____________________ se durmieron diez minutos.
2. ____________________ sirvió refrescos a los jugadores.
3. ____________________ perdiste las entradas del partido.
4. ____________________ pedisteis autógrafos a dos jugadores.
5. ____________________ me vestí con los colores del equipo.
6. ____________________ nos divertimos mucho.

B. ¡Qué confusión! Tomasito es un niño de 5 años que le cuenta a su madre lo que hizo el primer día de escuela… pero todo en el presente. Escribe la forma correcta del pretérito de cada verbo subrayado en el espacio en blanco correspondiente. La primera oración sirve de modelo.

Mami, los niños se divierten mucho. Sólo Sara se siente[1] mal y tiene[2] que volver a su casa temprano. A las 2:00 de la tarde, todos los niños duermen[3] la siesta. Guillermito llora[4] mucho porque pierde[5] su gorro[a] rojo. Después de la siesta, la maestra nos sirve[6] jugo de naranja.

[a]*cap*

MODELO se divierten → se divirtieron

1. ____________________
2. ____________________
3. ____________________
4. ____________________
5. ____________________
6. ____________________

❖ **C. Frases incompletas.** Forma oraciones completas usando la siguiente información y los verbos de la lista. Usa el pretérito de los verbos.

divertirse, dormir, morir, pedir, perder, sentarse, servir, vestirse

MODELO los niños / el parque →
Los niños se divirtieron en el parque.

1. Mi abuela / en el sofá
____
2. John F. Kennedy, Jr. / 1999
____
3. los clientes / la especialidad de la casa
____
4. Lidia / comida a los invitados
____
5. los estudiantes / el autobús
____
6. Juana (no) / porque estaba nerviosa
____

❖ **D. Una noche con amigos.** Escribe un párrafo sobre una noche divertida que pasaste con amigos. Usa los siguientes verbos y no olvides conjugarlos en el pretérito.

conseguir, decidir, divertirse, dormir, pedir, perder, preferir, sentirse, servir, vestirse

____
____
____
____
____
____
____
____

Pronunciación y ortografía

l; r and rr

Lee y estudia la información en el libro de texto antes de hacer estas actividades.

A. Comparación. Escucha las siguientes palabras para comparar la diferencia entre la *l* inglesa y la **l** española.

	INGLÉS	ESPAÑOL
1.	hotel	hotel
2.	mall	mal
3.	goal	gol
4.	dell	del
5.	alter	alto
6.	tilled	tilde

B. La *l*. Escucha y repite las siguientes palabras con la **l** al final de sílaba.

1. fútbol
2. fenomenal
3. jugar al tenis
4. el alcohol
5. voleibol
6. golf
7. alguien
8. ¿Qué tal?

C. La *r*

Paso 1. Primero, practica la **r** entre vocales. Repite las siguientes palabras.

1. para 2. los bares 3. me parece 4. jugar a los naipes 5. ver una película

Paso 2. La **r** es más difícil junto a otras consonantes. Repite las siguientes palabras.

1. parte 2. perder 3. partido 4. charlar

D. La *rr*. Escucha y repite estas palabras con el sonido **rr**.

1. aburrido
2. borracho
3. Enrique
4. reunirse
5. Puerto Rico
6. alrededor
7. burro
8. resfriado
9. ropa
10. rutina

E. *¿R* o *rr?* Escucha y repite cada palabra. Luego, indica la palabra que escuchaste.

1. ☐ coro ☐ corro
2. ☐ coro ☐ corro
3. ☐ ahora ☐ ahorra
4. ☐ ahora ☐ ahorra
5. ☐ varios ☐ barrios
6. ☐ varios ☐ barrios

PARTE 2 Vocabulario

Fiestas y diversiones

A. ¡Que se diviertan! Completa las siguientes oraciones con la expresión apropiada.

bailar pegados, bebida alcohólica, en ambiente, encontrarse, fuma, tiene prisa

1. Juana y Lorenzo son novios. Les gusta ______________________________ con música romántica.
2. Despues de sus clases, Blas va a ______________________________ con sus amigos a un café.
3. Pedro nunca compra cigarrillos, pero siempre ______________________________ en las fiestas.
4. Carlota no bebe más de una ______________________________ en una fiesta porque no le gusta estar borracha.
5. Jaime ______________________________ porque son las 9:00 y la fiesta empezó a las 8:00.
6. Celia volvió a casa porque no se encontró ______________________________ en esa fiesta.

B. Busca la intrusa. Indica la palabra intrusa (que no pertenece al grupo).

1. ☐ charlar con amigos ☐ pasarla bien ☐ molestar ☐ encontrarse con amigos
2. ☐ pegados ☐ prisa ☐ separados ☐ música
3. ☐ los invitados ☐ el anfitrión ☐ el bar ☐ la fiesta
4. ☐ la bebida alcohólica ☐ charlar ☐ borracho ☐ tomar bebidas
5. ☐ invitado ☐ en su punto ☐ tranquilo ☐ en ambiente
6. ☐ humo ☐ fumar ☐ molestar ☐ pasarla bien

C. En la discoteca. Escucha a Juana contar de una noche en la discoteca e indica la palabra o frase que completa las siguientes oraciones.

1. Juana fue a la discoteca _____.

   ☐ el sábado pasado ☐ anoche ☐ la semana pasada

2. Juana fue con sus _____.

   ☐ novio ☐ amigas ☐ padres

3. El _____ de Juana fue con ellas para cuidarlas (*take care of them*).

   ☐ hermano ☐ padre ☐ novio

4. Juana y sus amigas bebieron _____.

   ☐ refrescos ☐ cerveza ☐ vino

5. Juana y sus amigas _____ la salsa, el merengue y la cumbia.

   ☐ bailaron ☐ tocaron ☐ hablaron de

6. Juana y sus amigas _____ Álvaro y Rafael.

   ☐ bailaron con ☐ charlaron de ☐ se reunieron con

Entrevista 2

A. Sonido y significado

Paso 1: Sonido. Las siguientes oraciones se basan en la entrevista con José Veliz Román. Primero, lee cada oración y comprueba su significado. Después, escucha mientras el narrador pronuncia cada oración frase por frase. Repite cada frase en las pausas hasta que puedas decir toda la oración con fluidez.

José Veliz Román
San Juan, Puerto Rico

1. Mi hora favorita del día es la noche; yo no soy una persona diurna, me encanta la noche.
2. Anoche salí con unos amigos y fuimos a casa de unos compañeros a hablar. Luego, nos fuimos a una discoteca a bailar.
3. La fiesta estuvo increíble, o chévere, como decimos nosotros. Bailamos juntos, nos reímos y la pasamos increíble.
4. En la fiesta se tocó de todo tipo de música: música americana, música *hip hop*, pero sobre todo, música latina, salsa y un buen merengue.
5. Los americanos, cuando salen a disfrutar, el punto principal es el alcohol. Pero nosotros los puertorriqueños, cuando salimos, lo que queremos hacer es conocernos y bailar.
6. No hay prisa de llegar a tiempo a estas fiestas ni prisa de irse temprano.

Paso 2: Significado. Indica cuál de las siguientes oraciones *no* es cierta, según las oraciones del **Paso 1.**

a. ☐ A José le gusta más el día que la noche.
b. ☐ José fue a bailar a una fiesta con unos amigos.
c. ☐ Según José, hay una diferencia entre los puertorriqueños y los americanos cuando salen.

B. Respuestas lógicas. Primero, lee las preguntas y respuestas divididas de la entrevista con José. Luego, escucha la entrevista y empareja la primera y segunda partes de sus respuestas.

PREGUNTAS Y RESPUESTAS PARTE 1

1. ¿Cuál es tu hora favorita del día?

   «Mi hora favorita del día es la noche; yo no soy una persona diurna, me encanta la noche. _____.»

2. ¿Qué hiciste anoche?

   «Anoche salí con unos amigos y fuimos a casa de unos compañeros a hablar. _____.»

3. ¿Y qué tal estuvo?

   «Oh, la fiesta estuvo increíble, o 'chévere', como decimos nosotros. Fuimos un grupo de amistades a la fiesta. _____.»

4. ¿Qué música se tocó?

   «En la fiesta se tocó de todo. El *discjockey* nos puso música americana, música *hip hop*, _____.»

5. ¿Se divierten los puertorriqueños de manera diferente de los estadounidenses?

   «Yo encuentro que sí, que hay una diferencia. Los americanos, cuando salen a disfrutar, el punto principal es beber alcohol. _____.»

6. ¿Cómo son las fiestas en Puerto Rico?

   «Este… lo interesante de estas fiestas es que terminan cuando terminan. No hay prisa de llegar a tiempo _____.»

RESPUESTAS PARTE 2

a. ni prisa de irse temprano. Así que uno se siente a gusto en ambiente, todo el mundo disfrutando y pasándola bien
b. Pero nosotros los puertorriqueños, cuando salimos, lo que queremos es conocernos, bailar, reírnos. El alcohol está ahí, pero no es el punto principal
c. pero sobre todo, música latina: salsa y un buen merengue
d. No me encuentro en ambiente sino hasta las 11:00 ó 12:00 de la noche
e. Todos bailamos juntos y nos sonreímos y la pasamos increíble
f. Y luego nos fuimos a una discoteca a bailar

C. ¿Entendiste? Contesta las siguientes preguntas con oraciones completas, según la entrevista con José.

1. ¿Qué hora del día prefiere José?

   ____

2. ¿Qué hizo José anoche?

   ____

3. ¿Qué música se tocó en la fiesta?

   ____

4. ¿Qué les gusta hacer en las fiestas a los puertorriqueños?

   ____

❖ **D. Preguntas para ti.** Vas a escuchar tres preguntas. Escribe tus respuestas personales.

1. ____
2. ____
3. ____

Forma y función

8.3 Negative Words

Clínica de gramática

Here are the most commonly used negative words in Spanish and their English translations.

jamás	never	**nunca**	never
nadie	nobody, no one	**tampoco**	neither, not either
ni _____ **ni**	neither _____ nor	**nada**	nothing
ningún/ninguna	no, not any		

Note: Even if one of these negative words follows the verb, **no** or another negative word must precede the verb.

Ese equipo **nunca** va a ganar.

or

Ese equipo **no** va a ganar **nunca.**

Lo opuesto. Escribe la palabra opuesta.

MODELO siempre → jamás

1. nadie _______________
2. también _______________
3. nunca _______________
4. algo _______________
5. ninguna _______________

A. La noche y el día. Ángela y su hermana son como dos gotas de agua (*like two peas in a pod*) físicamente, pero sus gustos y personalidad son muy diferentes. Lee la descripción de Ángela y adivina (*guess*) las características de su hermana, quién es completamente lo opuesto. **¡OJO!** No te olvides de incluir las expresiones negativas para describir a la hermana.

ÁNGELA	SU HERMANA
1. Siempre ve la televisión.	_______________
2. Le gustan todos los deportes.	_______________
3. Tiene muchas fiestas en su casa.	_______________
4. Siempre le molesta algo de los políticos.	_______________
5. En las fiestas, habla con todos.	_______________
6. Come dulces y carne también.	_______________

B. Jaime jamás. Jaime es muy negativo y responde a las siguientes preguntas negativamente. Escribe sus respuestas.

MODELO ¿Siempre estudias por la noche? →
No, nunca estudio por la noche.

1. ¿Siempre escuchas música clásica?

____

2. ¿Alguien estudia español contigo?

____

3. ¿Te gusta algo de Puerto Rico?

____

4. ¿Estudias francés también?

____

5. ¿Tienes alguna amiga puertorriqueña?

____

C. **Por otro lado.** Cambia las siguientes oraciones negativas para formar oraciones afirmativas.

MODELO Jamás colecciono estampillas. →
Siempre colecciono estampillas.

1. Nunca juego a los naipes.

____

2. Nadie en mi clase cuenta chistes.

____

3. No tengo nada de dinero para jugar al billar.

____

4. Ni juego al ajedrez ni voy al cine tampoco.

____

5. Ninguno de los videojuegos es interesante.

____

8.4 Using Direct and Indirect Object Pronouns Together

Clínica de gramática

When both a direct and an indirect object pronoun occur in the same sentence, the indirect object (IO) pronoun always precedes the direct object (DO) pronoun.

—¿Quién **te** (IO) regaló este disco (DO)?

—**Me** (IO) lo (DO) regaló mi mamá.

Note: When both the direct and indirect object pronouns are in the third person, the indirect object pronoun **le(s)** becomes **se.**

IO DO
—¿Quién **le** regaló <u>este disco</u> **a tu hermano?**

IO DO
—**Se** <u>lo</u> regaló un amigo.

¿Quién te lo regaló? Luis le hace algunas preguntas a Encarna sobre los regalos que ella recibió el día de su cumpleaños. Completa las respuestas de Encarna, usando los dos pronombres juntos.

MODELO LUIS: ¿Quién te compró los discos compactos?
ENCARNA: Mi primo me los compró.

1. LUIS: ¿Quién te mandó el libro de García Márquez?
   ENCARNA: Una amiga ______
2. LUIS: ¿Quién te regaló las pulseras de plata?
   ENCARNA: Mis tíos ______
3. LUIS: ¿Quién te escribió este poema de amor?
   ENCARNA: Mi novio ______
4. LUIS: ¿Quién te dio la blusa de algodón?
   ENCARNA: Los vecinos ______
5. LUIS: ¿Quién te compró el abrigo de piel?
   ENCARNA: Mis padres ______

A. ¿Qué y a quién?

Paso 1. Escucha cada oración e indica el objeto que corresponde al pronombre de complemento directo.

MODELO (*escuchas*) Me lo regaló para mi cumpleaños.
(*ves*) la bolsa / el libro →
(*escoges*) el libro

1. ☐ el coche ☐ las estampillas
2. ☐ los tacos ☐ las estampillas
3. ☐ los tacos ☐ las enchiladas
4. ☐ las estampillas ☐ la composición
5. ☐ el coche ☐ la composición
6. ☐ los tacos ☐ las enchiladas

Paso 2. Ahora, vuelve a escuchar (*listen again to*) las oraciones del **Paso 1** para identificar a la persona que recibió cada objeto.

MODELO (*escuchas*) Me lo regaló para mi cumpleaños.
(*ves*) yo / tú →
(*escoges*) yo

1. ☐ él ☐ yo
2. ☐ tú ☐ ella
3. ☐ ellos ☐ nosotros
4. ☐ yo ☐ ella
5. ☐ tú ☐ yo
6. ☐ yo ☐ ellas

B. Los regalos. Usa la siguiente información para formar oraciones completas. Sustituye los pronombres correspondientes por los complementos directo e indirecto. **¡OJO!** Cada oración tiene complementos directo e indirecto.

MODELO mi padre / dar / disco compacto / a mí →
Mi padre me lo dio.

1. mis padres / compraron / coche / a mí

____

2. yo / compré / la pelota / a ti

____

3. nosotros / compramos / las bicicletas / a nosotros

____

4. tú / diste / los videojuegos / a mí

____

5. tus compañeros de cuarto / regalaron / el disco compacto / a ti

____

C. ¿Quién es? Lee las siguientes oraciones y luego emparéjalas con un regalo y recipiente a la derecha.

MODELO Se lo vendieron. →
el video musical a mi hermana.

1. _____ Se los regaló.
2. _____ Se la leyeron.
3. _____ Se lo dieron.
4. _____ Se las trajo.
5. _____ Se la compraron.

a. la bicicleta todo terreno a tu novio
b. el boleto a mi hermana
c. la novela a las muchachas
d. las pelotas de tenis a los jugadores
e. los libros a Juan

D. En la fiesta. Vuelve a escribir las siguientes oraciones. Sustituye los pronombres correspondientes por los complementos directo e indirecto. **¡OJO!** Recuerda que puedes colocar (*place*) los pronombres junto a los infinitivos y gerundios y que **le** y **les** cambian a **se** con **lo(s)** y **la(s).**

MODELO Nos están diciendo la verdad a nosotros. →
Nos la están diciendo. / Están diciéndonosla.

1. La anfitriona nos está mostrando la casa.

____

2. Nosotros les vamos a dar este regalo a los anfitriones.

____

3. El anfitrión le está sirviendo la limonada a Beatriz.

____

4. El anfitrión nos está tocando música excelente.

____

5. Voy a mandarles esta carta de gracias a los anfitriones.

____

E. Oraciones revueltas

Paso 1. Usa la siguiente información para formar oraciones lógicas. **¡OJO!** Usa el pronombre de complemento indirecto en tus oraciones.

MODELO compró / a mí / un videojuego / mi mejor amigo →
Mi mejor amigo me compró un videojuego.

1. dijeron / a Margarita / la verdad / sus amigas

 ____

2. la profesora / el material / explicando / está / al estudiante

 ____

3. voy a / un regalo / comprar / a mi madre

 ____

4. a mis hermanos / el disco compacto / di

 ____

5. preparó / a nosotros / una cena fantástica / Sergio

 ____

Paso 2. Ahora, vuelve a escribir las oraciones del **Paso 1.** Sustituye los pronombres correspondientes por los complementos directo e indirecto. **¡OJO!** Recuerda que **le** y **les** cambian a **se** con **lo(s)** y **la(s).**

MODELO Mi mejor amigo me compró un videojuego (a mí). →
Me lo compró.

1. ______________________________
2. ______________________________
3. ______________________________
4. ______________________________
5. ______________________________

❖ Análisis cultural

Lee la siguiente cita sobre la música del Caribe por Nicolás Kanellos. Luego, contesta las preguntas, basándote en la información de la cita y la información que aprendiste en este capítulo.

"**Salsa** is Spanish for *sauce*—in this case a term that refers to the hot, spicy rhythms of Afro-Caribbean music. When people talk about salsa music, however, they are actually referring to a generic term that includes a number of distinct types of Afro-Caribbean music, although one in particular, the **son guaguancó,** has predominated since the 1960s. Whatever the origins of the term **salsa,** the music has deep, even sacred, roots in its Afro-Caribbean context.

Clearly, for people of Afro-Caribbean descent—Puerto Ricans, Cubans, Dominicans, and others—what is now called **salsa** has that kind of summarizing power. **Salsa** stands preeminently for their special sense of Afro-Hispanic 'Caribbeanness.' But **salsa** obviously has an audience that extends far beyond its core Caribbean setting. As a cultural symbol, it spreads out with diminishing influence toward audiences whose contact with the music's cultural roots is at best casual. Among these audiences, the music's symbolic power is highly diluted or even nonexistent."

Source: *The Hispanic Almanac: From Columbus to Corporate America*

1. ¿Qué formas musicales son propias de tu cultura (himnos religiosos, música de baile, canciones patrióticas, etcétera)? ¿Conoces el origen de esta música?

   ____

   ____

   ____

2. ¿Se conocen estas formas musicales fuera de su contexto cultural? En tu opinión, ¿comprenden los otros esta música?

   ____

   ____

   ____

3. ¿Qué otros símbolos culturales se asocian con tu grupo o región (bailes, comidas típicas, costumbres sociales, etcétera)? Es decir, ¿qué costumbres distinguen tu grupo o región cultural?

   ____

   ____

   ____

4. ¿Qué sabes de la música salsa? ¿Te gusta? ¿Por qué sí o por que no? ¿Es posible aprender a bailar salsa en tu comunidad?

   ____

   ____

   ____

❖ PORTAFOLIO CULTURAL

Redacción: Querido diario

El diario nos permite recordar los momentos más importantes de la vida. En esta actividad, vas a describir los tres momentos más importantes o inolvidables de tu vida.

A. Antes de escribir

Paso 1. Primero, en una hoja aparte, apunta los tres momentos que quieres recordar. Puedes usar las siguientes ideas si quieres:

en un deporte	una fiesta
en la música	un viaje
en la escuela o en la universidad	un problema o una buena/mala experiencia con otra persona

Paso 2. Para cada momento, haz una lista de información relacionada:

el lugar	tus emociones
la fecha (*date*)	la importancia
otras personas	

Paso 3. Para cada momento, escribe una lista de las acciones y fechas que lo precedieron (*preceded*) y que contribuyeron al clímax.

MODELO

el 3 de julio de 1994	Hoy mis padres me compraron una bicicleta nueva.
el 4 de julio	Esta mañana mi padre me enseñó a andar en bicicleta. Pasamos tres horas en la calle y me caí muchas veces. ¡Uf!
el 5 de julio	Mi padre me ayudó hoy también. ¡Por fin pude andar en bicicleta yo solo!

B. ¡A escribir! Ahora, escribe las entradas (*entries*) relacionadas a los tres momentos que escogiste. Incluye las fechas (las puedes inventar) para organizar la información de **Antes de escribir.** Si quieres, puedes darle un título a cada momento.

C. ¡A corregir! Antes de entregar tus entradas, revisa los siguientes puntos.

- ☐ Las formas del pretérito
- ☐ El uso de palabras negativas
- ☐ La concordancia entre los adjetivos y sustantivos
- ☐ El uso de palabras y expresiones de transición entre ideas

WWW Exploración

Escoge y completa *una* de las siguientes actividades. Luego, presenta tus resultados a la clase o crea una versión escrita para incluir en tu portafolio, según las indicaciones de tu profesor(a).

1. Usa recursos (*resources*) de la biblioteca o del Internet para identificar deportes con orígenes en un país hispanohablante, por ejemplo, ¿dónde se juega? ¿es un deporte de equipo o individual? ¿cómo se juega? ¿cómo se gana un partido? ¿qué tradiciones se asocian con el deporte? ¿hay algunas reglas importantes o particulares a este deporte? ¿puedes compararlo con un deporte de otro país? Unos ejemplos son el jai alai del País Vasco en España y el batey de los taínos, indígenas de Puerto Rico.
2. Investiga la biografía de Roberto Clemente, de Orlando Cepeda y de otros deportistas hispanos. ¿En qué son similares o diferentes sus carreras? ¿Cuándo empezaron a practicar su deporte? ¿Cómo llegaron a ser jugadores profesionales? ¿Qué obstáculos tuvieron? ¿Cuánto tiempo duró (*lasted*) su carrera? ¿En qué actividades humanitarias participaron?
3. Entrevista a un hispanohablante de tu comunidad. Pregúntale sobre el ritmo de su día. ¿Cuándo está en ambiente? ¿en punto? ¿Prefiere las mañanas o las noches? ¿Sale mucho? ¿Cuándo fue la última vez (*last time*) que salió? ¿Adónde fue? ¿Con quién? ¿La pasaron bien? Compara su ritmo diario con el tuyo. ¿Son parecidos o diferentes? Explica.

4. Busca más información sobre Puerto Rico en el Internet o en tu biblioteca. Puedes usar las siguientes ideas y palabras clave para empezar tu investigación:
   - la selva tropical: el Yunque
   - el ecoturismo en Puerto Rico
   - las comunidades puertorriqueñas en Nueva York y Nueva Jersey
   - el Viejo San Juan
   - los taínos (los habitantes originales de Borinquen)
   - el «Estado Libre Asociado» de Puerto Rico
   - el movimiento por la independencia puertorriqueña
   - la salsa: invención puertorriqueña y norteamericana
   - los deportes acuáticos en Puerto Rico

Answer Key

Capítulo 1

Anticipación **A.** 1. b 2. a 3. c 4. d

Parte 1

Vocabulario **C.** 1. se llama; Me llamo; Igualmente (*or* Encantado) 2. Estoy (*or* Muy); usted; Bien (*or* Regular *or* Más o menos) 3. estás; tú; Adiós **D.** 1. automóvil (*automobile, car*) 2. símbolo (*symbol*) 3. historia (*history, story*) 4. computadora (*computer*) 5. entrevista (*interview*) **E.** 1. una mujer 2. hombre o mujer 3. un hombre 4. una mujer 5. una mujer 6. una mujer 7. un hombre **F.** 1. italiana 2. japonesa 3. puertorriqueño 4. chino 5. francesa 6. *Answer will vary.*

Entrevista 1 **A. Paso 2.** c **B.** 1. b 2. d 3. e 4. a 5. c **C.** 1. Jairo es de Bogotá, Colombia. 2. Sus apellidos son **Bejarano Carrillo.** 3. Sus padres no son de Bogotá, son de pueblos pequeños.

Forma y función

1.1 Clínica. 1. él 2. ella 3. nosotros 4. ellos 5. vosotros (*Sp.*), ustedes (*Span. Am.*) **B.** 1. él 2. ellos 3. ellos 4. ellos 5. ellas 6. ella 7. ellas 8. él *or* ella **C.** 1. tú 2. usted 3. usted 4. tú 5. usted 6. tú **D.** 1. nosotros/as 2. él 3. ustedes 4. ella 5. vosotras *or* ustedes 6. tú

1.2 Clínica. 1. eres 2. somos 3. son 4. es 5. es 6. soy 7. sois **B.** 1. somos 2. son 3. es 4. es 5. eres 6. sois 7. soy **C.** *Correct verb forms:* 1. soy 2. es 3. es 4. son 5. es **D.** 1. Andy García y Jimmy Smits son de los Estados Unidos. 2. Ricky Martin es de Puerto Rico. 3. Enrique y Julio Iglesias son de España. 4. Fernando Botero es de Colombia. 5. Julia Álvarez es de la República Dominicana. 6. Isabel Allende es de Chile. **E.** 1. eres 2. soy 3. son 4. es 5. es 6. somos **F.** 1. Pedro es de Perú. 2. ¿De dónde son tus amigos? 3. Tú eres de Atlanta. 4. Mi profesora de español es de España. 5. Ustedes son de México. 6. ¿De dónde sois vosotros? **G.** 1. Cómo te llamas 2. Se escribe 3. De dónde eres 4. De qué origen es tu familia *or* De dónde es tu familia

Pronunciación y ortografía

D. 1. cómico 2. idealista 3. eficiente 4. positivo 5. serio 6. estricto 7. independiente 8. liberal 9. origen 10. hospital

Parte 2

Vocabulario **A.** *Cards 2 and 3 are winning cards.*

B	I	N	G	O
1	3	6	8	10
4	7	11	12	13
15	18	14	22	16
23	20	24	26	17
27	31	30	28	19

B	I	N	G	O
2	3	6	5	7
5	11	8	10	17
9	15	12	14	18
21	19	13	16	20
22	25	29	30	31

B	I	N	G	O
1	5	3	2	6
8	10	11	9	12
13	16	18	17	14
19	21	23	20	22
25	30	24	26	29

B.

MARZO						
lunes	**martes**	**miércoles**	**jueves**	**viernes**	**sábado**	**domingo**
		1	2	3 **Javier**	4	5
6	7	8	9	10	11	12
13 **Pilar**	14	15 **Tomás María**	16	17	18	19
20 **Andrés**	21	22	23 **Sara**	24	25	26
27	28	29	30	31 **Felipe**		

C. 1. 31 − 10 = 21, veintiuno 2. 4 + 16 = 20, veinte 3. 9 + 15 = 24, veinticuatro 4. 28 − 3 = 25, veinticinco 5. 13 − 12 = 1, uno **D.** 1. 30, 17 2. 28, 22 3. 13, 4 4. 11, 0 5. 21, 6 6. 29, 12 **E.** 1. seis 2. dieciocho 3. nueve 4. treinta y uno 5. dieciséis *or* diez y seis 6. doce 7. cuatro **F.** 1. amable 2. mala 3. guapo 4. grande 5. trabajadora 6. delgado 7. bonita **G.** 1. perezoso 2. castaños 3. encantadora 4. corto 5. pequeño 6. bonitas **I.** Roberto (*Victoria said:* Bueno, me llamo Victoria. Tengo el pelo negro y los ojos verdes. Soy una mujer moderna. Soy independiente, enérgica y trabajadora. Busco un hombre responsable, lógico y romántico también.)

Entrevista 2 A. Paso 2. a **B.** 1. c 2. a 3. d 4. b **C.** 1. La ciudad de Stella se llama Duitama. 2. Es una ciudad moderna con un paisaje muy verde. 3. Los colombianos son amables, alegres, hospitalarios y trabajadores. 4. Stella tiene el pelo castaño, los ojos oscuros y la piel clara.

Forma y función

1.3 Clínica. 1. *m., s.* 2. *m., pl.* 3. *f., pl.* 4. *f., s.* 5. *f., s.* 6. *m., s.* 7. *f., s.* 8. *m., pl.* 9. *f., pl.* **B.** 1. La 2. El 3. Los 4. Las 5. La **C.** 1. una 2. un 3. unas 4. unos 5. un

Clínica. 1. alegres, antipáticos, encantadores, altos 2. alegre, antipática, encantadora, alta 3. alegre, antipática, encantadora, alta 4. alegres, antipáticas, encantadoras, altas 5. alegre, antipático, encantador, alto 6. alegres, antipáticos, encantadores, altos 7. alegre, antipático, encantador, alto **B.** 1. guapa 2. encantadores 3. rubio 4. azules 5. trabajadora **C.** 1. Son unas amigas amables. 2. El profesor es inteligente. 3. La clase es interesante. 4. Son unos cantantes famosos. 5. Los autores colombianos son de Bogotá. 6. Es una estudiante trabajadora.

Capítulo 2

Repaso y anticipación B. 1. quince 2. veinticuatro 3. doce 4. veintiuno 5. trece **C.** 1. Es de los Estados Unidos. Es estadounidense. 2. Es de España. Es español. 3. Son de Alemania. Son alemanas. 4. Es de Inglaterra. Es inglés. 5. Es de Italia. Es italiana. 6. Es de Puerto Rico. Es puertorriqueño. 7. Es de México. Es mexicano. 8. Es de China. Es china.

Parte 1

Vocabulario A. 1. diseño 2. *Answers may vary. For example,* sociología, antropología, psicología 3. *Answers may vary.* 4. literatura 5. informática 6. química 7. francés **C.** 1. optativo 2. aburridas 3. útil 4. obligatoria 5. fáciles **D.** 1. e 2. d 3. f 4. a 5. b 6. c **E.** 1. La clase de arte precolombino es a las ocho de la mañana. 2. La clase de introducción a la filosofía es a las seis de la tarde (noche). 3. La clase de química orgánica es a las diez y media de la mañana. 4. La clase de arquitectura posmodernista es a la una de la tarde. 5. La clase de psicología adolescente es a las siete y media de la noche. **F.** 1. Luz habla con una profesora a la una y media. 2. Luz practica deportes a las tres. 3. Luz escucha CDs en francés a las cinco y media. 4. Luz entra en la clase de informática a las nueve y media. 5. Luz dibuja triángulos y rectángulos a las once. 6. Luz regresa a casa a las ocho de la noche. **G.** 1. Dónde 2. Cómo 3. Quién 4. Cuándo 5. Cuánto 6. Cuáles

Entrevista 1 **A. Paso 2.** a **B.** 1. d 2. c 3. a 4. e 5. b 6. f **C.** 1. Silvana trabaja en la Universidad Nacional de Heredia. 2. El bachillerato en Costa Rica es de cuatro años. 3. Los costarricenses llevan seis cursos. 4. Llevan una clase de ciencias, una de letras y una de idioma. 5. Hay tres períodos de estudio: por la mañana, por la tarde y por la noche.

Forma y función

2.1 Clínica. 1. trabajo, trabajas, trabaja, trabajamos, trabajáis, trabajan 2. hablo, hablas, habla, hablamos, habláis, hablan 3. escucho, escuchas, escucha, escuchamos, escucháis, escuchan 4. practico, practicas, practica, practicamos, practicáis, practican 5. estudio, estudias, estudia, estudiamos, estudiáis, estudian 6. enseño, enseñas, enseña, enseñamos, enseñáis, enseñan 7. llego, llegas, llega, llegamos, llegáis, llegan **A. Paso 1.** 1. estudiante 2. estudiante 3. profesor(a) 4. estudiante 5. estudiante 6. profesor(a) **Paso 2.** 1. llevar 2. practicar 3. preparar 4. trabajar 5. estudiar 6. llegar **B.** 1. enseñamos 2. enseño 3. enseña 4. preparo 5. escucha 6. estudio 7. hablamos 8. llego 9. entro 10. participan 11. usan 12. entra **C.** 1. están 2. prepara, toman 3. escucha, practica 4. llevan 5. estudia **D.** 1. llevas 2. llevo 3. trabajo 4. Trabajas 5. llegas 6. Llego 7. Regreso 8. Llevas 9. llevo 10. Estudio 11. Hablamos **E.** 1. No, no estudio biología. Estudio psicología y francés. 2. No, no practico francés en el laboratorio. Practico francés con amigos franceses. 3. No, no hablo francés con mis amigos en la residencia. Hablo francés con mis amigos en la cafetería. 4. No, no llevo muchas clases. Llevo tres clases. 5. No, no trabajo en la librería. Trabajo en la biblioteca. 6. No, no regreso a la residencia estudiantil a las nueve. Regreso a las diez.

2.2 Clínica. 1. ¿Dónde? 2. ¿Cuándo? (¿A qué hora?) 3. ¿Cuánto/a(s)? 4. ¿Quién? 5. ¿Qué? 6. ¿Cuál? 7. ¿Cómo? **A. Paso 1.** 1. e 2. f 3. c 4. g 5. a 6. b 7. d **Paso 2.** 1. e 2. c 3. g 4. b 5. f 6. a 7. d **B.** 1. ¿Cuándo usan las computadoras los estudiantes? 2. ¿Quiénes practican alemán en el laboratorio de lenguas? 3. ¿Cuántas clases llevas este semestre? 4. ¿Cómo estás? *or* ¿Cómo está usted? 5. ¿Dónde estudia Nola? 6. ¿Qué enseña la profesora Quintero? **C.** 1. ¿Cuándo regresas a la residencia? 2. ¿Cuántas clases lleváis? 3. ¿Cómo están los estudiantes? 4. ¿Quiénes son Ricky Martin y Gloria Estefan? 5. ¿Dónde trabaja Lorena? 6. ¿Cuáles son las clases obligatorias?

Pronunciación y ortografía **C.** 1. ¿Dónde trabajas? 2. ¿Es muy grande la universidad? 3. ¿Cuántas clases llevas? 4. ¿Hay muchas clases obligatorias? 5. ¿Quién trabaja en un restaurante?

Parte 2

Vocabulario **A. Paso 1.** 1. la pizarra 2. la tiza 3. el pupitre 4. la ventana 5. la silla 6. el bolígrafo 7. el cuaderno **C.** 1. falso: La biblioteca está a la derecha del edificio de administración. *or* La Facultad de Ciencias está a la izquierda del edificio de administración. 2. falso: Las residencias estudiantiles están detrás del estadio. 3. cierto 4. falso: El estadio está detrás del edificio de administración. *or* El gimnasio está detrás de la biblioteca. 5. cierto **D.** 1. e 2. d 3. f 4. b 5. c 6. a

Entrevista 2 **A. Paso 2.** b **B.** 1. e 2. b 3. d 4. a 5. c **C.** 1. Érika estudia en la Universidad de Costa Rica. 2. Muchos estudiantes alquilan cuartos o viven con sus padres. 3. Los estudiantes comen en pulperías. 4. Los estudiantes van a la playa, van a cafés y van a conciertos.

Forma y función

2.3 Clínica. 1. voy 2. va 3. vamos 4. voy 5. va 6. vamos **B.** 1. voy 2. va 3. vamos 4. voy 5. van 6. vamos 7. voy 8. van **D.** 1. Leonardo va a trabajar a las tres de la tarde. 2. María y Dolores van a ir a clase a las nueve de la mañana. 3. Vosotros vais a llegar a la residencia a las dos de la tarde. 4. Yo voy a usar la computadora por la tarde. 5. Tú vas a escuchar música por la noche. 6. Nosotros vamos a hablar con la profesora a la una. **E.** *Answers may vary.* 1. Vamos al laboratorio de lenguas. 2. Voy a la biblioteca. 3. Vamos a la residencia estudiantil. 4. Va a su oficina. 5. Van a su oficina. 6. Va al laboratorio de química.

2.4 Clínica. *Answers will vary.* 1. La biblioteca está… 2. Yo estoy… 3. El bolígrafo está… 4. Tú estás… 5. Mis amigos están… 6. Luisa y yo estamos… 7. Ustedes están… 8. Juan y José están… **B.** 1. están 2. estoy 3. estamos 4. estás 5. está 6. están **C.** 1. está 2. están 3. estamos 4. estás 5. estoy 6. están

Capítulo 3

Repaso y anticipación A. Paso 1. 1. soy 2. es 3. soy 4. estudio 5. voy 6. vamos 7. está 8. regresan **Paso 2.** 1. Dónde/Cómo 2. Cuál/Cuándo 3. Qué 4. Cuándo 5. Quién/Cómo

Vocabulario A. Paso 1. 1. mi abuela 2. mi hermano 3. mi cuñado 4. mi tía **Paso 2.** *Answers may vary.* 1. el hijo de mi tío/a 2. la hija de mi hermano/a 3. el padre de mi madre/padre 4. los hijos de mis hijos 5. el hermano de mi padre/madre 6. la esposa de mi hermano/a **C. Paso 1.** 1. d 2. c 3. a 4. e 5. b **Paso 2.** 1. veintiún 2. sesenta y cinco 3. cincuenta y nueve 4. noventa y dos 5. setenta y un **D.** 1. Cien 2. quince 3. cincuenta 4. noventa y cuatro 5. veintiuna

Entrevista 1 A. Paso 2. b **B.** 1. e 2. c 3. d 4. a 5. b **C.** 1. Cynthia es de Quito, Ecuador. 2. Tiene dos hermanos. 3. El hermano de Cynthia se llama Manolo, y su hermana se llama Milene. 4. La familia es importante para Cynthia si alguien tiene algún problema o simplemente quiere conversar.

Forma y función

3.1 Clínica. 1. tengo 2. tenemos 3. tienen 4. tiene 5. tienen 6. tiene 7. tenéis 8. tienes 9. tenemos 10. tenemos 11. tiene 12. tiene 13. tienen 14. tienen **A.** 1. tenemos 2. tienes 3. tengo 4. tiene 5. tienen 6. tienen **C.** 1. Lisa tiene dos hermanos. 2. Samuel y Mary tienen tres sobrinos. 3. Mis padres tienen cinco hijos. 4. Mi madre tiene un primo. 5. Mi hermano y yo tenemos veinte primos. 6. Yo tengo quince tíos. **D.** 1. tiene sesenta y nueve 2. tienen veintitrés 3. tengo diecinueve 4. tenemos treinta y cinco 5. tienes cuarenta y siete 6. tenéis cincuenta y cuatro **E.** 1. Es de mis padres. 2. Son de Ana. 3. Son del padre de mi novia. 4. Es de mi hermano. 5. Es del profesor Martínez **F.** 1. Jorge tiene el gato de Gabriela. 2. Teresa y Rogelio tienen el perro de Juanito. 3. Tú y yo tenemos el coche de Heriberto. 4. Vosotros tenéis los libros del profesor. 5. Yo tengo la paciencia de mis padres.

3.2 Clínica. 1. mis primos, mi hermana, mis padres, mi tía, mis abuelos 2. tus primos, tu hermana, tus padres, tu tía, tus abuelos 3. sus primos, su hermana, sus padres, su tía, sus abuelos 4. nuestros primos, nuestra hermana, nuestros padres, nuestra tía, nuestros abuelos 5. vuestros primos, vuestra hermana, vuestros padres, vuestra tía, vuestros abuelos **B.** 1. Vuestra 2. Sus 3. Tu 4. Nuestras 5. su

Pronunciación y ortografía A. Paso 1. 1. familia 2. unico 3. comico 4. relacion 5. divoriciado 6. pesimista 7. trabajador 8. tolerante **Paso 2.** 1. familia 2. único 3. cómico 4. relación 5. divorciado 6. pesimista 7. trabajador 8. tolerante **B. Paso 1.** 1. Regla 1 2. Regla 2 3. Regla 1 4. Regla 1 5. Regla 2 6. Regla 1 7. Regla 2 8. Regla 2 **Paso 2.** 1. Regla 1 2. Regla 1 3. Regla 2 4. Regla 1 5. Regla 1 6. Regla 2 7. Regla 2 8. Regla 1 **C. Paso 1.** 1. sig-ni-fi-ca 2. ab-do-men 3. ca-lle-jón 4. ám-bar 5. e-le-men-tal 6. la-bra-dor 7. lí-der 8. au-to-mó-vil 9. in-fe-rior 10. cár-cel 11. cas-ca-bel 12. hin-ca-pié 13. te-nis 14. Pa-rís 15. úl-ti-mo

Parte 2

Vocabulario A. 1. divorciados 2. padrastro 3. soltera 4. jubilado 5. hermanastros **B.** 1. c 2. a 3. e 4. b 5. d **C.** 1. Los padres de Ester 2. Los padres de Ester 3. Los padres de Rosalinda 4. Los padres de Rosalinda 5. Los padres de Ester 6. Los padres de Rosalinda 7. Los padres de Rosalinda 8. Los padres de Ester 9. Los padres de Ester **E.** 1. llevar 2. mirar 3. bailar 4. beber 5. echar 6. dar, leer **F.** 1. e 2. b 3. X 4. f 5. a 6. X

Entrevista 2 A. Paso 2. a **B.** 1. b 2. a 3. d 4. c **C.** 1. En la casa de Gabriela están su padrastro, su madre, dos hermanos y tres hermanastros. 2. Es una familia muy unida. 3. Van a la playa, caminan, conversan y comen juntos. 4. La comunicación es un aspecto primordial (fundamental).

Forma y función

3.3 Clínica. 1. como, come, comemos, comen 2. bebo, bebe, bebemos, beben 3. escribo, escribe, escribimos, escriben 4. vivo, vive, vivimos, viven 5. leo, lee, leemos, leen 6. discuto, discute, discutimos, discuten **A.** 1. falso 2. cierto 3. falso 4. cierto 5. falso **B.** 1. Mi esposa y yo leemos el periódico todas las mañanas. 2. Yo bebo vino con la cena. 3. Mis hijos viven en un apartamento en Quito. 4. Mi hija y mi hermano discuten la política cuando hablan. 5. Mi hijo escribe cartas a su novia. **C.** 1. vivimos 2. leo 3. comemos 4. bebemos 5. discuten 6. escribe

3.4 Clínica. 1. doy, hago, salgo, veo 2. dan, hacen, salen, ven 3. dais, hacéis, salís, veis 4. dan, hacen, salen, ven 5. da, hace, sale, ve 6. damos, hacemos, salimos, vemos 7. da, hace, sale, ve 8. das, haces, sales, ves 9. da, hace, sale, ve **A.** 1. b 2. c 3. a 4. a 5. c **B.** *Answers will vary, but the following verb forms should be used:* 1. doy 2. veo 3. hago 4. salgo **C.** 1. ves 2. veo 3. vas 4. voy 5. haces 6. Hago 7. hacen 8. damos

Capítulo 4

Repaso y anticipación **A. Paso 1.** 1. visitar a los gemelos 2. dar un paseo 3. perros y gatos 4. paseo 5. vivir **Paso 2.** 1. c 2. e 3. d 4. a 5. b **B. Paso 1.** 1. j 2. i 3. d 4. c 5. b 6. f and h 7. k 8. a 9. g 10. e

Parte 1

Vocabulario **A. Paso 1.** 1. el balcón 2. la habitación, el dormitorio 3. el cuarto de baño 4. el salón 5. la cocina 6. el comedor 7. el pasillo 8. el jardín **C. Paso 1.** 1. el comedor 2. el jardín 3. el salón 4. la cocina

D. Paso 1.

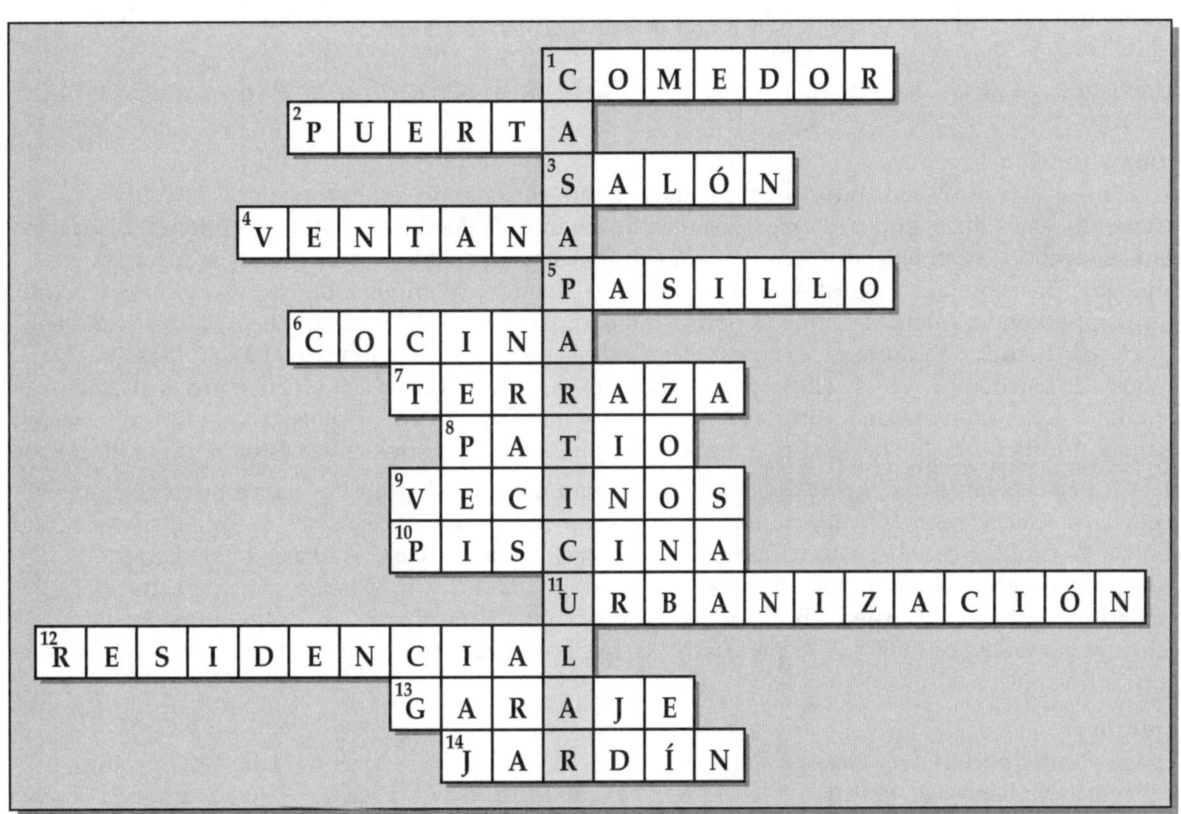

G. a

Entrevista 1 **A. Paso 2.** c **B.** 1. c 2. a 3. d 4. b 5. e **C.** 1. El pueblo donde vive María se llama Arcos de la Frontera. 2. Siete personas viven en la casa de María: María, tres hermanos, los padres y la abuela. 3. Hay ocho habitaciones: la entrada, el salón, cuatro dormitorios, la cocina y el comedor. 4. La familia de María comparte el patio con los vecinos.

Forma y función

4.1 Clínica. 1. este piso, ese piso, aquel piso 2. esta calle, esa calle, aquella calle 3. estos jardines, esos jardines, aquellos jardines 4. estas alfombras, esas alfombras, aquellas alfombras **B.** 1. Ese 2. Aquella 3. Esta 4. Aquellos 5. esas 6. Estas 7. esa 8. aquel **C.** 1. No me gusta ésta, pero me gusta ésa. 2. Me gustan ésos, pero no me gustan éstos. 3. Me gusta aquél, pero no me gusta ése. 4. No me gustan aquéllas, pero me gustan éstas. **D.** 1. esos 2. ésos 3. estas 4. eso 5. Aquél 6. Ése 7. esto 8. Esos

4.2 Clínica. 1. cierro, cierras, cierra, cerramos, cerráis, cierran 2. almuerzo, almuerzas, almuerza, almorzamos, almorzáis, almuerzan 3. puedo, puedes, puede, podemos, podéis, pueden 4. prefiero, prefieres, prefiere, preferimos, preferís, prefieren 5. quiero, quieres, quiere, queremos, queréis, quieren 6. vuelvo, vuelves, vuelve, volvemos, volvéis, vuelven **A. Paso 2.** 1. cerrar 2. dormir 3. soler 4. poder 5. jugar 6. querer **B.** 1. tenemos 2. puede 3. duermo 4. suelen 5. juegan 6. prefieren 7. vuelven 8. almorzamos **C. Paso 1.** 1. suelen 2. prefieren 3. quiere 4. puedo 5. almuerzan **Paso 2.** a. son (1) b. podemos (4) c. prefieren (2) d. suelen (3) e. almorzamos (5)

Pronunciación y ortografía **B.** 1. Vivo en aquella casa. 2. La silla está en el pasillo. 3. Me llamo Guillermo. 4. Llegamos a Sevilla a la una. 5. Vive en la calle Villanueva. **D.** 1. lápices 2. luces 3. cruces 4. voces 5. eficaces

Parte 2

Vocabulario **A.** *Fill-in-the-blank answers may vary.* 1. la secadora 2. el escritorio 3. la ducha 4. el horno 5. la bañera 6. el sillón

Entrevista 2 **A. Paso 2.** a **B.** 1. c 2. a 3. e 4. b 5. d **C.** 1. c 2. d 3. e 4. a 5. a 6. a 7. c 8. b 9. c

Forma y función

4.3 Clínica. 1. estoy tomando, estás tomando, estamos tomando, están tomando 2. estoy durmiendo, estás durmiendo, estamos durmiendo, están durmiendo 3. estoy leyendo, estás leyendo, estamos leyendo, están leyendo 4. estoy comiendo, estás comiendo, estamos comiendo, están comiendo 5. estoy jugando, estás jugando, estamos jugando, están jugando 6. estoy compartiendo, estás compartiendo, estamos compartiendo, están compartiendo **A. Paso 1.** 1. c 2. a 3. e 4. b 5. f 6. d **Paso 2.** 1. dormir 2. comer 3. leer 4. escuchar 5. mirar 6. tomar **Paso 3.** 1. ellos 2. ustedes 3. él 4. ellos 5. nosotros 6. yo **B.** 1. Javier está durmiendo la siesta. 2. Marta y Juan están tomando un café. 3. Yo estoy almorzando en la cafetería. 4. Los niños están jugando al fútbol. 5. El chef está preparando la comida. 6. Vosotros estáis estudiando la gramática.

4.4 Clínica. 1. lava, lave, lavad, laven 2. barre, barra, barred, barran 3. juega, juegue, jugad, jueguen 4. cierra, cierre, cerrad, cierren 5. piensa, piense, pensad, piensen 6. sueña, sueñe, soñad, sueñen 7. estudia, estudie, estudiad, estudien 8. lee, lea, leed, lean **A. Paso 1.** 1. cerrar 2. hablar 3. hacer 4. contestar 5. hacer 6. escribir **Paso 2.** 1. ustedes 2. tú 3. tú 4. usted 5. ustedes 6. usted **B.** 1. del cuarto de baño 2. la pizarra 3. ocho horas por la noche 4. a casa a las 10:00 5. el periódico 6. la pronunciación 7. en el comedor 8. por la puerta principal

Capítulo 5

Repaso y anticipación **A. Paso 1.** 1. la cocina 2. el comedor 3. el dormitorio 4. el salón 5. el cuarto de baño **B. Paso 1.** 1. c 2. e 3. d 4. a 5. b **C. Paso 1.** 1. c 2. e 3. b 4. a 5. d **Paso 2.** -ería; *store* **D.** 1. la piña 2. el limón 3. la sal 4. el jamón 5. el tomate 6. el azúcar 7. la sopa 8. la ensalada 9. la papa **E. Paso 1.** 1. b 2. d 3. f 4. a 5. c 6. e **Paso 2.** 1. La pizza es italiana. 2. El sushi es japónes. 3. El café es colombiano. 4. El chow mein es chino. 5. Los *croissants* son franceses. 6. Las enchiladas son mexicanas.

Parte 1

Vocabulario A. 1. carne 2. fruta 3. carne 4. postre 5. pescado 6. verdura 7. fruta 8. postre **D.** 1. viejo 2. agria 3. amargo 4. maduros 5. picante 6. tierno 7. frescas 8. fritas

Entrevista 1 A. Paso 2. b **B.** 1. c 2. f 3. d 4. a 5. e 6. b **C.** 1. Muchas personas hacen la compra en los supermercados. 2. En los pueblos mucha gente va al mercado para comprar frutas y vegetales. 3. Karina prefiere el mercado porque las frutas son más frescas. 4. El plato nacional se llama «la bandera nacional» y contiene arroz y habichuelas.

Forma y función

5.1 Clínica. 1. compran 2. colocan 3. distribuye 4. cubre **B.** 1. Se encuentran **caraotas** y **arepas** en todas las comidas. 2. Se comen mariscos y pescados diferentes. 3. Se va de compras con gusto porque las tiendas son muy lindas. 4. Se almuerza a las 2:00 en punto. 5. Se beben vinos importados de muchos países. **C.** 1. hace 2. baten 3. echa 4. mete 5. saca, deja

5.2 Clínica. 1. por 2. por 3. Para 4. por 5. para 6. por **A. Paso 1.** 1. *destination* 2. *purpose or goal* 3. *length or duration of time* 4. *through space* 5. *recipient* 6. *fixed expression* **Paso 2.** 1. para, *purpose or goal* 2. por, *duration or length of time* 3. por, *through space* 4. para, *recipient* 5. por, *through space* 6. para, *destination* **B.** 1. Por 2. por 3. por 4. por 5. para 6. para 7. por 8. para **C.** *Answers may vary.* 1. La comida venezolana es rica, por ejemplo, las arepas y las hallacas. 2. No me gusta la carne, por eso no como hamburguesas. 3. Es importante comer por lo menos una manzana por día. 4. Me gusta mucha sal en mi ensalada; por favor, ¿puedes pasarme la sal?

Pronunciación y ortografía B. 1. *general* 2. *pajama* 3. *correct* 4. *direct* 5. *geology* 6. *protect* 7. *genius* 8. *agent*

Parte 2

Vocabulario A. *Answers may vary.* 1. El limón es más agrio que las uvas. 2. La langosta es más cara que el pollo. 3. El té es tan amargo como (menos amargo que) el café. 4. El pastel de chocolate es más dulce que la manzana. 5. Los jalapeños son más picantes que los pimientos verdes. 6. Las piñas son tan deliciosas como (más/menos deliciosas que) las naranjas. 7. El ajo es tan esencial como (más/menos esencial que) la cebolla. 8. El desayuno es tan importante como (más/menos importante que) el almuerzo.

D.

					1 C	O	2 C	I	N	3 A				
		4 S					O			5 L	A	T	A	
6 F	R	E	Í	R			M			G				
		R			7 U	N	P	O	C	O	D	8 E		
		V					R					N		
9 P	R	I	N	10 C	I	P	A	L				T		
R		R		U			R	■	11 P			R		12 N
I				E		13 V	■	14 D	E	S	E	A		A
15 M	E	R	E	N	D	A	R		D			D		D
E				T	■	S			I		16 T	A	Z	A
R		17 P	L	A	T	O			R					

E. 1. Este plato no tiene nada de queso. 2. Este restaurante no sirve ningún plato vegetariano. 3. No hay nada en este menú para los niños. 4. Esta salsa no tiene ningún ingrediente exótico. 5. No me gustaría probar ninguna fruta tropical. **F.** 1. desean 2. recomienda 3. traigo 4. Me gustaría 5. trae

Entrevista 2 **A. Paso 2.** c **B.** 1. d 2. c 3. b 4. a **C.** 1. El pabellón criollo contiene arroz, caraotas, tajadas y carne. 2. El ingrediente principal es harina de maíz. 3. Las hallacas se preparan en Navidad con toda la familia. 4. Los venezolanos tienen el almuerzo entre mediodía y las 2:00.

Forma y función

5.3 Clínica. 1. sirvo, servimos, sirves, sirven, servís 2. frío, freímos, fríes, fríen, freís 3. digo, decimos, dices, dicen, decís 4. consigo, conseguimos, consigues, consiguen, conseguís 5. mido, medimos, mides, miden, medís **A.** 1. conseguimos 2. sirve 3. digo 4. fríen 5. pides **B.** 1. Nosotros pedimos hamburguesas en la cafetería. 2. Ellos sirven papas fritas con las hamburguesas. 3. El cocinero fríe las papas por quince minutos. 4. El cocinero frecuentemente no mide bien los ingredientes. 5. Muchos estudiantes dicen: «No me gusta la comida de la cafetería.» **C. Paso 1.** 1. fríe 2. dice 3. piden 4. sirven 5. consigue 6. miden **Paso 2.** 1. C, M 2. M 3. M 4. C 5. C, M 6. C, M

5.4 Clínica. 1. La 2. Los 3. Las 4. Lo 5. La 6. Las **A.** 1. <u>lo</u>, vino 2. <u>me</u>, yo 3. <u>las</u>, verduras 4. <u>la</u>, cuenta 5. <u>los</u>, platos exóticos 6. <u>la</u>, sopa 7. <u>te</u>, tú 8. <u>os</u>, vosotros/as 9. <u>las</u>, papas 10. <u>los</u>, tamales **B.** 1. Lo gasto. 2. Los llamo. 3. Las hago. 4. Lo leo. 5. Lo pido. 6. La pago. **C.** 1. Yo las hago. 2. Nosotros las compramos. 3. Raúl la trae. 4. Usted lo va a cocinar (va a cocinarlo). 5. Carmen lo prepara. 6. Esteban y Lidia los llaman. 7. Ustedes lo hacen. 8. Paloma la cocina. 9. Yo las traigo. 10. Marisol los va a comprar (va a comprarlos).

Capítulo 6

Repaso y anticipación **A. Paso 1.** 1. el tiempo libre 2. el trabajo 3. el trabajo 4. el trabajo 5. el trabajo 6. el tiempo libre 7. el tiempo libre 8. el tiempo libre 9. el trabajo 10. el tiempo libre 11. el tiempo libre 12. el tiempo libre 13. el trabajo 14. el tiempo libre **B. Paso 1.** 1. sí 2. sí 3. no 4. sí 5. no 6. sí 7. no 8. no 9. no 10. sí **Paso 2.** caminar una milla o más al día, hacer ejercicio con regularidad, desayunar bien, echar una siesta al día **C. Paso 1.** 1. tengo 2. trabajamos 3. salgo 4. lleva 5. vuelvo 6. suelo 7. prefiere 8. sirvo 9. tienen 10. podemos 11. estoy 12. Duermo 13. tengo 14. dice 15. es 16. trabajo 17. desayuno 18. almuerzo 19. como 20. ceno

Parte 1

Vocabulario **A. Paso 2.** 1. Son las nueve menos veinte. 2. Son las once y cinco. 3. Son las dos y diez. 4. Son las cuatro y cuarto. 5. Es la una y veinticinco. **B.** 1. h 2. f 3. b, a 4. c, g 5. d, e **C. Paso 1.** 1. c 2. d 3. a 4. e 5. b **Paso 2.** *Answers may vary.* 1. levantarse 2. ducharse 3. vestirse 4. maquillarse 5. cepillarse los dientes **D.** 1. sufres, copa 2. tomar una siesta 3. insomnio, café 4. divertirte 5. hacer ejercicio **E.** *Answers may vary.* 1. Debe acostarse más temprano. 2. Debe quedarse en la cama. 3. Debe ducharse por la noche. Debe levantarse a las seis. 4. No debe tomar café o refrescos con cafeína. Debe hacer ejercicio por la tarde. 5. Debe tener tiempo libre para divertirse y reunirse con amigos.

Entrevista 1 **A. Paso 2.** b **B.** 1. d 2. a 3. c 4. b **C.** *Answers may vary.* 1. En un día típico, Güido se levanta temprano, hace ejercicio, come con la familia, va al trabajo, toma una siesta y sale con los amigos. 2. Es aceptable llegar quince o veinte minutos tarde. 3. El ejercicio es bueno para los problemas de salud y los problemas psicológicos también. 4. Güido dice que la gente no hace planes y hay mucha inseguridad.

Forma y función

6.1 Clínica. 1. me despierto 2. os levantáis 3. te duchas 4. nos vestimos 5. se baña 6. se cepilla 7. se acuestan **B.** 1. me pongo la bata 2. me ducho 3. me visto 4. me cepillo los dientes 5. me acuesto **C.** 1. me levanto 2. me ducho 3. me visto 4. se acuestan 5. se quedan 6. se baña 7. nos maquillamos 8. nos ponemos 9. nos reunimos

6.2 Clínica. 1. Sé 2. Conozco 3. Conozco 4. Sé 5. Conozco 6. Conozco 7. Sé **A.** 1. Conoces, conozco, sé 2. Conocen, conocemos, sabemos 3. Sabe, sé 4. Sabes, Sé, conozco **B.** 1. sé 2. conoce 3. sabe 4. conozco 5. sé 6. sabe 7. conoce 8. sabe **C.** 1. saben, conocen 2. sabe 3. conoces 4. sabe 5. conocen **D. Paso 1.** 1. ¿Conocen ustedes a alguna persona famosa? 2. ¿Sabes hablar otra lengua? 3. ¿Sabe usted cuántos años tiene la profesora? 4. ¿Conoces la cultura indígena de Bolivia? 5. ¿Conocen ustedes bien la ciudad donde viven? **Paso 2.** 1. Sí, (No, no) conocemos a alguna (ninguna) persona famosa. 2. Sí, (No, no) sé hablar otra lengua. 3. Sí, (No, no) sé cuántos años tiene la profesora. 4. Sí, (No, no) la conozco. 5. Sí, (No, no) la conocemos bien.

Pronunciación y ortografía B. 1. museo 2. antropología 3. crían 4. serio 5. mutuo 6. ciencia 7. tabúes 8. ruido **C.** 1. Si tú no tienes tu libro, puedes usar mi libro. 2. No sé cómo vamos a llegar hasta La Paz. 3. Es difícil eliminar el estrés de la vida. 4. ¿Adónde vas para relajarte cuando estás cansado? 5. Sólo falta un día más para el sábado.

Parte 2

Vocabulario D. 1. d 2. a 3. b 4. e 5. c

Entrevista 2 A. Paso 2. a **B.** 1. c 2. f 3. b 4. d 5. a 6. e **C.** 1. El clima de La Paz es frío. 2. La gente prefiere los remedios caseros. No va siempre al médico. 3. Los remedios naturales se usan más en el campo. 4. Los síntomas del soroche son: dolor de cabeza y la falta de aire.

Forma y función

6.3 Clínica. 1. están 2. es 3. estoy 4. es 5. está 6. está 7. están 8. es **B.** 1. a 2. i 3. c 4. e 5. f 6. d 7. h 8. b 9. g **C.** 1. estamos, estamos 2. es 3. estoy 4. soy, están, es 5. estamos, Es

Capítulo 7

Repaso y anticipación B. Paso 1. 1. b 2. c 3. a 4. f 5. e 6. d **D.** 1. Son las once menos cuarto y están hablando con otros turistas en el parque. 2 Son las dos y están comiendo en un restaurante típico. 3. Son las tres y cuarto y están esperando el postre. 4. Son las cuatro menos diez y están leyendo un periódico de México. 5. Son las cuatro y media y están tomando un autobús a las ruinas aztecas. 6. Son las cinco y están viendo unas pirámides. 7. Son las ocho menos quince y están escuchando música en el parque. 8. Es medianoche (Son las doce) y están durmiendo en un hotel elegante.

Parte 1

Vocabulario B. 1. d 2. e 3. a 4. b 5. c **D.** *Answers may vary.* 1. Le muestro los vestidos formales. 2. Devuelvo los pantalones a la tienda. 3. Regateo.

Entrevista 1 A. Paso 2. c **B.** 1. f 2. d 3. e 4. b 5. a 6. c **C.** 1. Minerva fue de compras al centro comercial y al tianguis. 2. El tianguis es un mercado sobre ruedas. 3. A Minerva le gusta el tianguis porque puede encontrar todas las cosas que necesita, a un buen precio. 4. Minerva compró regalos para su hija y otros miembros de la familia.

Forma y función

7.1 Clínica. 1. llevé, llevaste, llevó, llevamos, llevasteis, llevaron 2. bebí, bebiste, bebió, bebimos, bebisteis, bebieron 3. recibí, recibiste, recibió, recibimos, recibisteis, recibieron 4. preparé, preparaste, preparó, preparamos, preparasteis, prepararon 5. conocí, conociste, conoció, conocimos, conocisteis, conocieron 6. decidí, decidiste, decidió, decidimos, decidisteis, decidieron **B.** 1. viajé 2. nos quedamos 3. salimos 4. gustaron 5. aprendí 6. compré **C.** 1. decidió 2. Llamó 3. almorzaron 4. salieron 5. compró 6. se probó 7. vio 8. entró 9. pagó 10. regresó 11. devolvió **D.** 1. Tomás y Paco salieron para el centro comercial. 2. Magda se probó unas botas de cuero en la tienda. 3. Jorge y yo compramos comida en el supermercado. 4. Tú cenaste en un restaurante con tu novio. 5. Yo llevé el perro a la veterinaria. 6. Ustedes cambiaron los pantalones por otros. **E.** 1. pasé, me quedé 2. tomamos, conocimos 3. llevó 4. recibí, aprendí 5. salió 6. volvimos **F.** 1. ¿Quién te mostró los vestidos formales? 2. ¿Qué devolvió Pedro? 3. ¿Cómo te quedaron los zapatos? 4. ¿Qué le regaló José a Luis? 5. ¿Cuánto costaron los aretes?

7.2 Clínica. 1. Mi amiga me devolvió el suéter. 2. La dependienta les mostró a ustedes unos vestidos. 3. Siempre les enviamos un recibo a nuestros clientes. 4. Mis padres te compraron un regalo en esta tienda. 5. Yo le abrí la puerta del probador a mi amiga. **A.** 1. Les 2. Me 3. Le 4. Nos 5. Les 6. Te **C.** 1. Le 2. le 3. les 4. Les 5. Le 6. Le **D.** 1. Les 2. Les 3. Te 4. me 5. nos 6. Le **E.** 1. Mi esposo les compró chocolates a los niños. 2. Tus padres nos regalaron ropa a nosotros. 3. Los niños me mostraron sus regalos a mí. 4. Te compré otro reloj a ti. 5. Le regalaste un abrigo a tu madre.

Pronunciación y ortografía **A.** 1. expliqué 2. ofrecí 3. llegué 4. llegó 5. ofreció 6. vio 7. almorzó 8. almorcé 9. explico 10. ofrecemos

Parte 2

Vocabulario **A.** 1. hechas 2. regatear 3. costar 4. alta calidad 5. pagar **B.** 1. Los aretes de plata cuestan ciento cincuenta pesos. 2. El poncho de lana cuesta quinientos veinte pesos. 3. Los alebrijes cuestan ciento cuarenta y cinco pesos cada uno. 4. La bolsa de cuero cuesta novecientos ochenta pesos. 5. La guayabera de seda cuesta cuatrocientos treinta y cinco pesos. **C.** 1. regalos para su familia 2. compra para hombres 3. hace calor donde vive 4. prefiere los regalos hechos a mano 5. carteras 6. $500 7. $600 8. $750

Entrevista 2 **A. Paso 2.** b **B.** 1. d 2. b 3. a 4. c **C.** 1. Hay centros comerciales, tianguis y mercados de artesanías. 2. Puedes encontrar sarapes, platos pintados a mano y artesanías de plata. 3. En México la gente no se reúne mucho con otra gente en el centro comercial como en los Estados Unidos.

Forma y función

7.3 Clínica. 1. me gustan 2. me gusta 3. me gustan 4. me gusta 5. me gustan 6. me gustan 7. me gusta 8. me gustan **B.** 1. gustan 2. gusta 3. gusta 4. gustan 5. gustan 6. gusta 7. gustan 8. gustan 9. gusta 10. gusta **C.** 1. A los profesores les gusta la ropa formal. 2. A nosotros nos gustan las camisetas de algodón. 3. A mí me gustan las camisetas de seda. 4. A los estudiantes les gustan los pantalones cortos. 5. A mi madre le gustan los centros comerciales. 6. A mi padre le gustan las zapaterías para hombres. 7. A ti te gusta el sombrero nuevo. 8. A ustedes les gustan los mercados al aire libre.

7.4 Clínica. 1. se 2. le 3. 0 4. nos **A.** 1. *to be located* 2. *to fit / to look good* 3. *to stay* 4. *to fit / to look good* 5. *to stay* 6. *to be located* 7. *to have left* 8. *to have left*

Capítulo 8

Repaso y anticipación **C.** 1. decidí 2. llamé 3. llegaron 4. salimos 5. invité 6. llegamos 7. bajamos 8. exclamó 9. señaló 10. tomó 11. vio 12. gritamos 13. llevó 14. compró

Parte 1

Vocabulario **A.** *Answers may vary.* 1. levantar pesas 2. bucear, esquiar, nadar, surfear 3. el baloncesto, el fútbol (americano), el voleibol 4. el baloncesto, el fútbol (americano), el golf, el tenis, el voleibol 5. correr, la equitación, escalar montañas **B.** 1. d 2. e 3. h 4. a 5. g 6. b 7. c 8. f **C.** *Answers may vary.* 1. Mi familia acampa. 2. Mi padre y mi tío juegan a los naipes. 3. José Alberto y Alejandra juegan al ajedrez. 4. Doña Pilar teje. 5. Santiago y yo escalamos montañas. 6. Mi hermana colecciona estampillas. **D.** 1. golf, tenis, naipes, ver partidos de béisbol 2. golf, tenis, ajedrez, ver partidos de béisbol 3. artes marciales, béisbol, ver partidos de béisbol 4. natación, billar, ver partidos de béisbol 5. ajedrez, estampillas, monedas, carteles, ver partidos de béisbol

Entrevista 1 **A. Paso 2.** b **B.** 1. c 2. a 3. e 4. d 5. f 6. b **C.** *Answers may vary.* 1. A Mitch le gusta ir a la playa, hacer barbacoas, nadar, caminar en el bosque y escuchar/tocar música. 2. La última vez que fue a la playa Mitch nadó, corrió, hizo una barbacoa con la familia y vio la caída del sol. 3. El deporte más importante de Puerto Rico es la pelota. 4. Los chicos juegan a la pelota, y las chicas suelen jugar al voleibol.

Forma y función

8.1 Clínica. 1. anduve 2. fue 3. hizo 4. quisiste, pudiste 5. dimos, trajeron 6. vinisteis **A.** 1. poder, nosotros/as 2. poner, yo 3. tener; usted, él/ella 4. venir, tú 5. traer; ustedes, ellos/as 6. querer, vosotros/as **B.** 1. estuvimos 2. pudo 3. Hizo 4. llevamos 5. hubo 6. hicieron 7. fueron **C.** 1. Tuvimos 2. pudo 3. dio 4. redujo 5. Fue 6. vino 7. Hicimos 8. trajimos 9. compramos **D.** 1. fue a un partido de béisbol 2. un amigo 3. comida 4. sentados 5. buenos 6. una pelota

8.2 Clínica. 1. sentí, sintió, sentimos, sintieron 2. morí, murió, morimos, murieron 3. volví, volvió, volvimos, volvieron 4. dormí, durmió, dormimos, durmieron 5. perdí, perdió, perdimos, perdieron 6. me vestí, se vistió, nos vestimos, se vistieron 7. me divertí, se divirtió, nos divertimos, se divirtieron 8. pedí, pidió, pedimos, pidieron 9. serví, sirvió, servimos, sirvieron **A.** 1. ellos 2. él 3. tú 4. vosotros 5. yo 6. nosotras **B.** 1. se sintió 2. tuvo 3. durmieron 4. lloró 5. perdió 6. sirvió

Pronunciación y ortografía **E.** 1. coro 2. corro 3. ahorra 4. ahora 5. varios 6. barrios

Parte 2

Vocabulario **A.** 1. bailar pegados 2. encontrarse 3. fuma 4. bebida alcohólica 5. tiene prisa 6. en ambiente **B.** 1. molestar 2. prisa 3. el bar 4. charlar 5. invitado 6. pasarla bien **C.** 1. anoche 2. amigas 3. hermano 4. cerveza 5. bailaron 6. charlaron de

Entrevista 2 **A. Paso 2.** a **B.** 1. d 2. f 3. e 4. c 5. b 6. a **C.** 1. José prefiere la noche. 2. Anoche fue a casa de unos amigos y luego fue a una discoteca a bailar. 3. En la fiesta se tocó de todo: música americana y música latina. 4. A los puertorriqueños les gusta bailar y conocer a la gente.

Forma y función

8.3 Clínica. 1. alguién 2. tampoco 3. siempre 4. nada 5. alguna **A.** *Answers may vary.* 1. Nunca ve la televisión 2. No le gusta ningún deporte. 3. No tiene ninguna fiesta en su casa. 4. Nunca le molesta nada de los políticos. 5. No habla con nadie en las fiestas. 6. No come ni dulces ni carne tampoco. **B.** 1. No, no escucho nunca/jamás la música clásica. 2. No, nadie estudia español conmigo. 3. No, no me gusta nada de Puerto Rico. 4. No, no estudio francés tampoco. 5. No, no tengo ningúna amiga puertorriqueña. **C.** 1. Siempre juego a los naipes. 2. Alguién en mi clase cuenta chistes. 3. Tengo algo de dinero para jugar al billar. 4. Juego al ajedrez y voy al cine también. 5. Algunos de los videojuegos son interesantes.

8.4 Clínica. 1. Una amiga me lo mandó. 2. Mis tíos me las regalaron. 3. Mi novio me lo escribió. 4. Los vecinos me la dieron. 5. Mis padres me lo compraron. **A. Paso 1.** 1. el coche 2. las estampillas 3. los tacos 4. la composición 5. el coche 6. las enchiladas **Paso 2.** 1. yo 2. tú 3. nosotros 4. yo 5. tú 6. yo **B.** 1. Mis padres me lo compraron. 2. Yo te la compré. 3. Nosotros nos las compramos. 4. Tú me los diste. 5. Tus compañeros de cuarto te lo regalaron. **C.** 1. e 2. c 3. b 4. d 5. a **D.** 1. La anfitriona nos la está mostrando. / La anfitriona está mostrándonosla. 2. Nosotros se lo vamos a dar. / Nosotros vamos a dárselo. 3. El anfitrión se la está sirviendo. / El anfitrión está sirviéndosela. 4. El anfitrión nos la está tocando. / El anfitrión está tocándonosla. 5. Se la voy a mandar. / Voy a mandársela. **E. Paso 1.** 1. Sus amigas le dijeron la verdad a Margarita. 2. La profesora le está explicando el material al estudiante. / La profesora está explicándole el material al estudiante. 3. Le voy a comprar un regalo (a mi madre). / Voy a comprarle un regalo (a mi madre). 4. Les di el disco compacto a mis hermanos. 5. Sergio nos preparó (a nosotros) una cena fantástica. **Paso 2.** 1. Sus amigas se la dijeron. 2. La profesora se lo está explicando. / La profesora está explicándoselo. 3. Se lo voy a comprar. / Voy a comprárselo. 4. Se lo di. 5. Sergio nos la preparó.